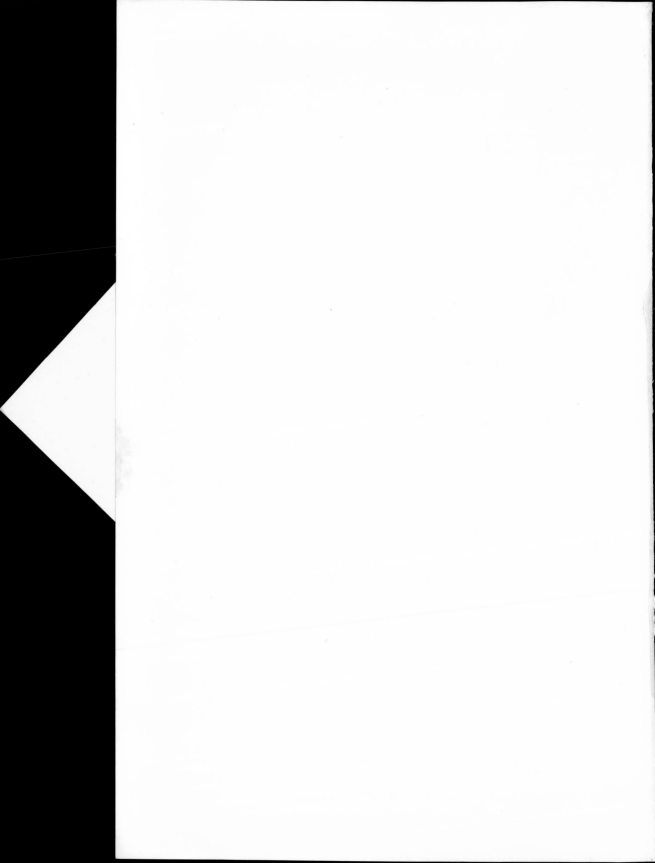

Home Care for the Elderly

A Complete Guide

JAY PORTNOW, M.D.
with MARTHA HOUTMANN, R.N.

McGraw-Hill Book Company

New York St. Louis San Francisco Toronto
Hamburg Mexico

This book is not intended to replace the services of a physician.
Any application of the recommendations set forth in the following
pages is at the reader's discretion and sole risk.

1 2 3 4 5 6 7 8 9   DOCDOC   8 7

ISBN 0-07-050582-9

Library of Congress Cataloging-in-Publication Data

Portnow, Jay.
  Homecare for the elderly.
  Bibliography: p.
  1. Aged—Home care—United States—Handbooks, manuals,
etc.   I. Houtmann, Martha.   II. Title.
HV1461.P673   1987   649'.8   86-21289
ISBN 0-07-050582-9

BOOK DESIGN BY JUDY ALLAN
ILLUSTRATIONS BY LAURA HARTMAN
EDITING SUPERVISOR: MARGERY LUHRS

To our parents,
Florence and Alfred E. Portnow
and
Mary and Edouard Houtmann

Contents

Acknowledgments

This book is not a simple collection of facts and advice about home care. It is an expression of a philosophy, of our view of life and of what is important in life. As such, it reflects the influence of all those who have shaped our lives—of friends, as well as strangers, who have reached out to help us. It is impossible to list or even to know all of these people. At the very least, we want to thank the following for their friendship, and to say that in countless, unrecorded ways they have contributed to the pages of this book: Jimmy Arthur, Maria Balsam, John Baskerville, Sandra Bergey, Bob Boote, Arthur Brown, Martin Cherkef, Lee Cooperman, Nate Daniels, Jack Dehovitz, Agnes Dwyer, Joe Gabel, Martin Goldberg, Doris Gormley, Gayle and David Halperin, Dan Hofstadter, Shep Houston, Edouard Houtmann, Gus Houtmann, Jane Houtmann, John Houtmann, Matthew and Nancy Houtmann, Mitsunari Kanai, Jeff and Roberta Kurland, Karen Kuykendall, Sarita Kuykendall, Al and Bev Landman, Jeff and Connie May, Masahilo Nakazono, Jacob Oltman, Richard Portnow, Ilya Prigogine, Looey Roby, George and Jeanine Rousseau, Melvin Singer, Harvey and Judy Strassman, Alan Tobias, Tom Waldman, and Fred Wagstaff.

1 Introduction

This was once a down-to-earth, no-nonsense country known for its independence and frontier spirit. We were a nation of rugged individualists with a healthy distrust for high-minded, authoritarian pronouncements. The word of authority was never a reason for doing anything. We expected everything that touched our lives, from a simple cold remedy to a complex gadget, to be understandable in commonsense terms. If you wanted people to believe what you had to say, you had better be prepared to make sense of it in simple terms. As for your degrees, academic appointments, awards, and professional standing—well, with the price of a ticket they could get you on a stagecoach going across the country. The average person was the important person. Experts and professionals existed to help the rest of us and make our lives safer, healthier, and more enjoyable. In the democratic traditions of our country, experts served the people.

Over the last century the situation has slowly changed. Today, specialists and professionals have taken over and intimidated the rest of us into silence. Nowhere is this more obvious than in the field of health care. We understand little about the diseases and medical conditions that affect the quality of our lives. Intimate details about our bodies and lifestyles are shared with experts, and strangers counsel us without explaining their reasons in understandable terms. The authority of the experts has become reason enough for people to alter their lives. Even life-and-death decisions are left to the experts because we do not know all the facts and details.

A hundred years ago our great-grandparents nursed and doctored human ailments on the frontier; only the complex and mysterious problems were brought to the specialists. Today no one makes a move without first checking with a specialist. No one fixes a sink without getting a plumber's opinion, or builds an addition to a house without consulting an architect. In medicine it's gotten so bad that no one takes a walk without first clearing it with a doctor. Our independence and freedom of choice have been sacrificed to the cult of the expert. Where have all the confident, commonsense men and women who built our country gone? Where is the old self-reliance, the Yankee ingenuity, the frontier spirit, the rugged individualism? Where is the old healthy distrust of professionals?

The truth is we don't need doctors, nurses, therapists, technicians, and all our other highly skilled and erudite medical professionals for run-of-the-mill problems. Their expertise is needed and their time is better spent with difficult-to-understand and hard-to-manage problems. For straightforward problems or situations that call for only basic knowledge and horsesense, an ordinary person can rise to the occasion and do a creditable job.

Most problems that send people to doctors' offices are not difficult. Often they disappear on their own in a few days or else respond to rest, dietary changes, or simple counseling. It has been estimated that half of the problems that send people to doctors would respond to nothing more complicated than reassurance and tender loving care. No one is better prepared to provide this than a close friend or family member. Of course, serious problems, even life threatening ones, can masquerade as minor ailments, and neglecting a serious problem just once can be devastating. However, common sense and basic knowledge can protect us against making such a mistake. If we know when a symptom, a complaint, a sign, or a change in behavior may signal a serious underlying illness, we can easily arrange for proper medical help. The idea is not for us to become doctors, or to duplicate a doctor's work; the idea is to do the simple things ourselves and to ask for help when we are overwhelmed. Experts have their place in the health care system, and we have ours. Our place is not to sit back passively waiting for experts to tell us what to do, it is to take an active role in providing our own health care. To do this effectively, we need common sense, which most of us have in abundance, and basic knowledge, which for a long time we were denied. The medical and scientific knowledge that has accumulated over the last century is rightfully ours, and the fundamentals, which are all we require to look after our own simple health care needs, are understandable and accessible to anyone with the opportunity and inclination to learn them.

We have reached a high-water mark in terms of science and technology. The scientific discoveries and technological break-throughs of the twentieth century have created a medical care system unparalleled in history. Unfortunately, in the wake of the meteoric rise of modern medicine lies the average person. When medical treatments involved little more than salves, balms, lotions, potions, and folk remedies, and causative agents were evil spirits and bad humors, doctors and patients shared a common language and understanding. When the analytical power of science was directed against human disease, a chasm was created between patient and doctor which has widened ever since and which becomes more difficult to bridge each day. Medical scientists, engineers, and physicians speak a language that is foreign to the rest of us. But behind the jargon are commonsense thoughts. As sophisticated and unfamiliar as medicine has become, its foundations are still in down-to-earth concepts. Medical scientists have been accumulating new knowledge and technologies for too long without returning the basic, commonsense store of knowledge to us. While progress in medicine continues, the common person deserves to know what has been learned over the last century that is now taken for granted by the professional.

This book was written to return some of the century's accumulated knowledge to its rightful owners: you and your friends and relatives. Information that doctors and nurses take for granted and use every day in caring for people is discussed in the following pages. Our intent is not to turn you into a doctor or a nurse or to convince you to turn your home into a hospital. This is not a book about diseases, nor is it a medical or nursing textbook. It's a book about the health of elderly people, and the idea is that anyone who wants to take care of an elderly person at home can do the job as well as, and often better than, any hospital or nursing home. All you need is the basic knowledge presented in the following pages, a willingness to help, and an ability to trust yourself.

Doctors and nurses are trained to treat diseases, but more often than not the health care needs of elderly people are social and psychological in nature, rather than disease-related. Your contribution will come, in part, from initiating changes in your friend or relative's social life, recreation, diet, and exercise, as well as from overseeing his or her health and safety.

The positive consequences of caring for an elderly person at home extend far beyond the well-being of that person. You have only to think back to the lives of your ancestors to realize that the isolation of the elderly and the separation of generations today is an unfortunate modern phenomenon. Many thoughtful social scientists have searched long and hard for reasons to explain the breakup of the American family, but while everyone has lamented the breakup and pointed to dire consequences, few have proposed remedies. Caring for an elderly friend or relative at home unifies a family and provides a common cause, a goal for everyone to work toward. Moreover, in the case of a relative, youngsters have the advantage of living with one of the founders of their family and experiencing the mellowness, contentment, and wisdom that years bring. Middle-aged adults benefit as well. They can see first-hand that aging doesn't mean dying and that if decline is inevitable, there is, nevertheless, a big difference between the need for occasional help and total dependence. Furthermore, the most dramatic and personal demonstration of the flow and continuity of life comes when you look out and see your child on one side and your parent on the other and realize that you are in the middle, nurturing one and comforting the other.

The moral argument for taking care of an elderly person at home is best made by asking a question that people have asked for centuries: How is it that one mother can care for three children, but three children find it difficult to care for one mother? The answer lies in what is expected of us and what we are willing to give. As society changes, its expectations of individuals change, but what we are willing to give up in our lives for the sake of another person will always remain a personal moral decision. It isn't the purpose of this book to convince you to take care of an elderly friend or relative. No one can or should do that. The decision is yours. If you want the job, there are deep satisfactions and lasting rewards; if you have the desire and commitment, you have the ability. This book will give you the necessary knowledge.

Taking care of an elderly person at home doesn't mean doting on the person or catering to his or her every whim. It doesn't even mean making life as easy as possible for that person. The idea is to preserve independence and encourage as much individual initiative as possible. As the years go by certain abilities are lost, while others remain. The goal is to help the person refine and elaborate the remaining abilities rather than mourn the lost ones and give in to dependence. It's better for an older person to do something slowly but independently than to have the same thing done more efficiently by someone else. Independence and responsibility are necessary for a meaningful life.

One last word about home care. Anyone who is cared for in the warmth and generosity of a friend's or family member's home is a fortunate person. Nothing can compare with the understanding and devotion of a loved one. Hospitals have their place, as do nursing homes, but they are last resorts. When you're too ill to stay at home, you need a hospital. When you're alone in the world and too incapacitated to stay at home, you need a nursing home. But when you can get around on your own with a little assistance, a warm and loving home is the best choice. Spiritually, emotionally, and physically you are way ahead at home.

2 Nutrition

Many old people who live alone eat poorly. Often they can't get the food they need because they don't have the money or the transportation. At other times they're too scared to go out because the streets are cold and slippery or because there are muggers and ruffians in the neighborhood. Elderly people also lose interest in food: as the sense of taste deteriorates with age, food becomes bland and uninteresting and eating becomes more of a chore and less of a pleasure. Finally, sometimes it's just easier for them to stay home and eat processed junk food than it is to go out and shop for nutritious food.

When an elderly friend or relative moves in with you, you may have the chance to reverse years of poor eating habits. Money, transportation, and motivation are no longer limiting factors, and while the person's sense of taste is still blunted, there are lots of ways to spice up a meal. The key is to make it a nutritious meal, and for this all you need are basic food facts and simple guidelines.

In 1977 the Senate Select Committee on Nutrition and Human Needs, chaired by Senator George McGovern, investigated the quality of the American diet and its relationship to the health of Americans. The McGovern Committee recommended a set of dietary goals for the nation that called for eating more complex carbohydrates and roughage and less fat, sugar, salt, and alcohol. The dietary goals were intended to reduce the incidence of, and the mortality from, major chronic diseases such as heart disease, stroke, arteriosclerosis, and cancer. Risk factors such as hypertension and obesity were targeted as well.

There is no evidence that good nutrition late in life will reverse the ills of a profligate, gluttonous youth. There is no proof that the damage of seventy years of high doses of refined sugar, saturated fat, and cholesterol can be overcome with a balanced diet in the later years. We don't even know if reducing the risk factors for chronic disease late in life will prolong life. Proper nutrition in old age is not meant to undo the past; it is meant to ensure as vigorous an old age as possible. Adequate nutrition keeps the immune system robust enough to ward off infection. Nutritious foods keep the cardiovascular system healthy, and it in turn keeps us fit. Growth and repair of body tissue, blood clotting, and wound healing are further examples of bodily functions that depend on good food. The mind too needs adequate nourishment. And at no time in life is good nutrition more essential to a person's vigor and sense of well-being than late in life.

PROPER NUTRITION

Over forty nutrients are essential for the growth and maintenance of the body. The major ones are protein; the vitamins A, B complex, and C; and the minerals calcium and iron—which, according to the National Institute on Aging, are consumed in inadequate amounts by many of the nation's elderly. But when you are trying to provide proper nutrition for an elderly person, it is senseless to collect charts and tables on the nutrient quantities in food, to check the Recommended Dietary Allowances (RDAs), and to calculate optimally nutritious meals. You'd run out of space storing all the charts and tables, you'd run out of patience keeping track of all the revised and updated editions, and your computer (if you have one) would run out of memory doing the calculations. More important, nobody knows for sure the nutritional requirements of the elderly. The RDAs themselves are the same for all elderly people, no matter what age: They are valuable as a research tool but of scant use in day-to-day meal planning at home.

Computed estimates of nutrient needs and elaborate schemes of menu planning may work for a few days, but they'll exhaust you and they're useless over the long haul. You can meet the nutritional needs of your entire family, elderly members included, by adopting the simple, practical goals of the McGovern Committee and following the more recent recommendations of the Human Nutrition Center of the U.S. Department of Agriculture.

DIETARY GOALS

1. <u>Eat a variety of foods.</u>
2. Eat foods rich in starch and fiber.
3. Maintain your ideal body weight.
4. Avoid too much fat, saturated fat, and cholesterol.
5. Avoid too much sugar.
6. Don't use a lot of salt.
7. Don't drink a lot of alcohol.

What is a lot? What is too much? It's up to you—the idea is not to prescribe exact amounts but to provide practical guidelines for a healthy diet. The ideal diet (again, a guide—please don't try to reproduce the numbers exactly at every meal) derives 30 percent of its calories from fat (10 percent each from saturated, monounsaturated, and polyunsaturated fat), 12 percent from protein, and 58 percent from carbohydrate (10 percent refined sugar and 48 percent complex carbohydrate). Table sugar is a simple carbohydrate. Complex carbohydrates are found in most plant foods, including fruits, vegetables, and foods derived from grain, such as pasta and breads. As for fats, the more saturated they are, the firmer they are at room temperature; for example, butter fat, with more than 50 percent saturation, is a solid at room temperature. More important, saturation is an inverse measure of chemical reactivity. The more saturated a fat is, the less reactive it is and the more it sits around your body damaging your heart and blood vessels. Saturated fats tend to increase the amount of cholesterol in your blood. The cholesterol, in turn, is deposited on the walls of your arteries, which increases your likelihood of developing atherosclerosis and having a heart attack or stroke. Certain foods, including organ meats (especially brains), egg yolks, and shrimp, are rich in cholesterol, and when eaten in excess they can raise your blood level dangerously high. Most Americans eat too much fat, cholesterol, and refined sugar and not enough fiber and complex carbohydrate—so you can't go wrong if you simply reduce the fat, cholesterol, and sugar content and increase the carbohydrate and fiber content of your whole family's diet.

Goal number one is underlined for good reason; it is the most important one. If you follow this rule alone, you'll probably eat well and have a nutritious diet. Eating a varied diet is the best way to avoid nutrient deficiencies, especially vitamin deficiencies, and it's the only way to guarantee a well-balanced diet. Snackers are often well nourished for this reason; the food they eat is not always the best (though no food is all bad if it's eaten in moderation), but they eat enough of an assortment to meet all their nutritional needs. Variety also protects us against accumulating toxic doses of the dangerous substances naturally found in many foods, such as arsenic in seafood and the poison solanine in potatoes. Even essential nutrients such as vitamins A and D become toxic when they're consumed in large quantities, and a varied diet guards against accumulating them as well.

In the past we were taught to obtain all our necessary nutrients from the "basic seven" food groups, and later from the "basic four" food groups. The basic four—meat, fruits and vegetables, milk and dairy products, breads and cereals—are still with us, and good meals can still be prepared by mixing and matching servings from them. But today we are interested not only in supplying the necessary nutrients, but also in avoiding them in excessive amounts. The American diet is unhealthy more because of its excesses than because of its deficiencies. That's why we need a scheme that classifies food with unwanted nutrients such as refined sugar, salt, and saturated fat in mind. The Center for Science in the Public Interest has done just this, replacing the "basic four" food groups with "anytime," "in moderation," and "now and then" foods (Table 2-1). Fat, including lots of saturated fat, accounts for at least 50 percent of the calories in "now and then" foods, while "anytime" foods have less than 30 percent fat. The virtue of this scheme is that it's simple and easy to use: Eat anything you want anytime from the "anytime" category, enjoy but don't overdo the "in moderation" foods, and treat yourself to "now and then" foods on special occasions. If you follow this guide and accept the seven dietary goals as a philosophy of nutrition, you will find yourself effortlessly preparing nourishing and appetizing meals for the entire family; and the basic family diet will be nutritious and easy to modify for any special needs of your elderly friend or relative.

Table 2-1 New American Eating Guide

ANYTIME	IN MODERATION	NOW AND THEN
	BEANS, GRAINS, AND NUTS *(4 or more servings per day)*	
Bread and rolls (whole-grain)	Cornbread[8]	Croissant[4, 8]
Bulgur	Flour tortilla[8]	Doughnut[3 or 4, 5, 8]
Dried beans and peas	Granola cereals[1 or 2]	Presweetened cereals[5, 8]
Lentils	Hominy grits[8]	Sticky buns[1 or 2, 5, 8]
Oatmeal	Macaroni and cheese[1, (6), 8]	Stuffing (with butter)[4, (6), 8]
Pasta, whole-wheat	Matzoh[8]	
Rice, brown	Nuts[3]	
Sprouts	Pasta, refined[8]	
whole-grain hot and cold cereals	Peanut butter[3]	
Whole-wheat matzoh	Pizza[6, 8]	
	Refined, unsweetened cereals[8]	
	Refried beans[1 or 2]	
	Seeds[3]	
	Soybeans[2]	
	Tofu[2]	
	Waffles or pancakes with syrup[5, (6), 8]	

White bread and rolls [8]
White rice [8]

FRUITS AND VEGETABLES
(4 or more servings per day)

All fruits and vegetables except
   those at right
Applesauce (unsweetened)
Unsweetened fruit juices
Unsalted vegetable juices
Potatoes, white or sweet

Avocado [3]
Coleslaw [3]
Cranberry sauce [5]
Dried fruit
French fries [1 or 2]
Fried eggplant [2]
Fruits canned in syrup [5]
Gazpacho [2,(6)]
Glazed carrots [5,(6)]
Guacamole [3]
Potatoes au gratin [1,(6)]
Salted vegetable juices [6]
Sweetened fruit juices [5]
Vegetables canned with salt [6]

Coconut [4]
Pickles [6]

(continued)

Table 2-1 (Continued)

ANYTIME	IN MODERATION	NOW AND THEN
	MILK PRODUCTS	
	(3 to 4 servings per day for children, 2 for adults)	
Buttermilk (from skim milk)	Cocoa with skim milk [5]	Cheesecake [4, 5]
Low-fat cottage cheese	Cottage cheese, regular [1]	Cheese fondue [4, (6)]
Low-fat milk (1%)	Frozen yogurt [5]	Cheese soufflé [4, (6), 7]
Low-fat yogurt	Ice milk [5]	Eggnog [1, 5, 7]
Nonfat dry milk	Low-fat milk (2%) [1]	Hard cheeses: [4, (6)]
Skim-milk cheeses	Low-fat yogurt, sweetened [5]	blue
Skim milk	Mozzarella, part-skim [1, (6)]	brick
Skim-milk and banana shake		Camembert
		cheddar
		muenster
		Swiss
		Ice cream [4, 5]
		Processed cheeses [4, 6]
		Whole milk [4]
		Whole-milk yogurt [4]

POULTRY, FISH, MEAT, AND EGGS

(2 servings per day; vegetarians should eat added servings from other groups)

Cod	Fried fish [1 or 2]	Fried chicken, commercial [4]
Flounder	Herring [3, 6]	Cheese omelet [4, 7]
Gefilte fish [(6)]	Mackerel, canned [2, (6)]	Whole egg or yolk (limit to 3 a week) [3, 7]
Haddock	Salmon, canned [2, (6)]	Bacon [4, (6)]
Halibut	Sardines [2, (6)]	Beef liver, fried [1, 7]
Perch	Shrimp [7]	Bologna [4, 6]
Pollock	Tuna, oil-packed [2, (6)]	Corned beef [4, 6]
Rockfish	Chicken liver [7]	Ground beef [4]
Shellfish, except shrimp	Fried chicken in vegetable oil (homemade) [3]	Ham, trimmed [1, 6]
Sole	Chicken or turkey, boiled, baked, or roasted (with skin) [2]	Hot dogs [4, 6]
Tuna, water-packed [(6)]	Flank steak [1]	Liverwurst [4, 6]
Egg whites	Leg or loin of lamb [1]	Pig's feet [4]
Chicken or turkey, boiled, baked, or roasted (no skin)	Pork shoulder or loin, lean [1]	Salami [4, 6]
	Round steak or ground round [1]	Sausage [4, 6]
	Rump roast [1]	Spareribs [4]
	Sirloin steak, lean [1]	Red meats, untrimmed [4]
	Veal [1]	

[1] Moderate fat, saturated.
[2] Moderate fat, unsaturated.
[3] High fat, unsaturated.
[4] High fat, saturated.
[5] High in added sugar.
[6] High in salt or sodium.
[(6)] May be high in salt or sodium.
[7] High in cholesterol.
[8] Refined grains.

Source: Developed by the Center for Science in the Public Interest. A full-color poster of this guide can be obtained from CSPI, 1755 S Street NW, Washington, DC 20009.

FIBER

Fiber is not a single substance; it is all the indigestible material in plant food: cellulose, hemicelluloses, pectins, gums, mucilages, and lignin. It's found in the leaves, stems, roots, and seeds of plant food. In the past, when America was a farming country and cereals, legumes, tubers, and roots were plentiful, our diet was rich in fiber, but with the introduction of food processing, canning, and freezing, the fiber content of our diet dropped to pitifully low levels. The milling process removes large quantities of fiber from cereals and grains, while peeling and boiling remove fiber from fruits and vegetables.

The low-fiber diets of industrialized western countries have been linked to the high prevalence of certain diseases in these countries. Heart disease, colon cancer, diabetes, cholesterol gallstones, hiatal hernia, diverticulitis, varicose veins, and hemorrhoids are virtually nonexistent in third world countries, where high-fiber diets are the rule. Fiber is apparently protective, and the return to a high-fiber diet could possibly eliminate many of the ills of western people.

Fiber from whole grains and cereals absorbs water—up to three times its weight—and forms a gel. This softens the stool, increases its bulk, speeds the transit of food through the digestive tract, and increases the frequency of bowel movements. This natural laxative effect of fiber protects against constipation and prevents straining during defecation, which has been implicated in causing, and which aggravates already existing, diverticular disease, hemorrhoids, and varicose veins. Fiber protects against colon cancer through its bulking action, which dilutes carcinogens, and by hastening the passage of food through the gut, which cuts down the contact time between carcinogens and the bowel. Fruit and vegetable fibers contain soluble gums and pectins that interfere with the metabolism of carbohydrates, fats, and cholesterol. These fibers, not cereal fibers, are important in preventing diabetes, heart disease, and gallstones.

Unfortunately, changing to a high-fiber diet late in life will not cure any diet-related disease already present, but it will reduce the discomfort from such disease and will possibly prevent flare-ups and further deterioration. Fiber-rich foods alleviate constipation and impaction, and protect polyps, diverticula, and hemorrhoids from additional irritation. Fiber has no calories, and fiber-rich food tends to be low in fat, so an added benefit is protection against obesity.

The highly fermentable fibers of fruits and vegetables produce gases, including hydrogen and methane, in the large bowel; this can cause discomfort during the first weeks of a high-fiber diet. Bloating and diarrhea can also occur during this period. Fiber can bind minerals as well as water, but this is seldom a problem for elderly people, as long as their diet remains well balanced and varied. If your family is presently eating a typical American diet, you can safely double the fiber content. Increase the fiber gradually over a period of weeks. But don't use it as a food additive, indiscriminately sprinkling bran (which is the worst diarrhea troublemaker) over all the dishes. Instead, use a variety of high-fiber foods: whole grains, cereals, fresh fruits, and raw vegetables.

Present evidence indicates that our diet is too high in fat, sugar, and salt and too low in fiber and complex carbohydrates. Dr. Denis P. Burkitt, the epidemiologist who brought the health benefits of fiber to the world's attention, has recommended doubling the amount of carbohydrates and fiber we eat, halving the amount of sugar and salt, and reducing the amount of fat by one-third. These simple and specific recommendations, which are consistent with the McGovern Committee's dietary goals, if followed, would go a long way toward preventing the diet-related illnesses that plague the western industrialized nations.

CALCIUM

Calcium is necessary for the normal contraction of muscles, the clotting of blood, the activation of enzymes, and the formation and maintenance of strong bones. Bones are actually a storehouse for calcium; when the diet is deficient in calcium, the body raids the skeleton to meet its needs. Too many raids will deplete the storehouse and eventually weaken the skeleton. Even with adequate calcium in the diet we lose bone throughout life. Beginning in the 20s and 30s and accelerating for women after menopause, bone loss leads to lighter, weaker, and more fragile bones in late life (a condition known as *osteoporosis*). The reasons are complex and incompletely understood. Many factors contribute to the absorption of calcium from the gut, to its survival in bone, and to its excretion in urine. Genetics and nutrition interact with exercise and medications to determine the fate of calcium in the body and the integrity of bone. Hormone deficiencies; nutrition factors; lack of exercise, and the use of cigarettes, alcohol, and drugs all speed the loss of calcium from bone, whereas hormone supplements, increased activity, adequate supplies of calcium, and reduced amounts of phosphorus prevent or at least slow the loss. Once bone is lost, it is gone forever. Estrogens, vitamin D, and fluoride supplements will retard the loss of additional bone. But estrogens increase the risk of cancer of the uterus, and vitamin D and fluoride are toxic in high doses, so before an elderly person begins taking these medicines, he or she should discuss the risks and benefits with a physician. At home, regardless of the physician's prescriptions, you can begin a program that will arrest or slow further bone loss. An increase in the person's daily activity level is critical. Bone responds to activity, movements against gravity, and weight bearing by growing—and it weakens and atrophies in response to immobilization and disuse. Phosphorus has recently been implicated in the mystery of bone loss, and elderly people are well advised to avoid excessive amounts. Junk foods, especially soda pop, are dangerously high in phosphorus. Finally, adequate amounts of calcium must be included in an elderly person's diet. Milk and dairy products are the richest sources of calcium, but certain seafoods—especially sardines, oysters, and salmon—and green leafy vegetables such as spinach, kale, and broccoli are also good sources. The official RDA of calcium is 800 milligrams per day, but this can and should be increased to at least 1 gram for elderly people who are at risk for loss of bone and who can ill afford a mineral deficiency. A varied diet that includes calcium-rich food will satisfy this requirement.

SALT AND OTHER FLAVORS

Ordinarily we enjoy the sight, the texture, the smell, and the taste of food. But with age our senses deteriorate, depriving us of the physical pleasures of food. Many elderly people thus lose their interest in eating. All four taste sensations—salty, sweet, bitter, and sour—deteriorate, but the sweet and salty tastes are probably the first and most profoundly affected, accounting for the frequent complaint from elderly people that their food is sour and bitter. To overcome blunted taste and smell sensations, you have to season foods liberally with herbs, spices, and condiments. It takes more seasoning for elderly people to obtain the same taste pleasures from food that young people obtain. The salty taste is a special problem because of the health hazards associated with high salt intake. Elderly people with diagnosed high blood pressure should be on low-salt diets, and the rest of the elderly would be wise to avoid excessive amounts of salt. Combinations of sodium and potassium chloride or potassium chloride compounds alone are salty tasting and are good alternatives to table salt, but they are dangerous for people with liver or kidney disease. The healthiest substitutes for salt are mixtures of herbs, spices, and juices; garlic, paprika, and pepper, which are readily available; and lemon juice and lime juice, which are especially good on green salads and fresh vegetables. Holly H. Shimizu, writing in the *FDA Consumer*, recommended the following herb blends to replace salt:

SALT ALTERNATIVES

SALTLESS
SURPRISE

2 teaspoons garlic powder and 1 teaspoon each of basil, oregano, and powdered lemon rind (or dehydrated lemon juice). Put all ingredients into a blender and mix well. Store in a glass con-

tainer, label, and add rice to prevent caking.

PUNGENT SALT SUBSTITUTE — 3 teaspoons basil; 2 teaspoons each of savory (summer savory is best), celery seed, ground cumin seed, sage, and marjoram; and 1 teaspoon lemon thyme. Mix well, then powder with mortar and pestle.

SPICY SALTLESS SEASONING — 1 teaspoon each of cloves, pepper, and coriander seed (crushed); 2 teaspoons paprika; and 1 tablespoon rosemary. Mix ingredients in a blender. Store in an airtight container.

For a copy of her article, "Do Yourself a Flavor," write to Department of Health and Human Services, Public Health Service, Food and Drug Administration, 5600 Fishers Lane, Rockville, MD 20857.

IT TAKES MORE THAN NUTRITIOUS FOOD

Nutritionally balanced meals themselves don't guarantee nutritional health—the meals must be eaten to work. And many elderly people are fussy eaters, resisting menu changes and refusing to try new foods. Often they have eating habits and food preferences which are nutritionally unwise but which they won't give up. Chewing difficulties are common, and medical and dental problems, poorly fitting dentures, and medicines all can change the taste of food and interfere with its enjoyment.

The most common cause of chewing dysfunction, poorly fitting dentures, is easily corrected with a trip to the dentist.

Other causes of chewing dysfunction, such as mouth sores, periodontal disease, muscle weakness, and jaw pain, are not so easily corrected, and the chewing problem must be overcome with specially prepared meals. Cook foods that are nutritious and easy to chew—boiled chicken, vegetable stews, tender meat stews, and the like. Remember that small pieces are easier to chew than large pieces—even sandwiches can be taken apart and cut into tiny slices. And mushy foods such as chopped and mashed vegetables, cooked cereals, and milkshakes (a lot of calories, but also a lot of nutrients) are trouble-free.

Snacking is a treat for everyone, and elderly people are no exception. Snacking can also be beneficial. For example, an elderly person who has trouble sleeping often benefits from smaller dinners and bedtime snacks. The trouble with snacking is the snacks, which are usually fattening or highly salted. Rather than discourage the practice, which is with us for good, get rid of the fattening and salty snacks and stock your cupboards and freezer with healthful foods. Avoid such standard highly salted snacks as luncheon meats, processed cheeses, crackers, pretzels, potato chips, and nuts. Fresh fruit, vegetables, and whole-grain breads are the best snack foods—high in nutrients and low in calories.

An elderly person's nutrition can go awry, in spite of sensible eating habits. Drugs are often at fault, sometimes decreasing the absorption of needed nutrients, other times increasing their excretion, and occasionally contributing excessive amounts. Effervescent drugs like Alka Seltzer and Bromo Seltzer are the worst offenders: A single dose of Alka Seltzer contains more than a gram of sodium. Over-the-counter antacids are also unexpected sodium providers. Riopan contains the smallest quantity (2 milligrams per dose) and is the antacid of choice for people on sodium-restricted diets. Mineral oil is an unacceptable laxative for elderly people when there are so many other fine products on the market. Mineral oil dissolves the fat-soluble vitamins A, D, E, and K and carries them through the digestive tract, preventing their absorption by the body. Aspirin, in high doses, increases the excretion of vitamin C and potassium. Most diuretics also increase the excretion of potassium, and possibly calcium, magnesium, and the B vitamins thiamine and pyridoxine, while digoxin may increase the excretion of calcium and magnesium. Anyone taking a diuretic should eat foods rich in potassium: most vegetables and fruits, but especially bananas and oranges.

DIETING

Elderly people need the same nutrients (protein, minerals, vitamins, carbohydrates, and fat) in almost the same quantities as younger people, but they need fewer calories. They are usually less active and need fewer calories to support their activities. Also, basal metabolic rate, which is a measure of the energy the body needs to keep itself idling, declines about 20 percent from ages 20 to 70, and this can account for differences of hundreds of calories. Therefore, food must be chosen that is nutrient-rich and calorie-poor; otherwise extra calories will be consumed in meeting the nutrient requirements. Eating calorie-dense and nutrient-free food—junk food—is always nutritionally pointless, but late in life it is also risky, since there's no room for empty calories: It's too easy to get shortchanged on nutrients and overstuffed with calories, and too many elderly people are overweight for this reason.

Carrying around extra pounds makes us feel tired and sloppy. It also jeopardizes our health. Extra pounds mean more work for the heart and lungs, and more weight on the bones and joints. Heart disease, breathing difficulties, diabetes, and arthritis are just some of the medical problems brought on or made worse by being overweight. When we're trim, we're healthier, and we look and feel better. But dieting is not the way to lose weight. For one thing, it's seldom helpful. For every 100 pounds Americans lose by dieting, 95 pounds go back on within the year. For elderly people, dieting can be harmful as well as ineffective. Since most diets rely on either the diuretic effect (fluid loss caused by restriction of carbohydrates) or the starvation principle (fasting), dieters lose a lot of fluid or a lot of protein along with the fat. Elderly people can't afford to lose fluid or protein indiscriminately. When drying you out and starving you don't work, diets simply bore you into losing weight with monotonous, unappealing meals. Elderly people can't compromise on their nutrition. They can't afford to lose needed nutrients while they're losing calories. Elderly people have to abandon nutritionally unbalanced crash diets and instant solutions to their overweight problems. They have to develop a patient, philosophical approach to weight loss and aim at losing no more than 1 to 2 pounds each week. The foundation for safe and successful weight loss is a way of life that incorporates nutritionally sound eating habits, preferably in accordance with the seven dietary goals we've listed. Then, when it's time to lose extra pounds, you don't alter your usual healthful diet— you simply eat less. Also, successful weight loss always combines an increase in activity level (to burn off extra calories) with a decrease in calorie intake.

MENUS

An example of a week's worth of good eating follows. The menus were prepared by the U.S. Department of Agriculture, which publishes them, along with recipes, in the pamphlet *Ideas for Better Living*. You can get your own copy by writing to the Superintendent of Documents, U.S. Government Printing Office, Washington, DC 20402. If your elderly friend or relative binges one day or skips a meal another day, don't worry. Good nutrition is measured over weeks not days. It's the adequacy of a week's worth of food that is important not the day-to-day ups and downs.

MENU 1

1600 CALORIES		2400 CALORIES

BREAKFAST

1600		2400
¾ cup	Orange juice (fresh or frozen)	¾ cup
None	Egg (soft-cooked)	1 large
2 slices	Banana nut bread	2 slices
½ cup	Milk (skim, fortified)	1 cup
	Water, tea, or coffee	

Banana nut bread is a change of pace from plain toast. The 2 slices have about the same number of calories as a sweet roll, but more vitamins and minerals. The banana nut bread can be low in fat and sugar and should be made with whole-wheat flour.

BROWN BAG LUNCH

1600		2400
1 sandwich	Tuna salad sandwich: 2 oz tuna, packed in water; 1 tbsp chopped celery; 1 tsp chopped onion; 2 tsp mayonnaise; 2 slices whole-wheat bread	1 sandwich
1 medium	Pear (fresh)	1 medium
1 cup	Milk (skim, fortified)	1 cup

DINNER

1600		2400
4 oz	Pot roast (chuck, lean only)	4 oz
¾ cup	Mashed potatoes	¾ cup

The tuna is packed in water. The beef is trimmed of fat. Both steps lower the overall fat content of the menu.

½ cup	Green beans (fresh or frozen)	½ cup
1 cup	Spinach salad	1 cup
1 tbsp	Italian dressing	1 tbsp
1 slice	Italian bread (enriched)	2 slices
1 tsp	Margarine (soft)	1 tbsp
½ cup	Orange-pineapple cup (fresh)	1 cup
	Water, tea, or coffee	

SNACKS

¼ cup	Chili bean dip	½ cup
1 cup	Raw vegetable sticks: carrot, celery, and green pepper sticks	1 cup
None	Whole-wheat crackers	5 to 6 average
None	Juice (or a piece of fresh fruit)	12 oz
	Water, tea, or coffee	

MENU 2

1600 CALORIES		2400 CALORIES
	BREAKFAST	
½ cup	Strawberries (fresh or frozen, unsweetened)	½ cup
2 biscuits	Shredded wheat	2 biscuits
½ medium	with sliced banana	½ medium
None	Sugar	1 tbsp
1 cup	Milk (whole, 2% lowfat; fortified)	1 cup
	Water, tea, or coffee	
	FAST FOOD LUNCH	
1 sandwich	Hamburger/cheeseburger:	1 sandwich
2 oz	ground beef	3 oz
None	American processed cheese	¾ oz
1 bun	enriched bun	1 bun
½ cup	Coleslaw, with mayonnaise-type salad dressing	½ cup
1 small serving	French fries	1 large serving
8 oz	Juice (or a piece of fresh fruit)	8 oz

The kind of milk is your choice. When you use whole milk in one meal, you might be more moderate in your use of other fats.

DINNER

1 serving	Chicken cacciatore	1 serving
1/2 cup	Spaghetti, enriched	1 cup
1/2 cup	Zucchini, cooked fresh	1/2 cup
1 1/2 cups	Mixed green salad: iceberg lettuce, spinach, green onions, cucumbers	1 1/2 cups
1 tbsp	Italian dressing	1 tbsp
1 slice	Italian bread (enriched)	2 slices
1 tsp	Margarine (soft)	2 tsp
None	Pear (fresh)	1 medium
None	Pineapple juice (unsweetened)	1 cup

SNACKS

None	Graham crackers	2 squares
1/2 cup	Milk (whole, 2% lowfat; fortified)	1/2 cup
1 medium	Tangerine (fresh)	1 medium

Check your recipe—the skin should be removed to lower the fat content. No fat or oil should be used in cooking the chicken.

No fat or salt should be added to the zucchini. For added zest, try lemon juice, caraway seed, or marjoram.

Salad dressings add calories and sodium. Be moderate in your use of them.

MENU 3

1600 CALORIES		2400 CALORIES
BREAKFAST		
¾ cup	Orange juice (fresh or frozen)	¾ cup
None	Scrambled egg	1 large
1 bagel	Bagel	1 bagel
1 tbsp	Cream cheese	2 tbsp
None	Jam	1 tbsp
1 cup	Milk (skim, fortified)	1 cup
	Water, tea, or coffee	
BROWN BAG LUNCH		
1 sandwich	Sliced chicken sandwich:	2 sandwiches
2 oz	sliced chicken	3 oz
1 leaf	lettuce	2 leaves
2 tsps	mayonnaise-type salad dressing	3 tsp
2 slices	whole-wheat bread	4 slices
1 serving	Bean salad	1 serving
None	Apple (fresh)	1 medium
	Water, tea, or coffee	

For safety's sake, keep the sandwich cold until you're ready to eat it.

The bean salad adds starch and fiber to the meal (so does the whole-wheat bread in the sandwich).

DINNER

	Food	
1 serving	Vegetable chowder	1 serving
1 serving	Baked fish with spicy sauce	1½ servings
½ cup	Broccoli spears (fresh or frozen)	½ cup
½ cup	Brown rice	½ cup
1½ cups	Mixed green salad: iceberg lettuce, spinach, green onions, cucumbers	1½ cups
1 tbsp	French dressing	1 tbsp
½ cup	Grapes (seedless)	1 cup
	Water, tea, or coffee	

SNACKS

	Food	
1 serving	Gingerbread	1 serving
None	Pear (fresh)	1 medium

Raw and cooked vegetables are good sources of fiber.

The brown rice and the whole-wheat flour in the gingerbread add starch and fiber to the day's menu.

Fruits with edible skins and seeds are good for their fiber.

27

MENU 4

1600 CALORIES	BREAKFAST	2400 CALORIES
¼ medium	Cantaloupe	¼ medium
1 large	Egg (soft-cooked)	None
1 average	Corn muffin	2 average
None	Margarine (soft)	2 tsp
None	Jelly	2 tsp
½ cup	Milk (whole, 1% lowfat; fortified)	1 cup
	Water, tea, or coffee	

Some sugars in the diet are easy to spot—jelly and marmalade, for example. Others are not so obvious, like the sugar in muffins and yogurt.

LOWER CALORIE LUNCHEON

1 sandwich	Ham and cheese sandwich: 1 oz lean ham, 1 oz natural swiss cheese, 2 slices rye bread, 2 tsp mayonnaise-type salad dressing, lettuce	
1¼ cups	Tossed salad: lettuce, tomato, carrots, green onions	
1 tbsp	Italian dressing	
1 medium	Orange (fresh)	
	Water, tea, or coffee	

HIGHER CALORIE LUNCHEON

Pork chop (lean only)	1 large chop
Black-eyed peas, rice (enriched)	½ cup each
Hard roll (enriched)	1 large roll
Margarine (soft)	1 tsp
Sliced peaches (canned in syrup)	½ cup
Apple cider	¼ cup

The higher calorie diet has more room for added sugar, such as the sweetened syrup in canned peaches.

DINNER

Flounder Florentine	1 serving
Baked potato	1 medium
Sour cream	2 tbsp
Green peas (frozen)	½ cup
Whole-wheat roll	1 small roll
Margarine (soft)	1 tsp
Vanilla yogurt (lowfat) mixed with strawberries (fresh or frozen, unsweetened)	4 oz / 8 oz ½ cup
Water, tea, or coffee	

The sugar in flavored yogurt raises the calorie count. Yogurt with fruit preserves has even more sugar in it. We have added our own fruit.

SNACKS

English muffin (enriched)	1 whole muffin
Margarine (soft)	2 tsp
Marmalade	1 tbsp

29

MENU 5

1600 CALORIES		2400 CALORIES
BREAKFAST		
½ medium	Grapefruit (fresh)	½ medium
2 slices	Whole-wheat toast	2 slices
1 tsp	Margarine (soft)	1 tsp
None	Jelly	1 tbsp
1 cup	Milk (skim, fortified)	1 cup
	Water, tea, or coffee	
BROWN BAG LUNCH		
6 oz	Tomato juice (canned)	6 oz
1 serving	Luncheon salad:	1 serving
None	turkey	2 oz
None	ham	1 oz
1½ cups	mixed greens	1½ cups
1½ oz	Swiss cheese (natural)	1½ oz

There's salt in the tomato juice, as there is in most canned vegetables.

Ham, like most cured or processed meats, adds salt—so a moderate amount should be used.

30

1 tbsp	French dressing	1½ tbsp
1 serving	Corn bread	1 serving
1 small	Peach (fresh)	2 small
	Water, tea, or coffee	

Check your recipe—go easy on the salt.

DINNER

4 oz	Broiled ground beef (lean)	4 oz
½ cup	Corn (fresh or frozen)	1 cup
½ cup	Green beans (fresh or frozen)	½ cup
None	Rye rolls	2 rolls
None	Margarine (soft)	1 tsp
1 serving	Baked apple with 2 tsp brown sugar	1 serving
	Water, tea, or coffee	

To keep the amount of sodium down, no condiments are added to the ground beef—no catsup, mustard, pickles, or the like. Try some chopped fresh onions or tomato for a do-it-yourself relish.

Instead of salt, experiment with lemon juice, spices, and herbs for flavor.

SNACKS

None	Peanut butter sandwich: 2 slices whole-wheat bread, 2 tbsp peanut butter, 2 tsp jelly	1 sandwich
3 squares	Graham crackers	None
8 oz	Juice (or a piece of fresh fruit)	8 oz

MENU 6

1600 CALORIES		2400 CALORIES
	BREAKFAST	
¾ cup	Orange juice (fresh or frozen)	¾ cup
2 cakes	Whole-wheat pancakes	3 cakes
½ serving	Blueberry sauce	1 serving
1 cup	Milk (1% lowfat, fortified)	1 cup
None	Margarine (soft)	2 tsp
	Water, tea, or coffee	
	LUNCH AT HOME	
1 taco	Beef taco	2 tacos
¾ cup	Fresh fruit cup: oranges, apples, banana	¾ cup
½ cup	Milk (1% lowfat, fortified)	1 cup

Orange juice, a rich source of vitamin C, improves the body's ability to use the iron in the whole-wheat pancakes.

DINNER

4 oz	Roast loin of pork (lean only) 4 oz
1 small	Sweet potato (baked) 1 medium
½ cup	Collard greens (fresh or frozen) ½ cup
1¼ cups	Tossed salad: lettuce, tomato, green onions, carrots 1¼ cups
1 tbsp	Italian salad dressing 1 tbsp
1 biscuit	Biscuits (enriched) 2 biscuits
None	Honey 1 tbsp
1 tsp	Margarine (soft) 2 tsp
	Water, tea, or coffee

The lean roast pork makes the iron in the sweet potato, collards, and biscuit more useful.

SNACKS

4 squares	Graham crackers 4 squares
8 oz	Juice (or a piece of fresh fruit) 12 oz
None	Apple (fresh) 1 medium

MENU 7

1600 CALORIES		2400 CALORIES
BREAKFAST		
1/2 cup	Pineapple chunks (packed in own juice)	3/4 cup
1/2 cup	Oatmeal with cinnamon and raisins	1 cup
None		3 tbsp
1 tsp	Brown sugar	2 tsp
1/2 cup	Milk (whole, 1% lowfat; fortified)	1 cup
	Water, tea, or coffee	
LUNCH AT HOME		
1 serving	Split pea soup	1 serving
1 serving	Chicken salad stuffed tomato: 2 oz cooked, chopped chicken; 1 tbsp chopped celery; 1 tsp chopped onion; 2 tsp mayonnaise; 1 medium tomato	1 serving

The lowfat milk used here reduces calories without reducing essential nutrients.

3 crackers	Rye crackers	6 crackers
None	Margarine (soft)	2 tsp
None	Lemon sherbet	¾ cup
	Water, tea, or coffee	

DINNER

1 serving	Beef with Chinese-style vegetables	1½ servings
½ cup	Rice (white, enriched)	¼ cup
1 serving	Apple crisp	1 serving

SNACKS

2 slices	Banana nut bread	2 slices
1 cup	Milk (whole, 1% lowfat; fortified)	1 cup
1 medium	Orange (fresh)	1 medium

At 1600 calories, you can't afford many foods that are high in sugar and low in vitamins and minerals.

Apple crisp will fit in if you use a recipe low in fat and sugar.

Snacks are for eating anytime. You could have the banana nut bread and milk at bedtime, and the orange in the afternoon. You could drink the milk at lunch or during your break, instead of coffee.

3 Exercise

Exercise is a buzzword today. Everyone is exercising. There are joggers, Nautilus Centers, and Universal Gyms in every town in America. Health spas and tennis, squash, and racquetball clubs are more popular than ever before. Every morning you can wake up to the pounding rhythm of an aerobic workout on television. Or you can work out, following one of the many exercise-your-way-to-health-and-beauty books written by Hollywood stars. There are also records, tapes, and video cassettes. All this action has even given rise to a new medical specialty, sports medicine, to treat all the physical problems created by the new enthusiasm.

Exercise is a great thing for most people. It keeps them fit, makes them stronger, increases their endurance, and lets them do more, more easily. There is even evidence suggesting that vigorous exercise, begun early enough in life, reduces the risk of heart disease. However, there is no evidence that exercise will turn back the clock, guarantee eternal youth, unclog blocked arteries, or cure chronic diseases. Exercise is preventive, not curative. And while it makes good sense for young people to incorporate vigorous exercise programs into their lives, there is no reason for elderly people to do the same. Elderly people need activity, not formal exercise programs and workout schedules. They have to keep moving, stay out of bed and away from their favorite chairs. An elderly person's heart, lungs, and circulation can't respond to added stress very well, and simple activities, such as walking a few blocks, that are done without thinking by young people, are actually serious exercises for the elderly. A slow walk for an out-of-shape elderly person can be the equivalent of an all-out run for someone younger.

In the following pages we'll discuss the differences between exercise and activity, why activity is so important, and the principles you should follow in setting up an activities program for an elderly person. Once again the virtues of common sense and the benefits of home care will be apparent.

EXERCISE VERSUS ACTIVITY

The only reason to take an elderly person to an exercise spa is for socializing, kibbutzing with friends and neighbors, talking about the weather, politics, health, or whatever. It's the nonexercising that's helpful. The exercise part can all be done at home with no equipment and at no expense. And, except during convalescence after a serious illness or hospitalization, there is no need for visits by physical therapists—you know enough to take your friend for a walk!

Exercise is physical activity codified, circumscribed, and packaged for specific training effects. Elderly people don't need the training effects, but they do need the activity. They need to do something physical that gives them pleasure, relaxation, companionship, and a sense of well-being: simple, unstructured physical activity chosen for its enjoyment. That's all—very simple and very easy.

Physical activity is vital. It improves psychological well-being; it also provides physiological benefits and prevents the total body deterioration that comes with prolonged inactivity. The body needs to be moved; if it isn't, it breaks down. The body's admonition to us is, "Use it or lose it." Muscles waste away if they aren't used; joints become less flexible. Protein breaks down, and calcium gets leached out of the bones. After a few weeks of bed rest, the bones actually soften and fracture more easily. Strength and flexibility are lost, and tasks that were once easy become formidable. Speed and coordination are lost as well, and fine motor skills deteriorate. Endurance rapidly disappears, and everything becomes a chore. The heart, lungs, and circulation show some of the most dramatic changes. When they are not challenged and forced to support an active body, their capacities to respond in unusual situations and to increased demands are lost. For example, a task as simple as standing up becomes a difficult and perhaps dangerous endeavor after a few weeks in bed, because the cardiovascular system loses its ability to pump blood fast enough to supply the brain when the body is in the upright position.

A sedentary life only aggravates the loss in physical capacity that naturally accompanies aging. Being active is the only way to prevent wasting away and to maintain the capacity for an involved, independent life. Inactivity and normal aging are a dangerous combination, because the physical capabilities necessary for an independent life—strength, endurance, speed, and coordination—are rapidly lost. Add illness to inactivity and aging and the situation is devastating.

We all know that it's easy to gain weight and practically impossible to lose it; on the other hand, it's difficult to gain strength and endurance but easy to lose them. Activity must be constantly maintained. Even a few days of inactivity take their toll. Inactive muscles, for example, lose their strength twice as fast as exercising muscles gain strength. Aerobic capacity, which is the maximal amount of oxygen that the body uses in an all-out effort, also deteriorates rapidly when not challenged, and is built up only slowly.

DAILY ACTIVITY LEVEL

As we've already emphasized, elaborate exercise programs for the elderly are a luxury and a matter of taste, not a necessity. The necessity for the elderly is activity, and a useful concept is the daily activity level. After age 65 we're not concerned with maximal oxygen uptake, submaximal heart rate, caloric expenditure, carbohydrate loading, and the like. Maintenance of an active life is all that counts, plain and simple, and this can be ensured by planning for a number of pleasant and useful activities throughout the day.

Don't forget that, since aerobic capacity decreases with age, the oxygen demands of an ordinary walk take a bigger chunk of the aerobic capacity pie every year. Simple activities such as walking often become aerobic exercise in disguise!

Dressing, bathing, and grooming also consume bigger pieces of the oxygen pie each year and should be included in any accounting of daily activities. Making the bed, helping with the dishes, preparing snacks, and light housekeeping are all useful, healthful activities. These household chores and personal hygiene responsibilities, combined with walks after meals or in the late afternoon, produce a solid, basic daily activity level.

The basic activity level can be modified for individual preferences and capabilities. Many elderly people still play squash
and enter marathons, and for them walking around the block
as a way of staying fit would be boring and almost silly. On
the other hand, for those who are housebound, confined to bed,
or ill, a walk would be too taxing.

A typical day for a healthy but normally and naturally slowed
down elderly person begins by eight in the morning. He or she
washes up, has breakfast, and gets dressed—all as independently as possible. The bed is made, and then it's time for a
rest, perhaps sitting with the morning papers in a favorite chair.
The only thing more important than activity for an elderly
person is rest. Rest periods must be liberally spaced throughout
the day. No activity should proceed more than an hour without
an interval for rest, and all activities must be followed by rest.
There is no reason to tax or fatigue elderly persons, and every
reason not to. They've paid their dues; now it's time for them
to relax and enjoy.

To continue with the day's activities, after the morning papers it's time for more activity—helping with the dishes, perhaps, or doing some light housework. Next is a leisurely lunch
followed by a short walk—about ¼ to ½ mile—and another
well-deserved and appreciated rest. Afterward the household
chores can be tackled. Pressing shirts, dusting furniture, peeling vegetables, setting the dinner table, or preparing a salad
for dinner are all possibilities. Dinner itself is a good time for
the family to catch up on the day's events. After dinner, help
with the dishes is always appreciated; and afterward, watching
television, listening to the radio, reading, or simply talking
makes for a pleasant and relaxing evening. A late-night snack
follows, and a bath before retiring is a soothing way to end the
day.

The only exercise in this typical day is the short walk after
lunch, yet the daily activity level is high. Dressing, grooming,
bathing, and doing the dishes and some light housework make
for a full day. Activity at this level will maintain the physical
fitness of an elderly person and prevent the dangers of inactivity. Moreover, it will keep the person involved, stimulated, and
helpful.

Think of your own life for a moment. The quality of your life
depends on being active and independent. For the elderly, the

physical capabilities needed for a vital, high-quality life can be guaranteed with a daily activity program maintained at a sufficiently high level and composed of individual activities chosen for pleasure alone. The idea is not to add years to life, which is impossible with exercise alone, but, in the words of the late George Morris Piersol, M.D., to add life to years. This is, in the last analysis, the relaxed, commonsense approach to fitness after age 65.

CLOTHING AND EQUIPMENT

Magazines are filled and billboards are plastered with advertisements for special exercise clothing and equipment. If there's lots of extra money lying around your house and if the social security checks are used only for pocket money, then the elderly person in your house can be outfitted in a designer sweatsuit (available in all colors of the rainbow) with matching headband and wristbands and a color-coordinated workout jacket. Fashion and Madison Avenue aside, however, the only article of clothing that needs special attention is shoes. Especially for exercise, shoes must be comfortable. Don't buy uncomfortable shoes that look great with the hope that they'll stretch and mold and, in time, come to tenderly caress your feet. Everyone should take the foot test, which is described in Chapter 6, "Grooming," before getting a new pair of shoes.

One additional word about clothing. Elderly people have less efficient temperature-regulating systems and decreased sensitivity to temperature changes, compared with young people. Therefore, they find it harder to tell when the temperature rises and falls, and their bodies have trouble adjusting to the extremes of hot and cold. To complicate matters, elderly people have impaired perspiration, which is a critical mechanism for dissipating heat and cooling the body. All this means that an elderly person must dress appropriately for the weather, especially when exercising. In hot weather, light-colored, loose-fitting permeable clothing should be worn to reflect the sun's heat, circulate air, and encourage evaporation. In cold weather, clothing should be layered so that an insulating layer of air lies between garments.

✝PRECAUTIONS

Like everything good, activity and exercise also have some bad sides. Activity and exercise, in spite of promoting fitness and health, have risks associated with them. We have already mentioned the elderly's poor response to the environmental extremes of hot and cold, which predisposes them to hypothermia (low body temperature) on the one hand and heat stress, exhaustion, and heat stroke on the other. Proper clothing and modifications of activity programs in the winter and summer months should eliminate these problems. Very often, mental changes are the first sign of both low and high body temperature. Confusion, agitation, and somnolence are warning signs, and the simplest way to check on these problems is to take the temperature! It's normal for body temperature to rise a few degrees Fahrenheit during exercise. Any drop in temperature, whether in the winter or summer, is a danger signal—the exercise should be stopped and the family doctor called. An increase of more than 3° or 4° Fahrenheit during exercise should put you on alert, and exercise intensity should be reduced, especially when there are also mental changes. Sweating must not be interfered with. Lots of drugs do interfere with sweating, the most common being the anticholinergics and antihistamines, which are especially common in over-the-counter cold remedies, drugs for Parkinson's disease, and drugs for psychiatric disorders. All activities in hot weather must be approached cautiously by a person taking any of these drugs. When a person is properly dressed, the normal activities of daily living should not throw his or her temperature-regulating system out of whack. Still, it is important to know the dangers, no matter how remote they are.

Problems with the heart and lungs are more common complications of excessive activity and exercise. You don't have to become a cardiologist to supervise housework, light activities, and walks in the neighborhood. Of course, if a more intensive exercise program is contemplated, a medical examination is required. If any activity becomes uncomfortable, your friend should stop it and rest. Difficulty in breathing, breathlessness, chest pain, dizziness, and faintness are warning signs and must be respected; the person should rest, start up again slowly, and if the symptoms return, stop, lie down, and relax. If light activities bring on these problems, it's time for your friend to see a doctor, since they are the body's way of saying that the heart is overworked and in trouble. Of course, chest pains and breathing difficulties can also come from muscle spasms, cramps, sprains, strains, and aching joints, but it's best to be careful.

If your friend insists on participating in a formal exercise program, make sure that all workouts start with a warm-up period of at least ten minutes duration and end with a cool-down period of another ten minutes. A person is most at risk for hurting muscles and joints at the beginning of a workout and for developing heart problems at the end of a session. Also, exercise should be approached cautiously. An elderly person who has been sedentary for a long time should begin exercising modestly and work his or her way up to a physically demanding session slowly over time. This is especially true for the aging athlete who, in a burst of enthusiasm, is apt to ignore the years of inactivity and expect to participate at his or her former level.

4 *Understanding the Elderly*

At birth we are almost indistinguishable from one another. As we grow and develop, our personalities emerge, and the challenges of life sharpen our individual differences in behavior, interests, and abilities.

This process of change naturally continues as we age. But we don't go mad or become stupid, cantankerous, nasty, or weird. Wisdom isn't guaranteed either. Well-adjusted men don't become dirty old men at age 65, and serious, responsible women don't turn into cute little old ladies on their 65th birthday.

Myths about old people and prejudices against them are widespread. But, in fact, it's impossible to generalize about elderly people because they are so different from one another. It's easier to generalize about adolescents and young adults, because the individualizing process of life hasn't had time to complete its work—the concerns, interests, and backgrounds of adolescents and young adults are fairly uniform. When it comes to the elderly, however, we can safely talk only about individuals, and the only thing we can say for certain is that people change as they age. Your elderly friend or relative is different today from what he or she was thirty years ago. An 80-year-old man is not the same person he was at 25. His sight and hearing have declined, and he's weaker, slower, and less coordinated. His immediate memory has declined, his recall ability is diminished, and it takes longer for him to learn new material. Nonetheless, he may be stronger, faster, and better coordinated than a 25-year-old neighbor, and he may also be more alert, have a better memory, and learn more quickly than his neighbor. The changes we undergo as we age can be great, but the differences between people of the same or different ages can be even greater.

Don't prejudge anyone over age 65. In America, more than 2000 people turn 65 each day. They don't all suddenly become slow, dim-witted, forgetful, and crotchety. Not only is there nothing magical about the 65th year of life, there's nothing characteristic about people over 65, except that they are all different from their former, younger selves—but people over 35, 45, or 55 are also different from their former selves.

The idea of grouping people into groups such as *adolescents*, *young adults*, or *elderly* is useful for demographic, sociological, and political purposes because it helps us understand averages and trends, but it's unfair and useless for communicating and relating on a one-to-one basis. Relating to a person as a member of a group imposes the group's identity and average characteristics on the person. Elderly people, like the rest of us, are individuals and should be treated that way. Your elderly friend or relative is not simply a live-in representative of the elderly; he or she is an individual with a unique identity.

Besides the fact that average traits are not individual traits, there is seldom agreement on what the averages are in the first place. Your perception of a group, influenced by your own background, prejudices, and experience, can be entirely different from your neighbor's view of the same group. For example, some people, ever hopeful for eternal life, optimistically deny the changes that accompany aging, while others, forever bitter over the loss of youth, pessimistically exaggerate the same changes. These different views, in turn, influence the optimist's and pessimist's response to elderly people (Table 4-1).

Throw away your preconceptions, your expectations, prejudices, and judgments. Find out what kind of person your friend or relative is. Take the time to listen and observe. Learn about his or her hopes, fears, and plans for the future. Make it your business to know your friend's likes and dislikes, and to understand his or her strengths and weaknesses.

MENTAL CHANGES

Surely you've heard someone remark, upon seeing a well-groomed, attractive older woman, "She's so well preserved." This is an expression of the prejudice against elderly people and a reflection of the widespread misunderstanding of aging

---

TABLE 4-1   OPTIMISTS AND PESSIMISTS

SITUATION	PESSIMIST THINKS	OPTIMIST THINKS
An old man fails to cross the street before the traffic light changes.	"Oh well, what do you expect of an old man?"	"If he exercised more, he could certainly do better."
An old woman starts to retell an account of the birth of her first child.	"I don't have time to waste hearing this story again."	"If I listen, she will feel better and become more able to deal with the present."
A senator, age 71, appears on the evening news as a result of making a speech against mandatory retirement.	"That man is a remarkable exception to the way most old people are."	"More old people could be like that man if they tried."
An elderly woman arrives at the Social Security office only to find it closed for a federal holiday.	"Forgetting to call is typical of old people."	"With wider publicity she would not have made that mistake."

Source: Anna Gera Yurick, Barbara Elliott Spier, Susanne S. Robb, and Nancy J. Ebert: *The Aged Person and the Nursing Process*, 2d ed., Appleton-Century-Crofts, Norwalk, Conn., 1984, p. 117.

and the aged. Mummies are well preserved, not attractive women. The point is that while all of us change in various ways throughout life, we all start from different places and change at different rates. Men and women don't look old for their age any more than they look young for their age—they look themselves. For some of us our youthful looks change imperceptibly over time; for others it is mental agility or athletic prowess that changes slowly. But eventually, the slow imperceptible changes add up and differences become apparent. Change is inevitable.

We've already talked about the muscles weakening, bones becoming fragile, and joints stiffening. But the mental changes are the most difficult for us to understand and accept.

Generally speaking, mental processes slow down with age. You don't become less intelligent with the years, but you do become slower, requiring more time to complete complicated mental tasks, assimilate new material, and learn new skills. Absorbing, organizing, and recalling new information become more difficult; response times increase; and mental processes of all types fatigue more easily. You become more distractible and less able to filter out irrelevant information, and at the same time you lose the ability to shift attention easily from one subject to another.

All these changes make for slower, more hesitant, and less decisive thinking, which is often mistaken for lack of intelligence—which it isn't. Mistaking the slow, cautious thinking of older people for stupidity or confusion is more a reflection of our own impatience than of their intelligence level. Old people are no less intelligent than their younger counterparts. They are more cautious and less nimble with new ideas, but they are no less able. They can learn new information, adapt to new environments, and even change old behavior patterns—it just takes them longer and there are more distractions and interruptions along the way.

What happens to memory with aging? You've probably noticed your friend or relative forget the name of a person or a place from the past day, only to remember it with ease the following day. This type of forgetfulness—minor memory lapses for the details, but not for the essentials, of the past—is common in the later years.

There are three types of memory, depending on when in the past the event being remembered occurred: Immediate memory covers events only a few seconds old, recent memory covers several days of the past, and remote memory stretches back for years. Memory, whether immediate, recent, or remote, is a complicated mental function that requires acquiring, storing, and recalling information. The normal decline of memory with age affects the storage and recall components, so that recent and remote memory are primarily affected. For example, forgetting names and places from the past, a problem in recall ability, is a disturbance in remote memory. Forgetting what you ate for breakfast or where you put the car keys is a disturbance in recent memory and is either a recall or storage problem.

Of course, if an older person doesn't pay attention to what's going on, or if he or she is too tired to concentrate, or if there are too many distractions, then the information to be remembered won't even be noticed, let alone be stored and recalled. That's why when you present elderly people with new information, it's important not to overload their circuits with useless information or long and fatiguing instructions, and to avoid interruptions and distractions. Keep it simple, direct, and unhurried.

Unfortunately, any disturbance of memory in an elderly person, however slight, terrifies us with the thought of dementia and the picture of a friend or the person slowly losing touch with reality. Most memory changes are part of the normal aging process, however, and are not signs of impending madness. Forgetting details from the past and misplacing everyday objects are normal occurrences in the later years, not warning signs of approaching senility. Sometimes the difference between normal and abnormal memory changes can be unclear. Normal changes are usually temporary and not serious, and they affect details rather than essentials. They don't interfere with work and social life, and, unlike the memory changes of dementia, they aren't part of a global pattern of mental deterioration and personality and behavior breakdown. To forget where you put your slacks is normal and inconsequential, but to forget to put them on is another, more serious story.

✕ DEMENTIA

Dementia is a terrifying condition that devastates the lives of those it affects. Judging from recent media coverage, one would think that dementia was a modern plague, an epidemic ravaging the minds of everyone over age 65. The truth is that about 5 percent of the elderly are affected, and while this amounts to nearly a million people, most of the elderly are unaffected and enjoy an alert, robust old age. Dementia is not the inevitable consequence of a long life. It is an abnormality, a radical departure from the minor memory lapses and shortened attention span of normal aging. It is not madness; it is an intellectual impairment severe enough to alter a person's daily life. Dementia is not a single disease; it is a collection of symptoms that affect memory, language, reasoning ability, personality, and behavior. There are hundreds of situations and diseases that can cause these symptoms, but Alzheimer's disease is by far the major culprit.

At least 50 percent of the elderly people with dementia are suffering from Alzheimer's disease, which was named for Alois Alzheimer, a German pathologist who first described the disease in 1907. In spite of intensive research efforts, the cause of this disease is still unknown. In the early stage of the disease, memory problems may be all that are noticed. The person affected may forget to turn off the oven or to take morning medicines; he or she may begin to repeat sentences, forget common names, or make mistakes balancing the checkbook. At this stage it can be difficult to identify the memory problems as symptomatic of a dementing illness and not simply as part of normal aging. But with dementia the memory problems worsen, and personality changes also occur. The person may become less spontaneous, apathetic, and even withdrawn. As the disease progresses, abstract thinking, language, and motor abilities deteriorate. The person may have trouble following a conversation and understanding explanations. He or she may get lost frequently. Reading becomes difficult, and even tasks that were once easy become difficult and are abandoned. Organizing the day's activities becomes next to impossible, judgment deteriorates, and language problems go from bad to worse until the person is no longer able to express himself or herself. Coordination may deteriorate, eating may become difficult, and even handwriting may change. The person may stoop while walking, walk more slowly, or walk with a shuffle. Concern for personal hygiene and appearance may also decline, and uncharacteristic behavior and mood swings, such as angry outbursts, irritability, and agitation, may appear. Late in the disease, the person may be unable to recognize family members or utter more than a few words. The demented person may wander; fall frequently, become uncooperative, inattentive, and incontinent. In the final stage of the disease the person is physically and mentally impaired and totally dependent. Alzheimer's disease leads to death in about ten years, though sometimes the inexorable decline is slower and sometimes more rapid.

Many conditions mimic the early symptoms of dementia. If

there is any question in your mind that your friend is suffering from more than normal aging, a complete medical evaluation is necessary. While Alzheimer's Disease is incurable at this time, many of the other causes of dementia are curable, or at least reversible, with proper treatment. Physical illnesses such as heart and lung disease, tumors, and metabolic disorders lead to dementia that is quickly reversed by correcting the underlying physical condition, but that persists and worsens if the physical problem is left untreated.

Sometimes a change in mental status occurs abruptly, consciousness becomes acutely impaired, and confusion sets in. This is delirium, not dementia, and there is always an underlying treatable cause for it. Alcohol, drugs, infections, metabolic disturbances, and cardiovascular disorders are some of the more common causes. Dementia does not develop overnight or in a few days, the way delirium does, and a demented person, though intellectually impaired, is alert and fully conscious, whereas a delirious person is drowsy, with decreased awareness and a clouded consciousness. If your friend or relative shows a decrease in his or her level of consciousness, get medical help immediately. Delirium is reversible, but long-term damage can occur if the underlying cause is left unchecked.

The most common and troubling dementia impostor is depression. A depressed older person is easily mistaken for a demented one, because the memory loss, decreased attention span, social withdrawal, apathy, and irritability of depression closely resemble the symptoms of dementia. Pseudodementia, which is a severe form of depression that affects the elderly, easily masquerades as the real thing. The crucial difference is that depression is treatable and the dementia-like symptoms it causes can be reversed. The key is to recognize depression for what it is and treat it appropriately. Whenever an elderly friend or relative begins to act out of character or show unexpected memory losses or mental deterioration, depression must be considered a possible cause and a search must be made for unresolved emotional conflicts.

A person with suspected dementia should be under the care of a physician. It is to be hoped that a reversible cause of the mental deterioration will be found and treated. But if not, if Alzheimer's disease or another untreatable cause is at fault, a physician is still needed to manage complications, treat other illnesses, and keep everyone informed about the latest research and treatment options. More important than the physician's counsel are the family's commitment, understanding, and expectation of what lies ahead. Men and women afflicted with Alzheimer's disease are transformed from vital human beings into helpless inhabitants of a private world. Peaceful men and women can become violent and flamboyant, and energetic ones can become meek and withdrawn; the person you have known and loved for so long can disappear behind a vacant look. Words cannot express the agony a family feels when a loved one is taken from them this way. But if the disease cannot be cured, the person can still be comforted, cared for, made secure, and loved.

All of the suggestions we've made in this book for helping elderly people adjust to their physical impairments and medical problems apply to people with Alzheimer's disease as well. For the special problems that this disease creates there are scores of resource books. Two of the best are *The 36-Hour Day* by Nancy L. Mace and Peter V. Rabins, M.D., and *Caring: A Family Guide to Managing the Alzheimer's Patients at Home* developed by Fredericka Tanner, M.P.H., with Sharon Shaw, C.S.W. (see Appendix F for details of publication). Another worthwhile resource is the Alzheimer's Disease and Related Disorders Association, New York City (1-800-621-0379).

Basically, when someone with a dementing illness is living with you, you should try to keep your home orderly and stable, with a place for everything and everything in its place. People with dementing illnesses are distractible, they're easily confused, and they have trouble learning new information. The last thing in the world you want is for your home to be distracting and frustrating, instead of soothing and comforting.

A PRACTICAL APPROACH

What can you do about the mental changes that accompany aging? Can they be stopped? Is there any way you can lessen their impact or slow their course? And what do you do when the hand of fate strikes your friend or relative with an irreversible disease like Alzheimer's disease?

In medicine there is an old proverb that says that we can cure rarely, relieve occasionally, but comfort always. This applies to all of us, regardless of our profession, when it comes to the mental changes of our elderly friends and relatives. Today, there is no cure for Alzheimer's disease or for several other dementing diseases, but that does not mean that we must give up and abandon our loved ones to cope with the ravages of the disease alone. We can be there to comfort them and make life easier.

As for the normal mental changes of aging, there is probably no way to stop them, but common sense tells us that a mentally stimulated, active, and vital person has a better chance of keeping his or her faculties intact than does an isolated and withdrawn person.

Elderly people are close to the end of their lives and they are aware of this fact, even when the rest of us are too timid or embarrassed to talk about it. Ambition and accomplishment give way to comfort and security as concerns of life. Reminiscing about past accomplishments takes the place of planning for future ones.

It's easy to provide a physically comfortable and safe environment for your elderly friend or relative. Many of the underlying principles will be discussed in Chapter 7, "The Five Senses," and practical suggestions for modifying your home will be given in Chapter 8, "The Environment."

But for assurance of a comfortable, high-quality, vital life for your loved one, psychosocial and emotional adaptations are as important as physical ones.

When it comes to a fulfilling emotional life, old people have the same needs as young people. They must feel good about themselves and feel loved and appreciated by others. They must be hopeful about the future and have as much control as possible over their destinies. Finally, the simple truth is that a fulfilling and vigorous life is possible only when self-esteem is high. Part of your job will be to support and encourage a positive self-image and a strong feeling of self-worth on the part of your elderly friend.

If your friend likes to reminisce about the past, encourage that activity. Keep old family albums around the house and display old pictures in prominent places, especially the ones that flatter your friend—vanity is one thing that never ages! Family heirlooms, familiar objects, and mementos can spark conversations that will make it easy for your friend or relative to talk about past successes without being criticized for bragging or clinging to the past. When young children are in the home, everyone benefits. Kids love to hear about their family's history from the older members who made the history. And older people relish the company of youngsters—it makes them feel younger, they enjoy the limelight, and they like sharing their experiences. But most of all, it shows them that someone is interested in their lives and cares about them. The attention and love promote positive, creative feelings for everyone.

Plants are another helpful addition to your home. Not only do they keep the air moist and decorate the house, but their care is fulfilling work that fosters a sense of responsibility and pride of accomplishment. And as everyone who has worked with plants knows, nurturing a plant's growth is a rejuvenating and comforting experience.

Pets also foster a sense of responsibility, and they're loyal companions as well. They are loving and affectionate, and their dependence on human care generates feelings in their masters and mistresses of being needed and valued.

As important as responsibility, meaningful work, and nurturing activities are for a person's self-esteem, nothing rivals the importance of control over one's destiny and independence in one's life.

When your friend moves in with you, your natural instinct will be to do whatever you can to help. You'll probably start organizing the day, planning meals, decorating the room, scheduling outings, and the like. Be careful not to foster a dependent attitude. Remember that your friend had a comfortable way of life for many years before moving in with you. Encourage that way of life in your home—it's easy and familiar and it has passed the test of time. Take every opportunity to champion self-reliance and independence. Too many well-intentioned sons and daughters, in efforts to help their parents live comfortably, have promoted dependent behavior instead, and have unwittingly eroded their parents' self-esteem. Don't overdo your help. If it's needed, provide it, but resist the temptation to do everything yourself. People feel best when they're in charge of their own lives.

Encourage your friend to develop outside relationships, to join special interest groups and service organizations, to visit friends away from home, and to invite friends back to the house. Help him or her to remain as independent as possible.

Another thing to remember is that although your friend is moving in with you, he or she can still be a help to you. How many sons and daughters have relied on their parents for babysitting? How many couples have gotten child-rearing, legal, or financial advice from their parents? Whenever experience and practical, commonsense advice are needed, give your friend or relative a chance to help. A half or three-quarters of a century of life give a person a unique perspective that is worth hearing about.

Many elderly people living alone are lonely and also realize that their physical condition limits their independence and restricts their world. Yet because of their pride, their reluctance to impose on others, and their will to remain in control of their lives, they hide their needs and endure a restricted world as an inevitable part of life. You can help, not by catering to every whim and whimsy, but by providing an environment and an atmosphere in which your friend can live as independently as possible within the limits of his or her physical capabilities. This is an evolving situation, because as the years take more and more away, you'll have to do more, but always with an eye toward letting the skills and faculties that remain compensate for the ones that are lost.

Diseases of the mind, such as Alzheimer's disease, are in the hands of fate, and until we know more about their causes, there is little we can do to avoid them. But the mental changes that accompany an inactive, unstimulated life are avoidable. And even the normal losses that the years exact can probably be slowed, if not entirely resisted, by maintenance of an active, alert, and challenging mental life. Use it or lose it applies to the mind no less than to the body.

Sophisticated neuropsychological methods aren't needed to help elderly people maintain active mental lives. Talking with them, soliciting their advice, and involving them in family affairs are simple day-to-day activities that keep the cobwebs away by stimulating and challenging the mind. A home that fosters a sharing atmosphere in which each person's unique talents and contributions are respected also inspires each person to remain alert, to organize projects, develop hobbies, read and talk about ideas, discuss current events and community affairs, or engage in whatever else strikes his or her fancy.

But what do you do when your loved one's memory starts

to slip in spite of a stimulating home environment? First off, put a large calendar and clock in the bedroom to remind him or her of the time, day, month, and year. If necessary, a list of the day's activities can also be hung in the bedroom. Frequently used objects can be labeled, and warning signs and safety instructions can be written out and displayed prominently. Anything that jars the memory is useful, from simple written reminders to flash cards, pictures, and even a rubber band tied around a finger. It's always easier to remember something if you have a cue than it is to remember on the spot without help. If things get very bad, you can even put up signs around the house identifying different rooms or reminding your friend of important activities: signs such as BATHROOM, BEDROOM, WASH YOUR FACE, TIE YOUR SHOES, and so on.

There are also tricks that anyone with a decline in memory should try. It's always easier to remember lists of things by classifying the items and remembering them as groups. It also helps to say out loud whatever you want to remember. And associating the things to be remembered with mental images— the stranger and more bizarre the images the better—always reinforces the memory. Who could forget a twelve o' clock appointment with Mr. Smith if the appointment evoked the image of a bearded man with twelve candles on top of his head sitting in the middle of a clock?

Your friend's memory may continue to slip away, in spite of your interventions and his or her efforts. This can be upsetting, but you musn't become discouraged or overwhelmed. Accept it as part of life, make the best of it, and, if you can, laugh at it. Enjoy the other aspects of your friend's personality, and encourage a positive, optimistic outlook. There is no better antidote for life's adversities than hope and a sense of humor.

SEXUALITY AND AGING

Sexual interest is one of the few things that doesn't decline with age. Sexual activity is another story, however, because it often does decline, though usually for psychological rather than physical reasons. Elderly people think about sex, they dream about it, they enjoy it, and they're biologically capable of it. The problem is that society has ignored or ridiculed their sexual interests for so long that many of them have come to feel guilty or embarrassed about their natural yearnings. It's true that our sexual responses slow down with age, but they are not obliterated, and our physical capacity for sex remains intact. All physical functions slow with age, but in matters of sex, slow responses may actually be an asset. The longer it takes to achieve an erection or reach an orgasm, the longer lovemaking lasts and the more time is available for physical intimacy and psychological closeness.

When problems with sexual performance do arise, more often than not they are psychological or social and no different from the problems that affect young people. Several studies, including ones by Kinsey and by Masters and Johnson, have identified the six most common reasons for waning sexual responsiveness: preoccupation with work and economic burdens, mental and physical fatigue, mental and physical infirmity, excessive eating or drinking, boredom with a monotonous sex life, and fear of failure. The simplest way to avoid most of these problems is to create an open and easy atmosphere at home where your friend or relative is at ease and comfortable enough to talk about personal problems and sexual concerns. When it comes to psychological problems, talking is the best, and often the only, medicine.

Of course there are other causes for decreased sexual functioning besides psychological and social problems. Medications, especially blood pressure and antidepressant drugs, are prime offenders. Your friend or relative should be informed about the side effects, sexual and otherwise, of any drug he or she is taking. Most doctors are more than willing to help in this regard. The American Medical Association publishes fact sheets on all the commonly prescribed drugs. And if the doctor is unavailable, the pharmacist is another resource.

Many chronic diseases are associated in the public's mind with the loss of sexual function. Only a few uncommon diseases actually destroy a person's capacity for sex, and heart disease and arthritis, the ones usually blamed, are not among them. Although anyone who has suffered a heart attack should get medical clearance for sexual activity, generally if a person can walk up two flights of stairs without trouble, he or she can have sex. As for arthritis, if the usual and customary positions are impossible, awkward, or painful, the only thing standing in the way of more comfortable positions is your friend's (and his or her partner's) imagination.

Also, don't believe the myth that good sex must be spontaneous. For people with arthritis or other painful conditions, planning is the key to a happy sex life. Sex should be planned for the time of day when they feel best. A warm shower or bath before sex will loosen up the joints, reduce pain, and make lovemaking easier and more enjoyable, and properly timed and planned medications will further reduce pain, ease discomfort, and improve sex.

Remember that the safest and surest way to preserve sexual ability is to maintain a pattern of regular sexual activity. Encourage your friend or relative to stay involved with the opposite sex, to talk about problems when they arise, and above all, not to be embarrassed about the natural human desire for companionship and physical closeness, or to feel guilty about the natural human need to be loved and feel wanted.

SLEEP PROBLEMS

Few things in life are sweeter than a good night's sleep. Sleep unburdens the mind, refreshes the body, and rejuvenates the spirit. For most of us it is a treat, a well-earned reward, a happily awaited pleasure at day's end. But for many elderly people sleep is more a problem than a pleasure. Insomnia is common, and complaints about unsatisfying sleep, fitful nights, and drowsy days abound.

Nobody knows for sure how much sleep we need each day. Some scientists suspect that America is a sleep-deprived nation, that we're all walking around drowsier and slower than we should be because we haven't slept enough. Since it's impossible, at this time, for anybody's sleep needs to be quantified, the most sensible approach is to sleep enough to be wide awake, alert, and refreshed throughout the next day.

Elderly people sleep about the same amount as young people, but their pattern of sleep is different. You've probably noticed your friend or relative napping in the afternoon, or perhaps he or she has complained to you about waking up too early in the morning or getting drowsy after dinner. These are all variations on the usual young and middle-aged scheme of one uninterrupted block of nighttime sleep. Several factors account for the changes, the most important of which is that our sleep gets lighter as we age, and the deep, difficult-to-penetrate stages of sleep occupy less and less time with each succeeding year. Consequently, brief awakenings during the night become common. All of us awaken during the night, usually only for seconds at a time, and we seldom remember these nighttime interruptions in the morning. But the number and length of awakenings increase with age, and by age 60 we're probably spending triple the time awake at night as we did at age 20. Sleep scientists have counted more than 150 awakenings during the night in elderly people, whereas the average 20-year-old awakens only 10 times. The need for sleep doesn't change much with age, but the ability to sleep changes dramatically.

If your friend is waking up hundreds of times during the night, there is no doubt about his or her need for an afternoon nap. You and your friend have to realize that the young and middle-aged eight-plus hour sleep block is no longer realistic at age 65 and that sleep time must be parceled out in smaller segments. Unfortunately, many elderly people, along with their friends and relatives, don't realize that fragmented sleep is normal in the later years. Not only do they insist on one long bout of sleep and try to do away with naps, they also view the changing sleep pattern as a problem, a sign of insomnia, or something worse. The point is that the adequacy of yesterday's sleep should be judged by today's sense of well-being, not by its resemblance to a young person's sleep pattern. As long as your friend feels refreshed and alert today, it's irrelevant whether he or she napped yesterday afternoon, slept only three hours last night, or woke up at four in the morning. Of course, if your friend had a nine-to-five job, he or she couldn't nod out in the afternoon, but in that case your friend would probably be so tired by nighttime that he or she wouldn't wake up so often during the night or so early in the morning, and consequently wouldn't need the afternoon nap. If your friend enjoys napping and it doesn't interfere with his or her work, household activities, or social life, why worry about it? Our bodies and physical needs change throughout life, and there is no reason to impose the sleep patterns (or anything else for that matter) of a working middle-aged person on a retired elderly person who, if given the chance, will respond naturally to his or her body's needs and gracefully adopt the sleep pattern most compatible with his or her own biology and lifestyle.

Moreover, insomnia is what you make of it. It is not a specific disorder; there is no simple treatment, no magic drug. It is a symptom, a personal feeling about the quality of sleep. The insomnia that your friend or relative complains about today could well be the same pattern of sleep that he or she has happily tolerated for years, only now a change has occurred in his or her life (added stress, an illness, new worries) that has made sleep more desirable and rendered the old pattern unsatisfactory.

When the need or desire for more sleep is genuine, a lot can be done to help. First of all, common sense tells us to make the bed and bedroom as comfortable and as conducive to sleeping as possible—which means no creaky bedposts, sagging or bumpy mattress, or broken, jabbing springs that attack during the night. It also means a firm, comfortable mattress, light, airy blankets, fresh sheets, and enough fluffy pillows to cradle the head and make breathing easy. Also, the bedroom should be well ventilated, neither too hot nor too cold, and at bedtime it should be quiet with the lights out or dimmed. Preparing for sleep doesn't hurt either. A glass of hot milk before retiring is an age old cure for insomnia. A warm bath or a light snack before bed can be relaxing. Listening to poetry or soft music or taking a short walk are soothing activities. And praying not only relaxes the mind but also soothes the spirit.

As helpful as some activities can be in promoting sleep, others can be just as harmful in preventing it. Caffeine (coffee, tea, and cola) may keep you up, as may a large meal or strenuous exercise before bedtime. Too much smoking is also harmful As for alcohol, while a hot toddy before bedtime reputedly induces sleep, too much of a good thing is definitely not good—excessive drinking before bedtime is dangerous. Drinking not only prevents restful sleep but also interferes with breathing and dulls the senses and protective reflexes. Medication can be another problem. For example, if your friend or relative is taking a diuretic (a water pill), it is best if the pill is taken early in the day rather than late at night so that he or she won't have to get up at night to use the bathroom. Pain pills should be timed to give relief during the night and prevent pain from awakening the person. But here again too much of a good thing is dangerous, because pain medicines can dull the senses, reduce reflexes, and interfere with breathing.

Sleeping pills are a mixed bag. A sleeping pill will initially help anyone fall asleep, but often the price is confusion, drowsiness, memory loss, or a hangover the following day. Also, continued use of sleeping pills can lead to tolerance and dependence. Tolerance means that as time goes on, more and more pills are needed to do the same job that took only one pill in the beginning, and dependence leads to a rebound phenomenon, which is the appearance of a sleep disorder more severe than the original problem when the pills are abruptly stopped. The message is clear: Sleeping pills will put you to sleep, but since they also do so many other dangerous things (such as interfering with your breathing and causing confusion), it's best to avoid them.

More sleep is lost in worrying about problems generated during the day than for any other reason. While worrying keeps more people awake than any other reason, worrying about emotional conflicts, unresolved arguments, and frustrations is only part of the problem. The biggest worry of all is whether tonight is going to be another sleepless night. An entire night can slip by while a troubled insomniac lies awake tossing and turning and wondering whether this will finally be the night for sleep. The tragedy is that fears about sleeplessness are self-fulfilling prophesies. Worrying about falling asleep tonight may keep your friend awake tonight, and, having stayed awake tonight, he or she will worry about falling asleep tomorrow night, and so stay awake again, and then worry again the following night, and so on until he or she eventually collapses. Rather than waiting to collapse, an insomniac can stop the cycle in other ways. Encourage your friend to go to bed when he or she is sleepy, not before. The bed should be used for sleeping, not for worrying. Trying to force oneself to sleep is a prescription for failure and frustration. Instead, your friend should wait until he or she is tired, and then unwind with a glass of milk, a nonalcoholic drink, or a snack; take a bath, listen to the radio, read a book, talk to someone, or just sit quietly in another room and clear his or her mind. Your friend can reduce the pressure to sleep by realizing that if tonight doesn't bring sleep, tomorrow night will. If your friend is worrying about lost sleep, encourage him or her to think about pleasant things such as grandchildren, past accomplishments, and favorite vacation spots.

If your friend or relative has a sleep problem that resists all commonsense approaches, he or she will have to consult a sleep specialist and probably be examined at a sleep laboratory or a sleep clinic. Since sleep disorders are being increasingly recognized as a major health threat, more and more sleep laboratories are appearing in all parts of the country. Ordinarily, a neurologist or psychiatrist will refer you to one, but you can also ask for a list of sleep clinics from the Sleep Research Center at Stanford University School of Medicine, Stanford, CA 94305.

DEATH AND DYING

Since elderly people are close to and aware of death, they're usually more accepting of it than the rest of us, who are far removed and either terrified or indifferent. By the time a person reaches the later years of life, he or she is prepared for death and no longer afraid of it. But the process of dying can still be, and often is, frightening. People are scared of dying alone. They're also afraid of dying in pain. But most of all, they're scared of losing control over themselves and their world when death finally comes. They want to be in charge of their destinies, make their own decisions, and meet their own needs, but they fear that at the end they will be overwhelmed by disability and dependence. Here is where you can help by being responsive to your own feelings, being sensitive to your friend's or relative's wishes, and striving to keep the lines of communication open. A person who is approaching death is eager to talk about it but often feels cut off, because the rest of us are too busy feeling sorry, embarrassed, or scared to carry on a conversation. Your first step in helping your friend or relative cope with death is to examine your own feelings and come to terms with your own fears about death. Only then will you be free to talk openly and to comfort someone who is facing death. You don't want to reassure your loved one by denying the inevitable—nobody is helped when you tell a dying person not to worry because death is still far off. Instead, face the truth directly and realize that your gentle presence itself is reassuring. And in addition, you'll be at home and available to protect your loved one's dignity, to provide strength in moments of weakness, and to help him or her maintain a life that is as free and independent as possible for as long as possible. When you're caring for dying people it's easy to forget that making them comfortable and pain-free isn't the same as catering to their every need. The temptation to do everything and to make life as easy as possible is great, but must be resisted. People need to be in control of their own lives. Taking care of your personal needs yourself, even when you take longer to accomplish them and are more inefficient than anyone else, is ultimately more rewarding than relying on other people. In later years efficiency is not the issue— dignity and self-worth are.

Dying with dignity means living with dignity, which means, among other things, remaining in charge of your life, having your concerns heard and your wishes met. When it comes to practical matters, such as getting finances and business affairs in order, it's often easier for the dying person to talk about them than for the rest of the family. Easy or not, it's important to talk about these things before the person dies, in order to know his or her wishes and to avoid fights, legal battles, and uncertainties afterward. As the care giver, you should know the location of your friend's or relative's bank books, certificates of deposit, securities, insurance policies, savings bonds, pension plans, valuables, will, and other important documents. Someone in the house should also know how to reach the attorney who drew up the will and should have power of attorney in order to expedite matters during emergencies.

A will is an important document that should be drawn up by a lawyer and reviewed, and if necessary revised, every couple of years. It guarantees that a person's worldly possessions— the estate—will be distributed according to his or her wishes. It also identifies a person to administer the will and distribute the estate: the so-called executor or personal representative. A will is a written document of a person's wishes, which also protects the beneficiaries from court battles, legal fees, and taxes.

Another type of will that is gaining popularity today is the living will. This type of will, an example of which is given on page 63, has nothing to do with material possessions. It is a document that recognizes and tries to protect a person's right to refuse medical treatment and to determine the nature of his or her death. By signing a living will, a person makes known to the world that, in the event of a terminal illness with no hope of a cure, he or she does not want life needlessly prolonged by medicines, artificial means, or heroic measures. A living will is a vote for quality of life, as opposed to quantity of life. If your friend or relative is interested in a living will, the following are helpful resources:

> Concern for Dying
> 250 West 57th Street, Room 831
> New York, New York 10107
>
> Society for the Right to Die
> 250 West 57th Street, Room 929
> New York, New York 10107
>
> American Protestant Hospital Association
> 1701 East Woodfield Road
> Schaumburg, Illinois 60195
>
> Catholic Health Association of the U.S.
> 4455 Woodson Road
> St. Louis, Missouri 63134

When it's time for the will to be signed, have it notarized and witnessed by two adults who are neither relatives nor beneficiaries, put the original away for safekeeping, and send off a copy to the family doctor. Many states have "right-to-die" laws which establish the legality of living wills, but the majority of states have no such legislation. In these states, living wills are not legally binding, and their only benefit is to give people the opportunity to express their wishes about dying, which they hope will be respected by their families and doctors.

When a person dies, whether at home or in the hospital, a

My Living Will
To My Family, My Physician, My Lawyer and All Others Whom It May Concern

Death is as much a reality as birth, growth, maturity and old age—it is the one certainty of life. If the time comes when I can no longer take part in decisions for my own future, let this statement stand as an expression of my wishes and directions, while I am still of sound mind.

If at such a time the situation should arise in which there is no reasonable expectation of my recovery from extreme physical or mental disability, I direct that I be allowed to die and not be kept alive by medications, artificial means or "heroic measures". I do, however, ask that medication be mercifully administered to me to alleviate suffering even though this may shorten my remaining life.

This statement is made after careful consideration and is in accordance with my strong convictions and beliefs. I want the wishes and directions here expressed carried out to the extent permitted by law. Insofar as they are not legally enforceable, I hope that those to whom this Will is addressed will regard themselves as morally bound by these provisions.

(Optional specific provisions to be made in this space — see other side)

DURABLE POWER OF ATTORNEY (optional)

I hereby designate _____ to serve as my attorney-in-fact for the purpose of making medical treatment decisions. This power of attorney shall remain effective in the event that I become incompetent or otherwise unable to make such decisions for myself.

Optional Notarization:

"Sworn and subscribed to

before me this _____ day

of _____, 19_____."

_____
Notary Public
(seal)

Signed_____

Date _____

Witness _____

_____
Address

Witness _____

_____
Address

Copies of this request have been given to _____

_____

(Optional) My Living Will is registered with Concern for Dying (No. _____)

Distributed by Concern for Dying, 250 West 57th Street, New York, NY 10107 (212) 246-6962 doctor must see the body, pronounce the person dead, and sign a death certificate. If your family doctor is unavailable, call the county coroner or medical examiner. Once you are rested and in control of yourself, you can begin notifying friends and relatives. The days immediately after a loved one's death are filled with numbness, confusion, and disbelief, and many things are apt to go undone that later will create hurt feelings, resentment, and even legal problems. Make a list of the things you have to do, and go through it calmly, one step at a time.

Your loved one may have indicated a preference for burial or cremation. If that is so, you can go ahead with planning the funeral or memorial service. If you are overwhelmed by the process, you can ask for help from a memorial or funeral society, which is a nonprofit group that helps arrange simple burials. There are more than 200 such societies throughout the country, and they are a good resource for information about legal requirements and funeral costs. Look in the phone book for a local chapter or contact The Continental Association of Funeral & Memorial Societies, 2001 S Street NW, Suite 530, Washington, DC 20009. Funeral homes and other burial or memorial services will pick up and bury the body, do all the paperwork, and take care of all the legal requirements. Only funeral homes can arrange for embalming and cosmetic work, but if the body is buried within twenty-four hours of death or refrigerated until the burial, embalming is not usually necessary. If for some reason you don't want embalming, check with the medical examiner or county coroner's office to learn about your state's burial requirements.

5 Bathing

As people grow older, their range of daily activities decreases. Aging inevitably imposes limits on all of us. Stiffened joints, less acute sight and hearing, memory loss—to name but a few—are common changes that occur as time progresses. Because of these increasing limitations many older people must spend their days at home without enjoying the various activities that were once a normal part of life. As a result, routine activities like bathing can assume dramatic importance.

A bath not only cleanses the skin, it also relaxes and refreshes the whole person. Taking a little extra time to make certain that the bath is organized, the bathing area is safe, and the proper bathing articles are available can turn this simple activity into a luxurious experience for your friend. Keep in mind that you don't have to fuss to bring happiness to an older person. The occasional addition of a fragrant powder, a new after shave lotion or, best of all, a little hug can create long lasting pleasure.

The critical ingredient in any bathing program for an elderly person is consistency. While uncertainty and spontaneity are pleasures of youth, planned activities and fixed schedules are preferred by the elderly. Baths are best taken either in the morning before the day's activities begin or in the evening before bedtime. But once a time of day is set, you should stick to it.

The frequency of bathing depends on the individual and on the weather. Dry skin stays cleaner than oily skin and therefore needs less attention; more active people need more frequent bathing. Also, the warmer the weather the more frequent the need for bathing. As a rule of thumb, a weekly bath should take care of the hygiene needs of most people in winter, and two baths a week should suffice in summer. Baths for relaxation, of course, are entirely an individual matter.

BATH OR SHOWER?

A complete bath for a mobile person (see Chapter12, "Caring for the Bedridden," for details on the bed bath) involves either a shower bath or a tub bath. Lying in a warm tub is a pleasure for anyone. The problem is that older people have trouble getting in, and once in, often can't get out! Muscle weakness and joint stiffness turn the walls of the bathtub into barriers. Lying down in the bathtub is difficult and dangerous for anyone who is weak and unsteady. And standing up and renegotiating the tub walls after a warming and relaxing bath can be next to impossible. By no means should an older person be left alone in the house while taking a bath. If you can't be there yourself, make arrangements for someone else to be available. In fact, we discourage tub baths for all but the most active and conditioned individuals. Shower baths are much safer and equally relaxing. They too have drawbacks, but these can be remedied with slight architectural modifications.

A shower stall, of course, eliminates the need to step over the bathtub wall. But when a shower stall is unavailable and stepping over the tub wall is a problem, a tub-transfer seat is the answer (Figure 5-1). Take a look at the tub-transfer seat in the illustration. It is really two seats joined together so that one is outside the tub and the other is inside. The bather sits down on the outside seat, lifts one leg over the wall of the tub, and edges onto the tub seat so that he or she is sitting half on the outside seat and half on the tub seat. The bather then lifts the other leg over the wall of the tub and completes the move to the tub seat. The curtain is drawn and bathing begins. Practice this sequence of steps with your elderly bather until it is completely understood. Tub-transfer seats cost between $100 and $150, but for people who can't get into a bathtub any other way, they're well worth the price. They can be obtained from most medical supply houses.

In bathtubs without built-in showers, a personal shower consisting of a shower head and a flexible hose can be fastened to the tub faucet. Sometimes you'll have to modify the faucet for the hose to fit. Special adapters can be bought in most hardware

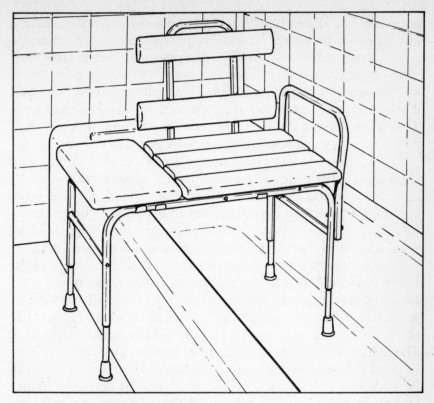

Figure 5-1. Tub-transfer seat.

stores. The shower head can be left on a wall bracket at any
convenient height.

SAFETY IN THE BATHROOM

The addition of an elderly friend or relative to your family
and home is usually accompanied by many anxieties and fears.
You worry about the person's getting proper nutrition, having
adequate rest and exercise, and avoiding illness. Most of all,
you probably worry about the person's safety. Although many
elderly people appear frail and unstable on their feet, appear-

ances can be deceiving. When the opportunity arises, take a few minutes to watch an elderly person maneuver around a room. Your fears will quickly disappear as you realize how much a weakened body can accomplish when there is determination and a strong will. Elderly people, when they are well motivated, will not let physical limitations stand in their way. They may have to slow their movements and shorten their steps, but they accomplish their tasks just like the rest of us.

Nonetheless, there are dangers involved in bathing and showering, and prudent ways of avoiding accidents must be discussed. If you take these precautions you'll acquire more confidence as well as bring comfort to the person you're caring for. The most useful safety measures are those suggested by your own self-reliance, common sense, and basic instincts.

The bathroom is potentially the most dangerous room in the house and the bathtub the most dangerous accessory. Therefore, the bathtub and shower stall must be made as safe as possible in order to minimize the risk of accidents. Every tub should have safety grip bars (Figure 5-2) fastened at one end. These bars are usually made of aluminum, and the best ones have rubber backing to protect the bathtub surface. Next, grab bars should be installed on the wall, one at standing height and the other at sitting height. These safety or security bars give an older person something to hold onto and make it much easier to maneuver in the tub. Showers should also be equipped with washable nonslip polyurethane carpets, and tubs should have safety bath strips with adhesive backing. All these supplies minimize the risk of falls; they are cheap, easy to install, and readily available. (See Appendix F, "Special Supplies," for a list of supply houses.)

Since older people often have slow reflexes and can't move quickly, it's important to make sure that the bathtub and shower faucets are always in good working order. For avoidance of painful mistakes, the faucets shouldn't allow sudden changes in water temperature. Also, hot and cold water taps should always be labeled clearly, and preferably in different colors.

For older people whose weakness or arthritis makes it hard for them to adjust to four-pronged, or star, water faucets, long-handled faucet turners are available. The long handles act as levers so that only minimal force is needed to turn on the faucet.

Outside the bathtub, make sure all the towel racks are well

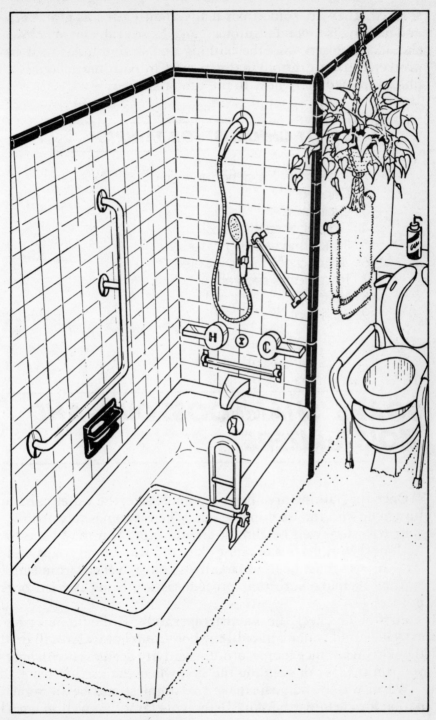

Figure 5-2. Bathtub safety aids.

secured. They are sometimes inadvertently used as grab bars, and nothing is more dangerous than a loose grab bar. Windows should be closed, and the bathing and drying area must be protected from drafts. Finally, a nonslip bath mat should be placed immediately next to the tub or shower.

SAFETY CHECKLIST FOR BATHING

1. Someone else at home
2. Grip bars
3. Grab bars
4. Carpet or safety strips
5. Faucets in working order
6. Hot and cold taps labeled
7. Towel racks secured
8. No drafts
9. Bath mat

SOAPS, SHAMPOOS, OILS, AND MOISTURIZERS

Once the bathing area has been made safe, the water can be turned on and the washing begun. When it comes to washing, your role may well be that of an educator. You may have to explain the properties of aging skin and why bland soaps and moisturizers must be used. You'll also have to check from time to time to make sure that procedures are being carried out properly.

First of all, check the water temperature: It should never be extreme. Cold water can chill the body, and hot water will dry the skin. Also, since temperature sensitivity decreases with age, you run the risk of scalding the skin when you use hot water.

Warm water and soap make the simplest and best combination for cleaning the skin. Detergents lather up well in hard water, but they are too harsh for old skin—keep them for the dishes. Aging skin is thin, fragile and easily irritated, so the best soaps are the mildest ones, especially oil-based soaps. Forget about colors, perfumes, and high-priced brands: mildness is the only consideration. Dove, Ivory, Neutrogena, and Camay are examples of good, mild, nonirritating soaps. "Soap on a rope" provides a clever way for an elderly person to avoid dropping the soap and risking a fall.

Soaps are good for the body but not for the hair. Here mild shampoos must be used. "Protein-enriched," "enzyme-fortified," and all the other appealing characteristics currently advertised are unnecessary. Once again, bland is best. Shampooing shouldn't be overdone—once weekly with the bath suffices. After the shampoo, an instant conditioner or cream rinse is a good idea. The conditioner should be liberally massaged into the hair and scalp, left on for one or two minutes, and then rinsed away. It helps prevent hair from drying out and makes brushing and combing much easier—long hair, especially, becomes more manageable.

Once the bath and shampoo are finished, skin moisturizer must be applied. Young people can bathe, dry themselves, and go on their way without worry. But older people's skin dries out easily. Because it is thin, its elastic properties are all but gone, and its natural lubricating oils are in short supply. When skin dries out, cracks and crevices form; the skin bruises easily and heals slowly; minor irritations quickly become infected sores. Thus, prevention through moisturizing is crucial. Moisturizers, by the way, don't actually add water or moisture to the skin; they simply prevent the skin from losing its own moisture. That's why moisturizers should be applied to damp skin rather than dry skin.

After the bath or shower, dry the skin gently until it is just a little damp. A terrycloth towel does well because its mildly abrasive surface helps to remove dead skin without irritating the healthy skin. While the skin is still damp, apply the moisturizer all over the body. There are hundreds of moisturizers on the market today. Some contain collagen and elastin; some are enriched with vitamins and minerals or are DNA- and RNA-fortified. Don't waste your money on these special ingredients, since they don't help moisturize the skin and are quickly washed away. Petrolatum is probably the best moisturizer money can buy: It isn't expensive (about \$2 for 8 ounces), and it's all that is needed. It should be applied in a thin layer, and it can be diluted with any of the mild commercial moisturizers (e.g., KERI LOTION) if grease stains on clothing become a problem. Lanolin is also good, as is Eucerin cream, which contains both lanolin and petrolatum. As a rule, the best moisturizers have water dissolved in oil, since it is the thin layer of oil spreading over the skin that locks in the body's moisture. Therefore, watch out for moisturizers that take a long time to rub in: Oil spreads very quickly, and a good moisturizer goes on easily. Also, watch out for alcohol: No matter how soothing it is to the skin, it's dangerous in excess. It dries the skin faster than the desert sun and dissolves away the body's natural fats and oils which serve as protection against bacterial invasion and skin infections.

Many people wonder if bath oils are helpful. The answer is yes, these oils help hold in the body's moisture. They are okay for showers when they can be applied with a washcloth, but they should never be used in a tub bath. The ingredients that moisturize the skin coat the bathtub, and the resulting slipperiness is too dangerous for older people. In addition, their use can lead to vaginal infections in women.

COMPLETE BATHS AND PARTIAL BATHING

Remember, even when your friend or relative is able to take a shower or bath alone, he or she can still benefit from your help. He or she may well have trouble reaching some body areas. These areas, usually the back, legs, and feet, can be saved for last, when you can be called in to help with their washing and drying. Long, firm strokes with a soapy washcloth and patting dry with a terrycloth towel feel best.

Day-to-day cleansing needn't be as elaborate as the weekly bath. Makeup (which will be discussed in detail in Chapter 6, "Grooming") can be removed daily with cold cream. The hands, face, underarms, and genital area should also be washed daily.

Once again, soap, warm water, and a washcloth are used for cleansing, and petrolatum for moisturizing. The feet can be troublesome for the elderly and therefore must be kept scrupulously clean. The spaces between the toes are often the site of skin breakdown and infection and should be checked daily; elderly skin, no matter where it is, must never be allowed to dry out. (See Chapter 6," Grooming.")

PLANNING THE BATH

For elderly people, planning the bath is as important as taking it. You must work out a routine with the elderly person you're helping and both of you must stick to it. A good idea is to write it out and tape it over the bathing area. You'll probably have to modify the routine as time goes on and physical capabilities change, but it's important to have one. Unplanned and unnecessary activity causes fatigue and increases the chance of an accident.

All the material that will be needed for bathing should be gathered beforehand and brought into the bathroom. A shower caddy hung over the nozzle keeps all the supplies immediately available in a safe place. A typical bathing routine is shown below:

TYPICAL BATHING ROUTINE

1. Wash body: face and trunk first followed by the arms and underarms, then the genital area, and finally back, legs, and feet.
2. Rinse.
3. Shampoo hair.
4. Rinse.
5. Apply instant conditioner, if necessary.
6. Rinse.
7. Dry with terrycloth towel.
8. Lightly moisturize entire body.

This type of planning is an example of work simplification, a concept introduced by medical researchers to help the elderly and disabled with their activities of daily living. When people are weak, when they tire easily, or when their joints are stiff, their activities must be organized to minimize energy expenditure and maximize efficiency. This requires eliminating unnecessary steps, sequencing the tasks, and getting into a routine. Rest periods should be incorporated into all activity routines, and strenuous activity should always alternate with lighter activity. It's surprising how much time and energy can be saved with a comfortable routine. Spontaneity might be exciting, but it can also be inefficient and tiring.

Another important principle to be kept in mind here is joint conservation. This principle applies to anyone with weak muscles or painful joints, but especially to people with arthritis. The goal is to maintain the health of the body's joints by keeping them active but at the same time protecting them. Holding an object in one position for a long time, or maintaining a fixed posture for a prolonged period, leads to early muscle fatigue. The joints are then prone to injury because their muscle support gives way easily. Bending any part of the body for a prolonged period is especially dangerous because it can lead to deformity as well as muscle fatigue. Here, as elsewhere, prevention is the best medicine: Elderly people should straighten their joints periodically and change positions often. Also, they should never hold or grip anything very tightly because the great internal forces generated by use of hand muscles can damage the joints of the hand. A loose but firm grip is better; when possible both hands should be used.

A special problem of the hands that usually affects arthritis sufferers is the tendency of the wrists and fingers to turn outward, toward the side of the little finger. In people with long-standing arthritis, this creates deformities and can make the hands useless. So, when an older person turns a knob clockwise, he or she should use the left hand, and when turning it counterclockwise, he or she should use the right hand. This means that most water faucets are turned on with the right hand, off with the left. In fact, "on with the right, off with the left" is a good maxim to remember. Preventive measures like this one increase the lifetime of the joints and make day-to-day activities more comfortable. The joints are like good tools that must be taken care of and used in the proper way. And you don't have to wait to reach age 65 to start using these methods. If you are weak or in pain, begin now.

WASHING AND DRYING AIDS

What if your friend or relative, despite all your planning, is too weak, too stiff, or in too much pain to bathe independently? What if weakness is so severe that bending over to wash is impossible? Or if arthritis is so disabling that holding a bar of soap is impracticable? You as the care giver can help. It is only natural to want to get involved and help whenever possible. But independence in simple activities is very important for an elderly person's dignity and self-respect. Before you get involved in direct care, like giving a bath, it is always best to try to modify the environment, to change the activity, or to introduce self-help aids to maintain the older person's independence. For the benefit of the elderly, direct hands-on assistance should be a last resort.

There are a multitude of aids and accessories which compensate for almost any disability and make troublesome activities manageable and comfortable. Some of the more popular devices are shown in Figure 5-3. As previously mentioned, the long-handled faucet turner helps with bathroom faucets. If weakness or incoordination makes holding a washcloth difficult, a wash mitt solves the problem. There are also brushes that fit over the fingers and others that can be attached to the wall or bathtub with suction cups. For squeezing tubes there are slotted rollers with oversized handles that slip over any tube and push the contents forward as the handles are turned. When limited reach or weakness makes the back inaccessible, long-handled back scrubbers and sponges can be used for washing, sling towels for drying. Long-handled toe and foot washers and driers help when the hips and knees are stiff and bending is difficult. The list of self-help aides and assistive devices is

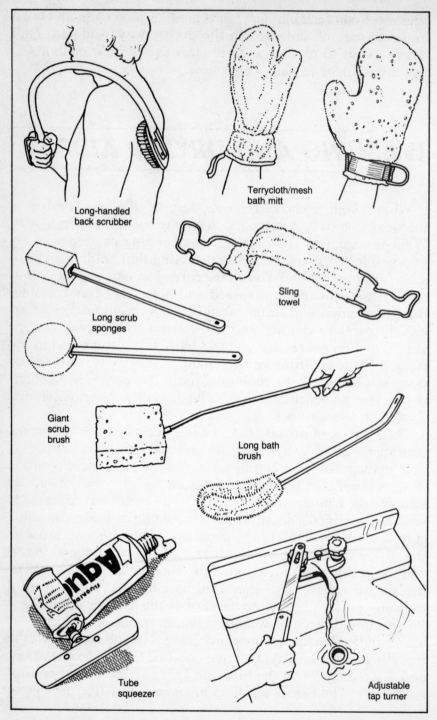

Long-handled
back scrubber

Terrycloth/mesh
bath mitt

Sling
towel

Long scrub
sponges

Giant
scrub
brush

Long bath
brush

Tube
squeezer

Adjustable
tap turner

Figure 5-3. Washing and drying aids.

endless. You can buy all of these aids from special supply houses (see Appendix E, "Special Supplies"), and most can be cheaply made at home. In fact, as new and unique problems arise in your household, there is nothing to stop you from designing your own devices.

6 Grooming

The desire to have a pleasing appearance never fades. Elderly people, like younger people, take pride in the way they look, and in a society in which personal appearance is so important, proper grooming plays a key role in self-esteem.

Good grooming accomplishes two things for elderly people. First, it gives them pleasure and a sense of well-being to look and smell good. Second, it makes them appealing to other people, who will mingle with them, seek them out, and provide welcome stimulation.

Your elderly friend or relative may feel far removed from the pleasures of life. He or she may feel no need or desire to improve personal appearance or look his or her best. This lack of initiative shouldn't be mistaken for stubbornness, rigidity, or lack of interest. Usually, all that is needed to reawaken an interest in good grooming is encouragement and gentle coaxing.

SKIN CARE

AGING SKIN

Unlike the character and spirit of most elderly people, aged skin is fragile and delicate. Through the years, skin ages and undergoes environmental wear and tear.

When we are young and our skin is healthy and resilient, it is a natural barrier that protects our bodies from the environment. As we age, the barrier properties deteriorate and our bodies become more susceptible to injury. The skin wounds more easily, takes longer to heal, and is more prone to infection. Sensation also declines, and the skin reacts more slowly to irritants: an older person may not even realize he or she is being injured until it is too late.

The skin normally plays a key role in regulating our temperature. As we age, this function of the skin is also altered, predisposing older people to both hypothermia (low body temperature) and heat stroke. Sweat production also decreases with age, further compounding the problems of temperature regulation.

The natural oils that lubricate and soften our skin when we are young gradually disappear as we age, leading to dry skin, one of the most common problems facing elderly people. Dry skin is almost inevitable in people over age 70 who live in temperate climates with cold winters. Although it isn't life-threatening, it can make life unpleasant. If dry skin is uncared for, it can become a health problem: Dry, itching skin leads to scratching, which in turn can lead to breaks in the skin, which can then lead to infection. The importance of frequent and liberal moisturizing of aged skin cannot be overemphasized.

THE SUN

Aged skin, like all skin, should be well protected from its number one enemy—the sun. A famous fashion designer introduced tanned skin on fashion runways in the early 1900s, and since then suntans have been considered chic, glamorous, and healthy. Nothing could be further from the truth. In fact, tanned or burned skin is damaged skin, and the harm done by long hours of basking in the sun is irreversible.

Bear in mind that ultraviolet radiation from the sun causes long-term damage even if the skin does not appear to burn. The fine, delicate fibers of normal skin are damaged not only by the sun, but also by use of sunlamps and tanning rooms. Darkly pigmented people may feel that they are spared the damage of ultraviolet radiation, but pigmentation is only a relative shield against the sun. It protects against immediate effects, like sunburn, but it does not protect against the long-term damage.

It can't be emphasized strongly enough that no one, at any age, should go into the sun without a sunscreen. Sunscreens are commercially marketed oils, creams, gels, or lotions containing chemicals that absorb or scatter ultraviolet light. They are sold according to their SPF, or sun protection factor. The SPF of a given sunscreen can range from 2 to 15, with 15 providing the greatest protection. Don't believe that a sun protection factor of 15 is a total sunblock, because a lotion with an

SPF of 15 will allow some tanning. To be optimally effective, sunscreen should be applied at least one-half hour before sunning and should be reapplied periodically during the day, especially after swimming or perspiring. It is now possible for people of all ages to enjoy sunshine and also be well protected against the aging effects of the sun.

Elderly people, when exposing themselves to the sun, should always wear a sunscreen with an SPF of at least 12. Hats and sunglasses should also be worn. Sunbathing in the early morning (before eleven o'clock) or in the late afternoon (after three o'clock) is much safer than in the middle of the day. Since the sun dries the skin as well as burning it, a moisturizer should be applied liberally after a day in the sun.

SKIN CHANGES

Probably the skin change that upsets aging women most, besides wrinkling, is the development of so-called liver spots (solar lentigos). After the skin has years of sun exposure, patches of excessive pigmentation appear in the form of freckles and blotches. Most commonly seen on the back of the hands, these pigmented areas are an attempt by the skin to protect itself against further sun damage.

There are many bleaching creams advertised today that promise to erase liver spots. Unfortunately, most of these are ineffective, because their active ingredient, hydroquinone, is present in concentrations too low to be useful. Until an effective bleaching cream is available, the best way to deal with liver spots is simply to conceal them with a good cover cream. Of course, to prevent the development of new freckles and blotches, remember to apply sunscreen before any further sun exposure.

~ Dilated blood vessels (telangiectasia) is another skin problem that plagues older people. Frequently found on the nose and cheeks, they look like tiny red spider lines and are usually caused by too much sun exposure. There is nothing that can be done to make them go away, but, again, a good cover cream will conceal them.

~ Seborrheic dermatitis, which causes excessive greasy scaling, usually on the scalp, is another skin problem prevalent among older people, especially men. It also causes scaling on the eyelids and eyebrows, along the sides of the nose, and in the ear canals. Seborrheic dermatitis is an inflammatory disease, so redness often accompanies the scaling. The well-known dandruff shampoos (e.g., selenium sulfides) are often helpful on the scalp. A low-strength hydrocortisone cream, which can be bought over the counter, can be used on the affected areas of the face. If there's no improvement in a week, consult your physician.

MOISTURIZERS REVISITED

The wide variety of moisturizers on the market today makes choosing the right one confusing and complicated, and lengthy lists of ingredients only add to the problem. But don't be overwhelmed. The task of selecting a good moisturizer is basically simple.

The two ingredients to look for, besides water, which is always a large component in a moisturizer, are petrolatum and lanolin. Three examples of good, simple, and relatively inexpensive moisturizers are KERI LOTION, Eucerin cream, and Lubriderm. Before trying any new moisturizer on the skin, apply a small amount on the inside of the forearm and wait twenty-four hours to ensure that no allergic reactions occur.

Moisturizers do not moisten the skin, they simply trap the water already present. Thus, the best time to apply them is immediately after bathing or washing, when the skin is still damp. Apply the moisturizer liberally, and massage until it is all absorbed.

Certain body areas require frequent moisturizing. The heels, elbows, shoulders, lower legs, and hands are areas that dry out quickly and need special attention. Keep a jar of a good moisturing cream accessible in several areas of the house. Always have one readily available in the bathroom, near the kitchen sink, on the nightstand, and in the laundry room. If it's easy to get to, chances are it will be used often. A good treatment for dry hands is to rub them liberally with petrolatum jelly before bed and put on cloth gloves for the night. In the morning the hands will be as soft as a baby's behind.

The discomfort of dry and itchy skin isn't something that elderly people should have to live with, since it can be prevented with proper care. Frequent moisturizing with a good cream should keep the skin soft and moist. If dry, red, scaly skin does not heal with good skin care, consult your physician.

SHAVING

Shaving should be done as often as necessary to keep the skin clean and comfortable. Most elderly women need not shave their legs and underarms, because the hair here gradually disappears with age. Men, however, must continue to shave their face into their later years.

A blade razor gives a closer shave than an electric one, but many men like electric razors because they are convenient and not as messy. When you are caring for an ill or bedridden patient, it's a good idea to use an electric razor for safety purposes.

Before shaving is done with a conventional blade, the beard should be softened. The easiest way is to lather the face with soap and water. Shaving should always be done in the direction the beard grows, and an after-shave lotion can be applied to help make the skin feel fresh. Alcohol, water, and fragrance are the main ingredients of these preparations, so it's unnecessary to spend a lot of money on them. If the skin is dry, a light moisturizer can be patted on afterward.

COSMETICS FOR THE ELDERLY

Although massive amounts of cosmetics and skin care products are marketed for young people, there are shamefully few for the elderly. Unfortunately, cosmetics manufacturers have failed to realize that millions of older women need and desire cosmetics specially designed for their skin. In spite of the indifference of cosmetics houses, with a little imagination elderly women can still find the right makeup.

Many elderly women don't wear cosmetics because they don't know how to use them or because they're afraid of being considered vain or frivolous. Your role, as care giver, can be to educate and encourage. If your elderly friend or relative doesn't know how to apply mascara or eye shadow, you can show her. If she is hesitant or uncertain, you can reassure and encourage her.

Wearing makeup is more of a necessity than a luxury because looking good makes you feel good. Study after study has shown that makeup improves one's self-image as well as the way one is perceived by others.

Essential makeup articles include concealer or cover cream, foundation, blush or rouge, eye shadow, mascara, and lipstick.

Makeup should be applied only after the face has been thoroughly cleansed with a mild facial soap and moisturized with a gentle cream. If an outing in the sun is on the day's agenda, a sunscreen should be applied before the makeup.

Makeup is best applied in the following manner: Apply concealer or cover cream first, over blemishes on the face and under the eyes to hide dark circles. Apply foundation next, to smooth and even the skin tone. It should be purchased in a shade slightly lighter than skin color and applied lightly and evenly over the entire face. Eye shadow comes next. Apply it lightly and evenly in a color that complements the eyes. Mascara can be applied on the upper and lower lashes now. Afterward, blush, which is available as a cream, gel, or powder, can be applied over the "apple" of the cheek and also lightly on the forehead and chin. Lipstick is the final touch. All makeup articles should be fresh: anything that is more than ten months old should be discarded.

For elderly women with pale, opaque skin, soft shades of pink and peach are best for blush and lipstick. For women with darker skin, light plums and gentle bronze tones work better. For skin that is thin and wrinkled, subdued makeup softly applied looks best. Stay away from harsh orangy tones, which make the face look hollow and wizened. When removing makeup, use cold cream and a tissue, and then wash the face as usual.

DEODORANTS AND ANTIPERSPERANTS

Many elderly people feel that deodorants and antiperspirants are a necessary part of good hygiene. They feel unclean without them and depend on them for a sense of well-being. In reality, deodorants are unnecessary.

Perspiration, a necessary part of everyone's temperature regulating system, is essentially odorless. People perspire when they are overheated, tense, or anxious. When the bacteria normally present on skin react with secretions from the body, the odors associated with perspiration occur. The best way to prevent these odors is to keep the body and clothing clean. For this, nothing is better than soap and water.

Antiperspirants are not a good idea for elderly people because they contain chemicals that decrease the amount of perspiration; thus they may prevent an overheated body from letting off steam. This is potentially dangerous for people whose temperature-regulating mechanisms are already compromised.

Feminine hygiene sprays and douches are also unnecessary, and at times unwise. Simply keeping the genital area clean prevents odors. If any unusual discharge, redness, or itching is present in the vaginal area, medical assistance is needed.

HAIR CARE

Healthy hair depends on general good health. No amount of lotions or potions will grow healthy hair if the body is sick. Once health is ensured and you can count on healthy hair, cleanliness and proper care will keep it looking attractive.

Hair should be washed as often as necessary to keep it clean. For an elderly person , this may be no more than once or twice a week. There is a tendency for hair to become dry with age, because the production of the body's natural oils decreases. To prevent hair from becoming excessively dry and brittle, frequent brushing is helpful, because it redistributes the reduced supply of natural oils and increases the blood flow to the scalp. Frequent brushing is also soothing and relaxing.

Personal preference will dictate what type of comb and brush to use. Wide tooth combs work well for curly hair and for detangling and combing hair after a shampoo. Avoid combs whose teeth are sharp or irregular, since they can scratch the scalp.

The best hairbrushes are made of natural bristles and can be bought in better pharmacies and department stores. If you find that the natural bristles aren't strong enough to go through thick hair, plastic bristle brushes are stronger and also less expensive. However, with a stronger bristle, you run the risk of tearing the hair. Make a point to wash the combs and brushes with water and dish detergent each time the hair is washed.

If your elderly friend's or relative's hair is dry, it doesn't require a lot of shampooing, but it does need frequent moisturizing. There are many inexpensive hair care products that moisturize and condition the hair. Oils such as castor oil, mineral oil, and olive oil are also good, but they can be messy, and often several shampooings are needed to remove them.

Oily hair, of course, needs more frequent shampooing and

less frequent conditioning than dry hair. Pillowcases need to be changed more often, and facial skin may need a little extra care to see that it doesn't blemish.

A woman's hair is often a large part of her identity. It is important to remember this when you provide personal care to your friend or relative. Find out how she likes to wear her hair, and style it this way for her. Keep it clean and well groomed. Although hair loss is a normal part of aging, it can be devastating for a woman. Try to minimize its effects by keeping the hair shorter, which will help it look fuller.

Elderly people, like the rest of us, need their hair cut from time to time. When your friend or relative wants a haircut, plan a trip to the barbershop or beauty salon or arrange for a beautician to come to the house.

ORAL HYGIENE

Good general health is essential for maintaining a healthy mouth and teeth. As with other aspects of good health, prevention is the best medicine.

For proper care of the teeth, a good toothbrush is a must. It should be the right size to fit the mouth. The bristles should be firm enough to clean the teeth but not so firm that they injure the gums. Oral-B is good, as is Py•Co•Pay Softex. If possible, teeth should be brushed right after eating or drinking. If this isn't possible, a thorough rinsing with warm water is the next best thing.

When brushing, your friend should be sure to reach all tooth surfaces, and should concentrate so that no teeth are missed. He or she should brush the teeth for at least three to four minutes and also brush the tongue. Flossing must be included as the next step, because brushing alone is not effective for ridding the mouth of decay-producing particles and bacteria. Make sure that your friend or relative flosses after all meals and snacks. The cleaner the teeth, the less potential for decay. To floss correctly, the person should start with a piece of floss about 18 inches long. The floss should be wrapped around the two forefingers of each hand, with the fingers controlling the floss no more than ½-inch apart. The floss should be inserted between the teeth using a gentle sawing motion and then moved back and forth five to six times. After all the teeth are flossed, the mouth should be rinsed well with water. Caution your friend or relative not to injure the gums with overzealous flossing.

As far as toothpastes go, everyone, regardless of age, should use a toothpaste containing stannous fluoride. Many people brush their teeth with homemade concoctions that are mainly sodium bicarbonate and salt. These are harmless but contain no active ingredient to fight tooth decay.

There is a home technique that is recommended for the prevention of periodontal, or gum, disease. It consists of spreading a thick mixture of bicarbonate of soda and hydrogen peroxide at the gum margins, usually with a rubber tip (like the kind found at the end of certain toothbrushes), followed by rinsing with a mild salt solution. Mouth washes are also helpful in preventing periodontal disease and destroying the plaque-forming bacteria that cause the disease. One should rinse the mouth twice a day with 2 tablespoonfuls of mouth wash, swishing it around the teeth for about thirty seconds before spitting it out.

Many elderly people have lost their natural teeth and replaced them with dentures. The importance of properly fitting dentures cannot be overstressed. Loose or poorly fitting dentures can cause irritation and soreness in the mouth, which, in turn, can create chewing difficulties. The worst thing that could happen is for your friend or relative to avoid eating because of uncomfortable or painful dentures. Dentures shouldn't be worn at night, because severe inflammation of the mucous membranes under the denture base can occur from excessive use. When not being worn, dentures should be immersed in a liquid. They can soak in a commercial cleansing preparation overnight, and tap water is fine during the day . If dentures are allowed to dry out, they can warp and become useless; they can also be destroyed by hot water. Dentures should be cleaned with a denture brush and toothpaste after each meal and at bedtime. Before scrubbing dentures, always fill the sink with water. If the dentures are accidentally dropped, the water will cushion the fall.

A denture wearer should see a dentist at least once a year. The dentist will check the dentures for fit, occlusion, and soft tissue irritation. He or she will also examine the tongue, lips, cheeks, gums, palate, and throat for signs of cancer—an exceedingly important exam for the elderly.

Elderly people with natural dentition should continue their regular semiannual dental visits. While it is true that the incidence of cavities decreases with age, the incidence of periodontal disease increases. In older people, many more teeth are lost because of periodontal disease than because of cavities.

While caring for your friend or relative, there may come a time when you are faced with the problem of bad breath. *Halitosis*, as it is called in scientific circles, is often caused by a problem far removed from the mouth. For example, if the odor of onions and garlic is on the breath, it is coming from the lungs where the oils are being removed from the bloodstream and eliminated with breathing. When bad breath is created by problems in distant parts of the body, oral treatment will never eliminate the odor, it will only mask it. When bad breath is caused by poor oral hygiene, cleansing the mouth well will decrease the odor. Mouth washes only mask the odor, they don't eliminate the problem.

HANDS AND FEET

NAIL CARE
The nails are an accessory structure of the skin, and, like the skin, they require proper care to keep them in good condition. With age they become thick, yellowish, dry, and brittle, so that caring for them becomes increasingly difficult.

Fingernails and toenails require trimming when they are cracked, jagged, or so long that they scratch the skin. Trimming the fingernails can be done by filing or clipping the nail to an oval shape. Avoid cutting the nail down the sides, to prevent injury to the cuticle. If you're using scissors, be careful to avoid injuring the tissue around the nail.

Cuticles can be pushed back with the blunt end of an orange stick, which is a wooden or plastic stick that has a pointed end and a blunt end. A pack of a dozen sticks costs about $1 in a local pharmacy. Cuticle care should be done after the area has been moisturized or soaked, so that the cuticle is soft and pliable. Hangnails, which are broken pieces of cuticle, should always be cut away. Their occurrence can be prevented by keeping the cuticle pushed back and moisturized. To clean under the nails, use a soft fingernail brush and soap and water.

Always apply moisturizing lotion to the hands after washing them. Be sure to include the nails, since this will lessen splitting and cracking.

You, as the care giver, may find that giving a periodic manicure to your elderly friend or relative will do a great deal to lift his or her spirits. It also provides an excellent opportunity for physical contact, which is so important for the elderly.

HEALTHY FEET

Now it's time to take a good look at our poor, tired, neglected feet. In a lifetime they carry the average person 70,000 miles. (That's three times around the world.) Though such an important part of our body, the feet are often neglected.

First and foremost on the list of rules for good foot care are properly fitting shoes. In the choice of shoes, fit is as important as style. Shoes that are too small lead to crowding of the toes, which in turn leads to bunions, corns, callouses, blisters, and hammertoes. If the shoe hurts, don't buy it! In a properly fitting shoe, the back of the shoe should fit snugly but not tightly. The arch of the foot should lie comfortably over the arch of the shoe, and there should be enough room in the front of the shoe to wiggle the toes. A quick and simple test to help you find a shoe that will not crowd your toes is the foot test: Stand on a piece of paper in stocking feet or bare feet. With a pencil, trace around your foot, and then place your shoe directly over the tracing. Your foot should fit in the shoe.

An elderly person, or anyone for that matter, should go shoe shopping in the late afternoon, because feet swell throughout the day and should be fitted at their largest size. Nothing is perfect, and neither are the feet. The right and left are usually different sizes, and shoes should be fitted to the larger size. Also—and this is important for elderly people who too often get set in their ways—under the constant stress of supporting the body for years, feet spread with age and shoe sizes change. Every time you buy shoes, recheck the size, and don't be afraid to buy shoes with a new size.

Shoes should be made of leather, because leather breathes and lets air circulate around the feet, keeping them cool and dry. Cloth shoes that are well made and have good support are also OK. In fact, the better sneakers, such as Nike and New Balance, are becoming increasingly popular with the elderly. Sandals are fine for short periods of time around the house, but they leave the feet too exposed and unsupported for long periods of outdoor walking. A well-constructed leather shoe with a low or mid-sized heel is the safest type of shoe for elderly people. High heels are attractive but dangerous. Worn occasionally for special events, they're OK, but they throw the body's alignment off, aggravate backaches, and encourage foot problems. They should never be worn for long periods of time. Strong arch supports are important, because they protect the feet from sudden shocks by helping to distribute weight and impact over a large area. Soles should have nonslip surfaces to grip the ground firmly, and insoles should be well padded.

Socks or stockings are also important. Not only do they protect the skin from shoes, especially poorly fitting shoes that rub and pinch, but also they keep the skin dry by absorbing excess moisture and perspiration. Elderly people with poor circulation should avoid colored hosiery, because the dyes in colored socks and stockings can sometimes irrritate their skin or cause a rash.

Besides the use of properly fitting shoes and socks or stockings, good foot care in the elderly involves washing, drying, and moisturizing the feet often, trimming the toenails when necessary, and changing the socks or stockings daily.

Feet should be washed daily. Make sure to rinse them well so that no trace of soap remains. Dry the feet thoroughly and be careful not to forget the spaces between the toes. After the feet are dried, a light moisturizer can be applied, especially on the soles and the heels, where the skin is often dry and cracked. Rub the moisturizer into the skin well and wait for the feet to feel dry before putting on socks or stockings.

Toenails should be trimmed when necessary. If your friend or relative is diabetic, this chore should be saved for the podiatrist. Elderly people's toenails are usually thick, brittle, and striated, so you'll have to look in your drugstore for a good pair of toenail clippers. To make the trimming easier, soften the toenails by soaking the feet in a basin of warm, sudsy water.

Adding bath oil to the water will help soften dry, scaly skin. The nails should be trimmed straight across and not too short. (You should be able to see a little white.) Don't cut out or dig in the corners.

It is inevitable that some people at some time in their lives will develop problems with their feet. Among the more common foot problems that trouble elderly people are ingrown toenails, blisters, corns and callouses, bunions, and athlete's foot. These foot ailments can usually be treated at home safely and easily.

—Ingrown toenails result from improper toenail trimming or tight-fitting shoes. They are common and almost always involve the big toe. Home care involves trimming the nail straight across, as previously mentioned, and temporarily wearing open shoes or sandals. Soaking the feet in warm water for thirty minutes twice a day helps. A doctor's care is required if home care measures fail or if an infection, which is manifested by swelling and redness, is present.

—Blisters develop where shoes repeatedly rub against the skin. To protect the feet, apply moleskin pads (Dr. Scholl's makes them) to protect the areas where blisters may form. Wash blisters daily, and, most importantly, don't pop them. They are protection for the young sensitive skin below, and popping them may cause an infection. If a blister happens to break, clean it with an antiseptic such as hydrogen peroxide and cover it with gauze or a plastic bandage. Remove the bandage at bedtime to let the air promote faster healing. If any redness or swelling develops, contact your doctor.

—Corns and calluses are also the result of poorly fitting shoes that repeatedly rub or press against the skin. Hard corns are found on the upper surface of the toes, usually over the joints. Soft corns form between the toes where one toe presses against another.

—Hard corns are prevented by using a corn pad (the nonmedicated type), a moleskin, or a thin piece of foam rubber over any area that is repeatedly rubbed. Soft corns are best prevented by placing a small piece of cotton or lambswool between the toes that rub together. Warm soaks and moisturizers can soften them. Never use over-the-counter medications to dissolve corns. These medications contain chemicals that attack healthy tissue as well.

~ Calluses form on flat surfaces, usually the sole of the foot, and particularly the ball and heel. They, too, result from shoes that are either too loose or too tight. They can be treated by rubbing the hardened areas with a pumice stone after a bath or soaking the foot, and applying a moisturizer afterward. Don't expect a callus to be eliminated with one treatment. Several treatments may be needed, because only a small amount of dead skin can be removed at a time.

Never cut a corn or a callus. This is dangerous and can cause an infection. If corns and callouses do not heal with a commonsense, home care approach, or if they are very painful, see your doctor.

—Bunions are swollen, painful, inflamed protrusions that occur on the side of the foot at the base of the big toe. They occur when the joints of the big toe are out of line, and they usually result from wearing shoes that don't give the toes enough room. Heredity can also be a factor. A smaller protrusion, called a *bunionette*, can develop on the outside of the foot.

If a bunion is not severe, self-care can begin with wearing shoes that don't cramp the bunion and that allow ample room for the toes. Remember, you should be able to wiggle all your toes freely in a well-fitting pair of shoes. A warm-water soak will soothe painful inflamed areas.

If a bunion is severe, surgery known as *bunionectomy* may be required. A bunionectomy is performed in the hospital with use of a general or spinal anesthetic. The big toe is realigned, and a small portion of bone is sometimes removed. Bunionectomies are performed by an orthopedic or podiatric surgeon.

—Athlete's foot, one of the many fungal conditions that can affect the feet, occurs because the feet are usually housed in a warm, dark, and damp environment, which is an ideal growing place for fungi and bacteria. Athlete's foot, a fungal infection that usually starts between the toes, can spread to the toenails and soles. Symptoms are redness, blisters, painful itching between the toes, and cracking and scaling of the skin. It is important to treat this condition promptly. Left unattended, it can become chronic and difficult to cure. Home care starts with prevention. Remember to wash and dry carefully between the toes. Expose the feet to the sun and air whenever possible, and change shoes and socks daily. Scratching can spread the infection. Fungicidal powders, such as Tinactin, can be dusted on the feet daily and usually eliminate the problem. But continued good foot care is required to prevent recurrence.

— Ingrown toenails are caused by improper trimming and, to a lesser degree, by wearing tight-fitting shoes. They occur when skin grows over the nail or when the nail pierces the skin. Ingrown toenails can be prevented by cutting the nail straight across and leaving a thin line of white nail on the top. A doctor's care is required if an infection is present.

—Hammertoes result from a muscle imbalance which causes the end joints of the smaller toes to bend down while the joint closest to the foot bends up. The second toe, being the longest, is usually affected. Where the hooked toes rub against the shoes, corns, callouses, and redness generally develop. Home care calls for wearing shoes that give toes adequate space (high toe boxes), and for use of adhesive doughnut-shaped pads for cushioning pressure spots. Splints and exercises also help. As a last resort, surgery is available for long-standing hammertoe problems.

GROOMING AIDS

Aids for washing and drying have already been discussed in Chapter 5, "Bathing." In general, elderly people have trouble either with grip strength or with loss of motion. Built-up handles are one way around the problem of grip strength. ADL (Activities of Daily Living) cuffs are another. Developed at the Institute of Rehabilitation Medicine in New York City, these cuffs are usually made of leather, with velcro closures. They fit over the palm of the hand and have compartments to hold the handles of most objects. For example, if your friend is having trouble holding onto a toothbrush, simply slip it into the pocket of an ADL cuff. ADL cuffs usually cost no more than a few dollars. Specially designed holders for selected items are also available, such as plastic-molded electric shaver holders.

When shoulder motion is restricted, long-handled or angled combs and brushes bring the hair into reach. When loss of elbow and wrist motion is the problem, pegged or notched

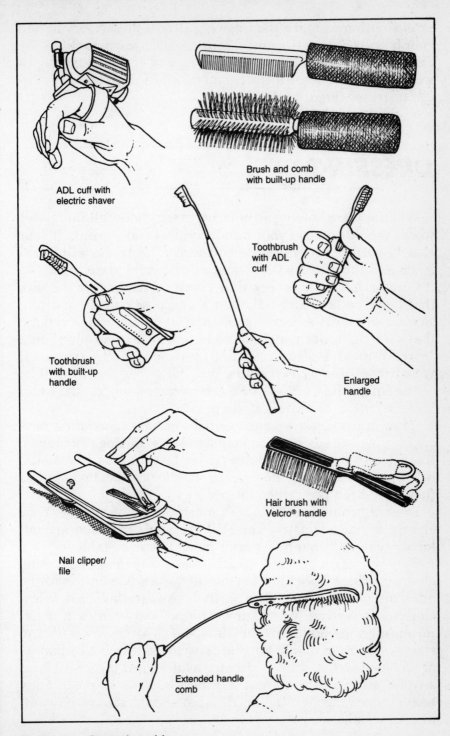

Figure 6-1. Grooming aids.

extension handles are the answer. Almost any grooming aid your friend will need—combs, brushes, sponges, razor blades—can be held by the adjustable notched end of these long, light-weight handles. Some handles can even be folded for easy storage or travel (Figure 6-1).

DRESSING

When you are helping an elderly person choose clothing, two words should come to your mind: comfort and warmth. If your elderly friend is comfortable and warm, he or she will be relaxed and the world will be a more enjoyable place.

Comfort means clothing that is not restricting. Make sure that belts, collars, and waistbands are loose enough and that sleeves and cuffs are long enough. Stay away from anything that's too tight. Garments should have a little room and should "give" a bit. It's also important to avoid scratchy fabrics. If your friend likes woolen pants, buy those that are lined. If he or she enjoys the warmth of woolen sweaters, suggest the wearing of a cotton turtleneck underneath.

Caution an elderly woman against wearing constricting garters or tying her stockings in knots. Besides causing discomfort, this can also stop the circulation to her feet and legs. She should not wear constricting hose, such as elastic stockings, unless they have been prescribed for her.

Dressing comfortably doesn't mean dressing sloppily. Your elderly friend or relative can still dress in styles that are tailored, neat, and snappy without being uncomfortable.

Staying warm in cold weather basically means layering clothing. Three light shirts or blouses worn one on top of the other are warmer than a heavy woolen sweater by itself. When clothing is layered, warm air is trapped between each layer, insulating the body from the outside. It's a very good idea to start with cotton or silk long underwear, followed by a flannel or woolen shirt. A woolen sweater as the third layer will keep anyone warm in the coldest weather. Because so much body heat escapes through the head, a hat should always be worn in cold weather.

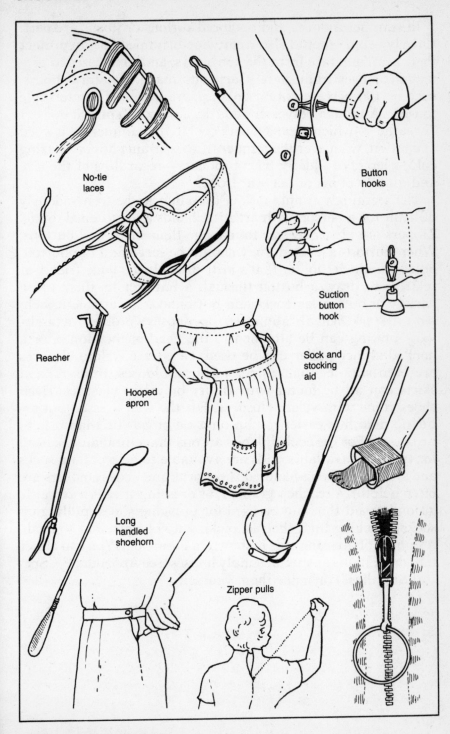

No-tie laces

Button hooks

Suction button hook

Reacher

Hooped apron

Sock and stocking aid

Long handled shoehorn

Zipper pulls

Figure 6-2. Dressing aids.

In summer months, light-colored cottons or linens are best. Elderly people should also wear wide-brimmed hats to protect their head and face from the sun's rays, and sunglasses to protect their eyes from glare. Garments made of natural fibers, such as 100 percent cotton or wool, are the most comfortable to wear. Although polyester adds durability to fabric, it doesn't "breathe"—which means it isn't cool in the summer. As a word of caution, whenever the temperature is stifling hot or freezing cold, keep your elderly friend indoors—regardless of the size and quality of his or her wardrobe.

The seemingly simple task of dressing can be tremendously difficult for a person with arthritic hands and stiffened joints. Zippers are always easier to manage than snaps and buttons. When buttons are used, they should be large and the buttonholes should be loose. If it's still difficult for your friend or relative to draw a button through a buttonhole, there are a variety of button fasteners and buttonhooks available to help with the task. When grabbing a zipper poses a problem, a tassle, loop, or ring can be attached to the head of the zipper, or a hooked zipper puller can be used. Of course, velcro closures are even simpler than zippers. Shirts, blouses, trousers, and skirts can all be found with zipper or velcro closures. Even shoes come with velcro closures. For the well-dressed but arthritic man, it's easier to clip on a tie or bowtie than it is to tie one on. For the cook, hooped aprons that eliminate the need for tying are available. Aids are available to help pull up socks and stockings. Long-handled shoehorns and shoe removers are often helpful. A reacher, grabber, or dressing stick is a versatile grooming aid that can be used for unlacing shoes, pulling up socks, reaching high shelves, picking up objects, and so forth. A sample of dressing aids is shown in Figure 6-2. You can either buy these items at special supply houses (see Appendix F, "Special Supplies") or make them yourself.

7 *The Five Senses*

Put on a pair of earmuffs, a pair of mittens, a nose clip, and underwater goggles. Wrap Ace bandages around your knees, and sit down for dinner. You'll be too stiff to sit comfortably for long, but what about the tastes and aromas you ordinarily enjoy? Can you still savor them? Can you hear the dinner conversation? Can you even see the food or use the silverware? This is the world of the elderly.

All five senses—sight, hearing, taste, touch, and smell—begin to decline in mid-life and gradually lose their sharpness and sensitivity. From year to year the losses are slight and unapparent, but after many years they accumulate and make themselves felt. The world becomes darker and quieter, and simple pleasures such as reading the newspaper, listening to a conversation, and tasting food become difficult and uncomfortable.

You can help your elderly friend or relative cope with these losses by learning about them, by appreciating the difficulties they impose, and by being available with advice, reassurance, and emotional support. You can also modify your home to make it safer and more comfortable. With minor repairs and modest redecorating, eliminating distracting signals and clarifying and sharpening the remaining ones, you can accident-proof your home and compensate for your loved one's failing senses.

HEARING AND HEARING AIDS

Hearing, like other senses, functions on three levels: a background level of which we are usually unaware, a signal level, and a symbol level. After age 50, hearing declines for most of us, and the loss occurs on all levels. Background-level hearing (e.g., city noises) helps us identify our surroundings, and its loss leads to a sense of isolation and feelings of depression. Signal-level hearing (e.g., a wolf's cry) alerts us to dangers in the environment, and its loss leads to feelings of inadequacy and insecurity. The loss of symbol-level hearing (language) limits our communication and fosters social isolation.

We seldom hear pure tones. Most sounds contain a multitude of tones (pitches or frequencies). As we age, the high-pitched ones disappear, so elderly people have their earliest problems with the upper registers, hearing only the low-frequency parts of words and having trouble distinguishing speech from background noise. Vowels are made up of low-frequency tones and carry much of the energy or intensity of conversational speech. Consonants, on the other hand, are high-frequency tones and carry little energy, but lots of information. An elderly person misses consonants and has difficulty understanding anyone who favors the higher registers, including most women and children. He or she will often hear you speaking but will have trouble distinguishing the words. You can't improve things by raising your voice, because loud sounds are painful and aggravate the situation. If you whisper, you won't be heard; if you shout, you'll create pain. To get your message across, raise your voice slightly and speak slowly and distinctly. When you speak to an elderly person, look at him or her and try to direct your voice to the better ear. This reduces background distractions and gives the person a chance to lipread. When you're speaking, make sure there is good light on your face, and keep your voice evenly modulated, neither raising nor lowering it. Since elderly people take longer to process information and respond appropriately, short sentences with pauses between them are better than long ones that are difficult to follow.

If you've done your best to speak clearly and distinctly but your elderly friend or relative still has trouble understanding you, it's time to think about a hearing aid. Make an appointment with an otorhinolaryngologist—an ear, nose, and throat (ENT) specialist—for a thorough medical evaluation. Some types of hearing loss are medically or surgically correctable, and the doctor will be able to determine this. He or she will also arrange for an audiologist to do a complete hearing evaluation. If a hearing aid is necessary, the audiologist will refer your friend to a hearing aid dealer.

Hearing loss is the commonest physical impairment of the elderly. Despite the fact that many elderly people need hearing aids, relatively few use them. Elderly people rarely mind using eyeglasses, but hearing aids are another matter. Perhaps eyeglasses are more acceptable because many young people use them, while hearing aids have come to symbolize deterioration and declining vigor. It is to be hoped that the recent acquisition of a hearing aid by the President of the United States will offset these images, which are themselves a manifestation of ageism, the subtle but widespread prejudice against the elderly. Regardless, the fact remains that an elderly person will use a hearing aid only if he or she wants to use one. There are thousands of elderly people today who sit in silence with their hearing aid stored in the closet—pride, misinformation, and prejudice preventing them from using the device. You can help by being supportive and patient.

Bear in mind that no hearing aid can restore normal hearing, so you mustn't encourage false expectations. A hearing aid only amplifies sound. All frequencies are amplified to some extent, even the ones that don't need it, like background noise. Therefore, the sounds heard through a hearing aid are unlike normal sounds, and your elderly friend or relative will need time to adjust to the aid. When talking with him or her, keep away from distractions such as the television and other conversations. Pick a quiet area in the house and talk slowly in a normal voice. If you're not being understood—which will happen often when a person with a hearing aid is tired, upset, or ill—talk more slowly and more distinctly, and rephrase your remarks rather than repeating them indefinitely. An elderly person who is using a hearing aid for the first time should wear the aid for no more than one hour a day initially, and gradually, over a month, increase the time to twelve hours a day.

All hearing aids have the same basic components: a receiver that picks up the sound signal, a battery-powered amplifier that strengthens it, a tube that transmits it, and an earmold that directs it into the ear. There are four major types of hearing aids, depending on where the receiver and amplifier are located:

TYPES OF HEARING AIDS

1. Body hearing aid—Large, bulky, and uncosmetic. Because of its size, it is capable of

large amplification. Useful for the severely impaired individual.
2. Eyeglass hearing aid—Useful for the so-called
   contralateral routing of signals (CROS): Sounds
   directed to the impaired ear are amplified
   and rerouted to the good ear.
3. Behind-the-ear hearing aid—Compact and
   cosmetic. The most popular type.
4. In-the-ear hearing aid—The smallest and least
   powerful. Useful only for the mildly impaired
   individual.

The batteries should be inserted with the hearing aid in the
"off" position. Once the earmold is inserted in the ear, the aid
can be turned on and the volume adjusted to a comfortable
level. Comfort is based on listening to someone talk in a normal
voice from about three feet away. A hearing aid is a precision
instrument and must be properly cared for. The table that follows tells you and your elderly friend how to do this. The most
common cause of hearing aid malfunction is a dead battery,
and the second most common cause is an improperly positioned
battery. Batteries will last one week if the hearing aid is used
twelve hours a day, and one set of extra batteries should always
be on hand. Earmolds usually need readjustment every two or
three years. The hearing aid itself should last between five and
ten years with proper care. Hearing aids range in price from
$300 to $800; unfortunately, they are not covered by Medicare
insurance.

A hearing aid, no matter how good the quality of its sound,
is helpful only if it can be used. The hearing-aid user must have
the concentration, understanding, and memory to operate the
aid. Vision, manual dexterity, and strength must be adequate
to put the aid on, take it off, manipulate the dials, and change
the batteries. Large, color-coded, and built-up dials are available for physically and visually impaired people. Your hearing-
aid dealer, the local chapter of the Arthritis Foundation, the
American Foundation for the Blind, or the local Speech and
Hearing Society can help you find these special hearing aids.
And, of course, you can always offer assistance and help with
complicated adjustments.

Some hearing-impaired elderly people are not helped by hearing aids. They must depend on other senses and on special sensory communication devices to compensate for their hearing loss. For example, alarm clocks, doorbells, and burglar alarms can be equipped with flashing lights and low-frequency buzzers. Even bed vibrators can be hooked up to alarm clocks and doorbells, and radio and television sets can be modified with special amplifiers. The telephone companies offer an assortment of rings, amplifiers, and flashing lights. All of these devices and modifications help with the ordinary activities of living, such as being awakened in the morning by the alarm, answering the doorbell to welcome a guest, or talking on the telephone with a friend. Most of us take these pleasures and conveniences for granted, but they are challenges for elderly people with poor hearing. Anything you can do to ease the burden is useful. Your local Speech and Hearing Society is the best source for additional information and help.

X CARE OF THE HEARING AID

1. Check the earmold regularly. Clean it with warm, soapy water and remove wax with a pipe cleaner. Never use alcohol for cleaning—it can dry and crack the mold.
2. Never shower while wearing a hearing aid. Keep the earmold and tubing dry at all times. A single drop of water can muffle the sound.
3. Avoid extremes of temperature. Never use a hair dryer while wearing a hearing aid.
4. Keep all sprays and aerosols away from the hearing aid.
5. Turn off the hearing aid when you're not using it.
6. Store the hearing aid in a dry, safe place. Remove the batteries and keep it in the "off" position.

VISION

Vision begins to decline around age 45. For some people the decline is steep, leading to early and severe vision loss, but for most of us it is slow and gradual and leads only to minimal, easily correctable loss. Still, even minimal losses are important to elderly people who rely on their remaining healthy senses to compensate for the declining ones. Vision lets an elderly person communicate by lipreading when hearing fails, and vision and touch together help an elderly person identify and enjoy food when taste and smell fail. The loss of vision, especially in combination with hearing loss, contributes to the vulnerability of elderly people. And vision loss, no matter how slight, can lead to social withdrawal, isolation, and depression. While there are a variety of ways to overcome the visual losses that accompany aging, perfect vision, as an end in itself, is unimportant. Remaining involved in the world, continuing a daily routine, and participating in familiar activities are important. A librarian doesn't need a hunter's far-ranging vision, nor does a sportsperson need the fine vision of a jeweler, but a women who likes to knit needs the ability to focus her eyes on the yarn.

The eye is a complex organ with a multitude of functions that affect the activities, tasks, and needs of daily life. Some of the more important functions that deteriorate with age are visual acuity, accommodation, color discrimination, and light sensitivity. The best way to think of the eye is as a camera with a self-adjusting lens and shutter. The pupil, which is the shutter, adjusts the amount of light entering the eye and the lens transmits and bends the light to focus it on the retina.

As we age, the pupil shrinks in size and the lens enlarges and thickens. These effects reduce the amount of light falling on the retina: In ordinary daylight, a 60-year-old receives about one-third the amount of light that a 20-year-old does! Moreover, with age, yellow-brown pigments accumulate in and discolor the lens. Blues and greens become harder to see and more difficult to discriminate between, and even less light is transmitted. Because so much light never reaches elderly people's eyes, extra light and high illumination are needed for close tasks such as reading and sewing.

The aged eye is caught between a rock and a hard place. While it ordinarily receives too little light, it responds poorly to too much light. Glare, the dazzling, sometimes blinding effect of bright light, is an ever-present problem. Most of us recover quickly after being exposed to bright light, but the elderly recover slowly. They are temporarily blinded by bright light. Glare arises from reflected light as well as from direct light such as sunlight in the afternoon or a car headlight at night. An elderly person can be temporarily blinded by the glare in a bright sunlit room with waxed floors, polished furniture, and white walls and ceilings. You would have a similar experience in a room filled with flashbulbs popping continually in all directions.

The elderly also have trouble adapting to the dark. If a small amount of light gets through the eye in daylight, even less gets through at night. Ordinarily, when you enter a dark room, having been outside or in a brightly lit room, it takes a while before you can see clearly. It takes elderly people much longer to adapt—not only because there is less light available to them, but also because their response times are delayed and their processing of visual information is slowed. Elderly people have double trouble driving at night, because while they are slowly adapting to the dark, they are being blinded by the glare from oncoming traffic.

Discriminating between colors is another problem for elderly people. All the colors of the rainbow seem to fade with the years, regardless of the amount of light available. Blues and greens are the most difficult colors to distinguish because of the yellow pigments in the lens of the eye; warm reds and oranges are the easiest colors to distinguish. Color contrasts and shades help us see the outlines of objects and appreciate their depth in space. For elderly people with limited ability to sense color contrasts, objects lose their depth and outlines lose their sharpness. The edges and corners of a room painted one color can "disappear" from view, and steps all painted the same color can blend together, losing their depth and height.

Visual acuity is the resolving power of the eye, the ability to discern fine details. It's what the doctor measures with an eye-chart in his or her office, and it too deteriorates with age. Having 20-20 vision means that at 20 feet the person being tested can identify the same letters that an average person can see at 20 feet. Only about one in ten people over age 80 have 20-20 vision. Having 20-50 vision means that at 20 feet the person can identify only letters that are large enough for an average person to see at 50 feet. Reading newspapers, as well as warning labels, becomes difficult with 20-50 vision, and about one-third of the over-80 population has vision this bad or worse.

Accommodation, the ability to focus an object on the retina, also deteriorates with age. *Presbyopia*, literally "old eyes," refers to the failure of accommodation and affects nearly everyone over age 60 . You've probably heard elderly people say that their arms are too short for reading, meaning that they can't focus more closely than the length of their arms—which is a long way to go from the 3 inches at which a child can focus. As we age, focusing on near objects becomes difficult, and accommodating quickly to different distances is troublesome. Have you ever said hello to an elderly women who was knitting and gotten only a blank stare in return? She wasn't being unfriendly—she was simply trying to bring you into focus. Having accommodated her vision to her work at close range she needed time to refocus on you—and also time to redirect her attention and reposition her body.

Present-day ad copy and product labels underscore the difficulties elderly people face in the marketplace. It takes nearly perfect vision to read this type of print, and accumulated and combined impairments in accommodation, visual acuity, and color contrast ability make reading it virtually impossible for many elderly people. How many times have you had to read small print, colored instructions, or warning labels on the inside of plastic bottles through similarly colored solutions? Or dark-blue instructions on light-blue paper? Elderly people might well ask, why bother with safety stickers and warning labels if they can't be read? Until publishers and manufacturers change things themselves, you'll have to rewrite the important notices in your home in large, clear, black print on white paper.

In addition to accommodation, visual acuity, color discrimination, and light sensitivity, other visual functions also deteriorate with age. The field of view accessible to an individual shrinks with age, visual memory declines, and depth perception, the ability to estimate relative distances (and often the culprit in the messy eating habits of some elderly people), also declines.

In the following chapter we will use all of this basic knowledge to rearrange, redecorate, and, in some cases, remodel your home to make it more accessible and comfortable for an elderly person.

Before we leave this section on visual changes we need to mention three common eye disorders that affect the elderly: cataracts, glaucoma, and senile macular degeneration. A *cataract* is the most common eye disorder of old age. While there is no medical treatment for a cataract, surgical removal is easy, painless, and highly successful—and accounts for the largest number of operations performed each year on the elderly. A cataract is any opacity in an otherwise transparent lens. Cataracts scatter light, cast shadows, and generally interfere with the focusing of images on the retina. Well-developed cataracts distort, blur, and cloud the image. But the mere presence of a cataract is not in itself a cause for alarm, or a reason for an operation. A cataract is treated by removing it, which should be done only when vision has deteriorated to the point of interfering with day-to-day activities. A cataract is removed by extracting the entire lens, so the eye can't focus until it's equipped with an artificial lens. An intraocular lens can be implanted during surgery, or cataract glasses or a contact lens can be provided afterward. The glasses are thick, they restrict the field of view, and they magnify and distort objects, sometimes to the point of creating a safety hazard. A contact lens produces much less distortion and is easier to wear, but an elderly person needs good hand dexterity and fine motor control to insert and remove it. The new plastic intraocular lens comes closest to restoring normal vision and is probably the best choice for elderly people. It eliminates the need for cataract glasses or a contact lens, and it's easy to adjust to, since vision through it is similar to vision through the unoperated eye. However, since intraocular lenses are the newest artificial lenses and implanting them requires additional surgery time, you or your friend or relative should discuss the pros and cons of all three types of lenses with your doctor before choosing one. Cataract surgery itself, regardless of the lens chosen, calls for special postoperative precautions which can be summarized as follows:

PRECAUTIONS AFTER CATARACT SURGERY

1. Realize that complete healing takes several months.
2. Wear an eye patch when sleeping to protect the eye.
3. When wearing an eye patch, seek assistance when moving around, since depth perception is reduced.
4. Move slowly, especially going up and down stairs.
5. Do not sleep on the operated side.
6. Whenever possible, avoid activities that increase the intraocular pressure—bending, lifting, sneezing, coughing, vomiting, or straining on elimination.

Chronic, open-angle *glaucoma* is an insidious disease. It is painless and affects peripheral or side vision first, so that it can do a lot of damage before anyone is aware of it. The very existence of a disease like glaucoma, which affects about 2 percent of the over-40 population, is reason enough for a yearly eye exam. It is caused by a buildup of pressure inside the eye, which can be diagnosed and treated easily and safely—and the earlier the treatment, the less damage is done. Lowering the eye pressure is the treatment, and medications in the form of eyedrops are usually successful, though laser surgery to drain off some of the fluid creating the pressure in the eye is sometimes necessary. Glaucoma is a chronic, incurable condition, an imbalance between eye fluid production and removal, and the use of drops must be continued for life. The following chart summarizes a safe, simple, and effective method for administering eyedrops. Another form of glaucoma, acute, narrow-angle glaucoma, is a sudden increase in pressure that can create severe pain, blurring, or loss of vision. It must be treated immediately. Medications lower the pressure temporarily, and laser surgery prevents further attacks. Glaucoma is one cause of impaired vision that can be completely overcome with proper treatment.

The problem is getting everyone to a doctor's office for an annual physical exam that includes an eye check.

Senile macular degeneration is a degeneration of the cells in the macula, the area of the retina responsible for central vision. It is the least treatable of the common eye diseases, though laser surgery can help when done early. Senile macular degeneration spares the periphery of the retina, so people with the disease never go totally blind—they always have peripheral vision. Close work such as reading or sewing becomes difficult because there is a shadow in the center of the field of view, but a low-vision aid such as a magnifying glass can extend the visual image over a large enough area of the retina for it to be detected by the healthy cells at the periphery.

USING EYEDROPS

1. Wash hands thoroughly.
2. Clean the eyelids with moist cotton balls.
3. Make sure the correct eye is being medicated!
4. Check the label on the bottle.
5. Check the label again.
6. Gently pull the lower lid down and out.
7. With the patient looking up, quickly place the drops in the cul de sac formed by the inside of the lower lid and the eyeball.
8. Close the eye to distribute the medication.
9. Never allow the tip of the dropper to touch the eye.
10. Never apply pressure to the eye.
11. For self-administration, the patient pulls the skin below the eyelid down with the index finger of one hand and instills the medication into the cul-de-sac with the other hand.

TASTE AND SMELL

The five senses are busy even when we're unaware of their activity. The eyes receive images whether or not we're "looking" at anything, and the ears register sounds whether or not we are "listening" to anything. And the background smells of the world, of which we are usually unaware—for example, the smell of spring or the smell of country air—help us identify our surroundings and connect us to the world. There is also a smell memory that is often charged with emotion: Think of or "smell," for a moment, your childhood Christmas tree. The sense of smell, like the other senses, is an early warning system that protects us from toxic fumes and poisons. It's also a source of unending pleasure—from the aroma of the morning coffee to the bouquet of an old wine. And, together with the sense of taste, it lets us identify and enjoy the flavors of foods.

Smells are sensed when individual molecules interact with specialized cells in the nose. The cells fire off information to the brain and an odor is perceived. These cells degenerate with age and eventually succumb to the accumulated irritations and injuries from colds, seasonal allergies, environmental pollutants, and occupational odors.

Our sense of taste is highly dependent on our ability to smell, so a deterioration of smell affects taste as well. There are four basic tastes: salty, sweet, sour, and bitter. These tastes are recognized by specialized cells housed in the taste buds that line the tongue, palate, and pharynx (the back of the throat). The palate is most sensitive to sour and bitter, the tongue to sweet and salty, while the pharynx has no favorites. Taste sensitivity declines with age, again for a variety of reasons. In addition to the atrophy and loss of taste buds, the flow of saliva slows (saliva is needed to dissolve the taste-stimulating molecules), the elasticity of the mouth decreases, the gum linings recede, and the tongue fissures. Also, the loss of teeth, the use of dentures (which cover the hard palate and hide its taste buds), and poor oral hygiene interfere with taste sensation, sometimes actually producing their own unpleasant tastes.

It's always a good idea to stimulate the declining senses, to challenge them and keep them alive. Fresh flowers in the house are always welcome, and your elderly friend or relative would certainly enjoy after-shave lotion or perfume. The pleasure a tasty meal can provide goes without saying.

TOUCH

The sense of touch provides us with the physical pleasure of human contact. With it we demonstrate our feelings of affection and belonging. Of course, the sense of touch also lets us identify and handle objects, and when it's impaired, simple tasks can become impossible challenges. But more than any other sense, touch allows us to share the human condition with each other, to demonstrate empathy, and to comfort one another. The simple act of touching can ease pain and relieve suffering, and a sure hand gently placed on a shoulder is calming and therapeutic.

The sense of touch declines with age, and with it a caring, humanizing connection to other people weakens. Touch is the sensation that arises from microscopic indentations of the skin. All five senses arise from specialized receptors picking up signals from the external world and transforming them into electrical information that gets processed by the brain. Chemoreceptors in the nose and mouth pick up and transform molecular smell and taste signals into electrical information, while the rods and cones of the eye transform visual signals, and the inner ear cells transform sound signals. The list of mechanoreceptors in the skin that transform mechanical indentations into electricity sounds like an international collection of scientific bric-a-brac: Meissner's corpuscles, Merkel's complexes, Ruffini's end organs, Krause's bulbs, and pacinian corpuscles. But touch, like the other senses, is a complex neurological affair, and its decline in sensitivity is due to more than changes in the receptors. The elasticity of the skin changes, the circulation to the skin is altered, and, most important, the time required for signals to be received and transmitted to the brain increases, as does the time needed to process the information and respond to it.

The decline in touch sensitivity leaves the elderly individual vulnerable to additional dangers. Tight belts or corsets can go unnoticed yet still cause skin damage. Tight shoes can pinch the toes and cause skin breakdown, again without warning. Particles of food can be overlooked and left in the mouth to aggravate tooth decay. Blunted responses to deep pressure can lead to pressure sores from sitting or lying too long in one position. And when sensitivity to vibration declines, unsteady tables, chairs, and footstools become hidden hazards.

It's difficult to compensate for the loss of touch. Loose clothing and scrupulous oral hygiene can prevent some of the problems, and textured materials stimulate and enhance the sense of touch. Smooth plastics and other synthetic materials are usually without much character or tactile interest. Above all, though, it is important to touch elderly people. Let them know that you care, that they are wanted, and that we are all connected and responsible for one another.

8 The Environment

When your elderly friend or relative gets ready to move in with you, you'll want to make sure that your house is as safe and as comfortable as possible. Usually, this requires some redecorating and minor house repairs, but none of it is very expensive or time-consuming. As you know by now, all five senses decline with age, which makes the world less accessible and more dangerous for elderly people. They can't rely on strong senses to compensate for weak ones, because by late life all the senses have usually lost their sharpness. The only way to make the world more inviting for elderly people is to modify the environment to meet their special needs. For example, if your elderly friend or relative has trouble seeing blues and greens, you can substitute reds and oranges; and if he or she has trouble adapting to the dark, you can install night-lights and easy-to-reach switches for overhead lights. With imagination and effort you'll be able to modify your home to overcome most age-imposed limitations and make it a safe, pleasing, and comfortable home for your loved one.

TEMPERATURE

In the winter months elderly people like the temperature high, often in the high 70s, but since the rest of your family would probably swelter in such heat, it's best to set the thermostat between 65° and 68° Fahrenheit. Not only will this keep everyone comfortable, but it will also save on fuel bills. Anything below 65° Fahrenheit is in the danger zone because it can trigger accidental hypothermia, an abnormally low body temperature to which elderly people are at risk and which can be deadly if untreated. Be especially careful if your friend or relative can't shiver or is too weak to move around to generate body heat, or if he or she is taking medications such as phenothiazines (Elavil, Mellaril, etc.) which interfere with temperature regulation. Since elderly people are so susceptible to hypothermia, they must always be kept warm. Make sure your friend dresses warmly. If he or she is still cold at 65° or 68° Fahrenheit, use throw blankets or shawls for further warmth. Accidental hypothermia can begin during sleep, so it's important for him or her to dress warmly for bed and to use enough blankets on the bed. There's nothing warmer than a down or feather comforter.

Often the air dries out when the heat is on for a long time. Plants help moisturize the air and protect against dry skin in the wintertime. If you don't like caring for plants, fresh flowers will do the same thing, and if flowers turn you off, a pot of water will do the job.

The summer months are less of a problem for elderly people, because they don't mind the heat. Nonetheless, they should stay indoors during the hottest hours of the day, and all day when a scorcher comes along. If you don't have an air conditioner, keep the windows open, shade out the sun, and use a fan to circulate the air. When the elderly do go out they should dress in lightweight, loose-fitting, and light-colored clothing, and avoid direct sunlight.

STAIRWAYS

It's a good idea to make a safety check of your house before your friend or relative arrives, and after he or she is settled in you can check for comfort and accessibility as well as safety. A house and its contents should "fit" the people inside. Watch your friend walk up and down the stairs to determine if there is a good fit on the stairs, watch him or her open and close doors, walk down hallways, sit down and get up from chairs and sofas, get on and off beds, and so forth. If the fit is poor but easy to correct, make the adjustments yourself. On the other hand, if extensive repairs are needed, like remodeling a staircase, talk with an architect or designer who knows the special needs of elderly people before doing anything yourself. Extensive repairs can be costly and time-consuming, and professional advice pays off in the long run.

Start your safety and comfort check on the staircase, which is where most home accidents occur. Slippery steps, short steps, and steep steps are the usual culprits. Often the steps and handrails are in disrepair, the lighting is inadequate, and the carpets are frayed or loose. You can begin accident proofing your home on the staircase by repairing the cracked steps, loose handrails, frayed carpets, and the like. Make sure the lighting on the staircase is adequate, and since elderly people have trouble adjusting to changes in light and dark, adequate lighting in the hallways and approaches to the staircase is equally important. Soft, nonglare, or frosted 100-watt light bulbs on the staircase and 75-watt light bulbs in the hallway will serve everyone well. The light bulbs should be shaded and placed above the line of vision to eliminate further glare. Avoid fluorescent lighting, since it's harsh and the flicker is unpleasant for elderly people. Light switches on the top and bottom of the staircase are helpful and will save on electric bills.

Because of the decline in depth perception with age, the first and last steps of a staircase are always troublemakers, and they should be highlighted in bright colors. Coloring the edges of the remaining steps is also helpful. The steps must all be the same size—not too narrow (less than 10 inches), too low (less than 4 inches), or too high (more than 7 inches). Nonskid surfaces, without carpeting, are the best, while overpadded carpeting is a nightmare. There should be at least one handrail on the staircase, though it's best to have them on both sides with enough space for the hands between the rail and the wall. Don't polish the handrails to a high sheen, because this will only produce hazardous glare. If there are rest landings or balconies on the staircase, the railings should be sturdy and always higher than your elderly friend's or relative's center of gravity, which usually means higher than 3½ feet. If there are any doors that open directly onto the staircase, they should be bolted shut.

HALLWAYS

Like the rest of the house, the hallway should be diffusely lit, with light coming from many directions; directly from shaded lights and indirectly from reflected surfaces. Light-colored walls and ceilings are a good source of diffuse light. You can color-code the doors along the hallway for easy identification, and they can also be set off from the walls in bright colors. Lever handles on the hallway doors—on all doors, for that matter—are easier to use than knob handles and cost only a few dollars more. Plain hardwood floors with a low-gloss finish are safe and easy to manage. Color contrasts help identify edges and borders, and since depth perception declines with age, it's easier for an elderly person to determine where the wall ends and the floor begins when the two are colored differently. If you have carpeting, make sure it's tacked down, and get rid of any scatter rugs, which are only hazards waiting to be tripped over. If your elderly friend uses a cane or walker, try to avoid shag carpeting: The bottoms of these walking aids get caught easily in the pile of the carpeting. Make sure that the hallway stays uncluttered: no broken or wobbly furniture, no loose extension cords, and no low-hanging plants or chandeliers (7 or 8 feet from the floor is a safe head clearance). Also, if your friend is too weak or unsteady to move around alone, you can install handrails along the hallway. You can get them at any medical supply house, and they take only minutes to put up.

THE KITCHEN

Your kitchen expresses your personality. It has evolved, over the years, to reflect your likes and dislikes and to meet your special needs and requirements. But it may not be the best kitchen for an elderly person whose needs are different from your own. Imagine your kitchen stripped bare and think about reorganizing it so that an elderly person would be able to use it safely and comfortably. As people get older, they tire more easily, and it becomes important for them to conserve their limited strength. In reorganizing your kitchen, the idea is to arrange things in such a way that wasted motions are eliminated, energy is conserved, and accidents are prevented. Store commonly used equipment close to where it will be used, in easy-to-reach cabinets. Keep glasses for cold drinks near the refrigerator and mugs for hot drinks near the stove. If you eat in the kitchen, keep the dishes near the stove for ease of serving or near the sink for ease of clearing, but if you serve family-style in the dining room, keep the dishes there to make table setting easier. Keep frequently used food in the front of the refrigerator, and make sure the refrigerator light is working. Frequently used utensils such as whisks, wooden spoons, and spatulas can be kept in a basket next to the stove to eliminate the need to hunt for them in drawers. If you have a cutting board, keep it near the sink to get rid of the unwanted portions of food more easily. Don't waste precious centrally located cabinet or drawer space for rarely used supplies. Keep frequently used pots and pans, such as skillets and saucepans, within easy reach, and store infrequently used ones, such as baking dishes, in the out-of-the-way cabinets. You can color-code the cabinets for easy identification, and even though manufacturers recommend storing spices in a cool, dry place, it makes for easier cooking if they're stored next to the stove.

The stove, and any other frequently used work area, should have its own overhead lighting, in addition to the upper lights for the room. Whether the kitchen floor is wooden or is covered with linoleum, use only nonskid, low-gloss polish to avoid unnecessary glare. It's best to have a stove with burner and oven knobs in the front, to avoid the possibility of your friend's reaching across lit burners.

In spite of all our efforts, sometimes fires still occur. Make sure your kitchen has a smoke detector. A fire extinguisher is also a good idea. Many home fires are electrical in origin, so check the electrical outlets, cords, and equipment regularly for frayed wires and loose connections. Try to keep your electrical appliances away from the sink, because in safety terms, electricity and water don't mix. Too many electrical burns and accidental electrocutions have occurred from electrical appliances falling into bathtubs or sinks. Also, since elderly people often have reduced temperature sensitivity, to prevent scalding set the maximum on your hot water heater near 120° Fahrenheit.

Many elderly people are weaker than they'd like to be. And even though they may have spent most of their lives preparing meals, as they get weaker and tire more easily they get discouraged from continuing to help in the kitchen. Many have trouble bending, their hands are often arthritic or stiff, and their grips are often weak. You can encourage your elderly friend's or relative's continued help by stocking your kitchen with utensils and equipment that are specially suited for the elderly.

A good place to start is with a countertop toaster oven, which will eliminate the need to bend over while baking or broiling small portions of food. There are dozens of specially designed jar and can openers to help people who have weak hand grips. They range from wall-mounted electric can openers for vacuum-sealed tin cans to hand-held jar wrenches for screw-type jar lids. There are even tab grabbers for twist-off bottle caps and special openers for milk cartons. If your elderly friend or relative has trouble peeling, slicing, or chopping fruits and vegetables, you can either buy a paring board or make one yourself with aluminum nails to secure the food and rubber suction cups to steady the board. You can do the same thing with a cutting board for meats. And you can use suction cups to steady any kitchen equipment. If turning on the water faucet is difficult for your friend, you can either buy or make a long-handled faucet turner; if lifting pots is difficult, you can buy double-handled pots; and if pouring liquids is difficult, you can build a pouring stand. The number of kitchen aids on the market today is practically infinite, and the type of aid you can build yourself is limited only by your imagination. A sampling is shown in Figure 8-1. If you suspect that weakness or incoordination is keeping your friend or relative away from the kitchen, browse through a few home health care catalogs to get some ideas. Fred Sammons, Inc., of Illinois, and Sears, Roebuck and Co. publish excellent catalogs with lots of pictures. Also, your local arthritis society is always a good source of information on self-help aids of any type. Check Appendix E, "Special Supplies," for names and addresses of supply houses and distributors.

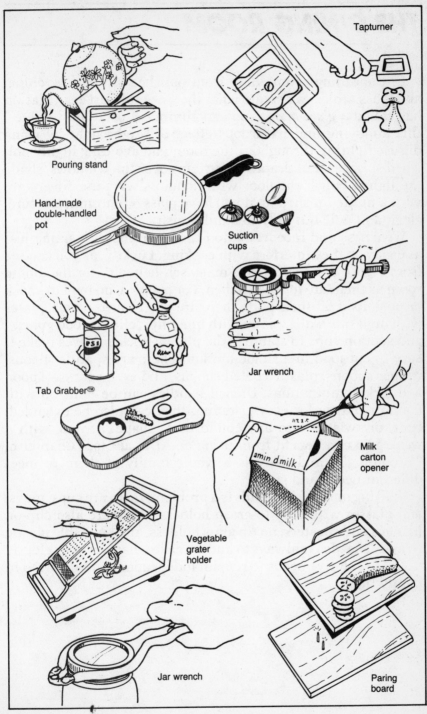

Figure 8-1. Kitchen aids.

THE DINING ROOM

In the dining room, glare from polished silverware, china, and glass tables can create what the gerontologist Jean Hatton has called *a glare-mare*. You can eliminate, or at least reduce, this annoying and hazardous effect of bright light by using diffuse lighting throughout the room and avoiding highly polished surfaces. Put drapes or curtains over the windows, shade the lights, polish the floor with nongloss wax, use silverware with a matte finish, and, if you have glass or chrome furniture, clean and polish it only to a dull finish.

Weakness and incoordination can interfere with eating just as easily as they interfere with cooking. Luckily, as you can see from Figure 8-2, there are as many self-help aids for the dining room as there are for the kitchen. For people who tend to knock or push food off their plate there are partitioned plates, plates with high side walls, plates with inner lips, clip-on food guards, and suction cups to stabilize the plates. Rocker knives make it easy to cut food in a single motion. There are spatula spoons, rubber spoons, plastic coated spoons, and even sporks—spoon and fork combinations. Utensil handles can be built up with foam or plastic for easy gripping; they can also be extended, bent, or twisted into any comfortable shape. Anyone with a weak grip can benefit from using an ADL cuff (see Chapter 6, "Grooming"), and there is a whole family of them to meet different needs and styles.

If lifting or drinking fluids is a problem, there are cups, mugs, and glasses with easy-to-grasp holders; there are also clip-on handles and coasters, no tip glass holders, and bendable plastic straws. The idea is always to find or make whatever your elderly friend or relative needs to remain independent and involved in family life.

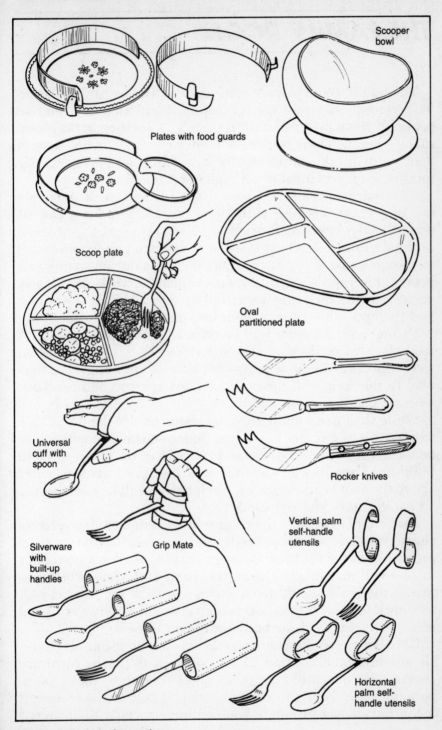

Figure 8-2. Aids for eating.

THE FAMILY ROOM

The family room is for leisure-time activities, and it should be arranged to encourage relaxation. Your friend or relative probably has a favorite chair. If there's a television in the room, make sure the chair is close enough for easy viewing; keep a floor lamp or table lamp nearby for reading; and in the winter months keep a blanket or an afghan on the chair.

The chair itself should be easy to get into and out of. Armrests are important, because with them an elderly person can sit down slowly, lowering himself or herself into the chair instead of falling into it. It's best if the armrests are padded and easy to grip, because they also support the arms during sitting and provide leverage for getting out of the chair. A weakened elderly person can use the armrests to pull up into a semierect position and then push off against them into a standing position.

Rising from the chair will be difficult if the chair cushion is too soft, low, or deep; if the seat slopes back it will be even more difficult. The best seats—for ease of standing—are parallel to the floor, and the best cushions are firm and resilient, with no sagging in the middle.

While sitting in a chair, anyone, young or old, should be able to place his or her feet flat on the floor and leave enough space between the edge of the seat and the back of the knees to avoid build-up of pressure behind the knees. A seat height of 16 inches above the floor is a good average height that will let most people sit comfortably and rise easily.

A footstool in front of the chair will let your friend or relative change sitting positions easily and also redistribute sitting pressures on the backside. Most important of all, a footstool or legrest will promote healthy circulation in the legs. The backrest of the chair should have a firm low-back support, as well as a neck support if the chair is high enough; it's always a good idea for the areas of the body that bend to be supported.

Upholstery for the chair should be easy to clean, flame-resistant, and nonirritating. Don't bother with plastic furniture covers: They produce glare, they don't "breathe," they're slippery, and they're hot in the summer and cold in the winter. If incontinence is a problem, you can buy specially upholstered furniture with interior moisture guards from a durable medical equipment company. (See Appendix E, "Special Supplies.") Alternatively, you can simply put a Chux (a popular brand of absorbent underpads available at most pharmacies) on the seat before it is used.

Once you've made sure that your friend's or relative's favorite chair is well positioned, safe, and comfortable, check to see that the pathway from the chair to the door is clear and uncluttered. Since so much of an elderly person's time is spent sitting, it makes sense to provide the best possible sitting arrangement.

Plants or flowers in the family room are a nice touch and keep the air well hydrated, especially in the winter. Drapes, wall hangings, and rugs are pretty, and they absorb background noise which could interfere with your friend's or relative's hearing. The rule for decorating the family room is to encourage relaxation and promote safety.

THE BEDROOM

The bedroom is a private space that reflects a person's taste and personality and is a refuge from the clamor of the rest of the household. When an elderly person moves into your home, he or she moves in with memories of the past and a life full of experiences. Often your elderly friend's or relative's home, brimming with possessions accumulated over a lifetime, must be condensed into a single room. Moving in with someone else, no matter how close the relationship, is a traumatic experience. But the bedroom can ease the transition with furnishings from the past. Nothing can match the warmth and security that old, treasured furniture brings to a new room. Let your friend or relative furnish the room and choose the colors. Early on, your only job will be as a safety inspector, making sure that the room is uncluttered and that there are no scatter rugs, shag carpeting, unshaded lamps, loose wires, high gloss surfaces, and the like (Figure 8-3).

A night-light is essential, but since it is only for orientation, a switch for the overhead light should also be close at hand. A

Figure 8-3. Model bedroom.

flashlight on a sturdy nightstand is another good idea. A desk or tabletop lamp for close work and high overhead lighting for general illumination meet most lighting needs, though a closet light is also important. If you can manage it, a two-way light switch is useful, so that the lights can be turned on and off from both the doorway and the bed. The light switch at the doorway should be between 3 and 4 feet above the floor.

If there is a telephone in the room, place it within easy reach of the bed; if your friend or relative has trouble seeing, you can get an oversized dial from the telephone company. Colorful calendars and wall clocks help elderly people stay aware and involved in day-to-day activities. Everything we've already said about chairs for the family room applies equally well to chairs for the bedroom. In addition, a rocking chair, though not essential, would provide both relaxation and gentle exercise. Try to provide a table or desk for close work, and make sure that it fits the chair. Working for a long time at a table or desk that is too low for its chair requires bending and strains the lower back, while working at a table or desk that is too high raises the elbows and strains the upper back and neck. As a rule of thumb, allow 1 foot between the seat and the top of the work area. The height of the bed is also important—for you as well as your friend or relative. If the mattress is less than 17 inches off the floor, making the bed can strain the back, while if it is more than 21 inches off the floor, sitting down on it can be impossible.

A night table next to the bed is another inessential but useful addition. You can arrange the telephone, a water pitcher, a flashlight or light switch, and eyeglasses within easy reach on the table. In this way your elderly friend or relative won't have to grope for essential items in the dark, and the chances for a nighttime accident will be reduced.

One final word: Never tidy up an elderly person's room yourself. Elderly people depend, psychologically and physiologically, on knowing where things are. They need the security, and with poor vision, compromised motor skills, and failing memory, they don't do well with redecorating surprises. Remember, one person's clutter is another person's filing system—and if there's no safety hazard, there's no harm.

THE BATHROOM

The bathroom is the one remaining room to be modified for your friend or relative. Make sure that the approach to the bathroom is uncluttered. If someone is using a wheelchair, there mustn't be any doorsills or steps leading into the bathroom. The width of the door must be wide enough for the wheelchair or any other walking aid. A heavy person with crutches would have to shimmy through a narrow door sideways, and someone in a wheelchair would be locked out of an open room if the entranceway were too narrow. A 34-inch door is common in most houses and provides 32 inches of uncluttered entrance space when it's swung open. The door itself must swing free and have an easy-to-use lock to guarantee privacy. Often someone in a wheelchair gets into a room easily only to discover that there isn't enough room inside to pull the door open to get out. It's best if the door swings in both directions. If you have to choose, out is better than in; better still are sliding doors. If your doors are too narrow, take them off, remove the doorjam strips which themselves restrict the space by another 1½ inches and improvise a door with curtains.

The toilet must be high enough for easy use. Too often elderly people become prisoners of low seats—they fall into them and can't get up because they are too weak. The toilet must be at the right height: A distance of 15 to 16 inches from the floor to the seat is customary, and it's adequate for most elderly people. If your friend is too weak or in too much pain to use an ordinary toilet safely, nearby guardrails and grab bars can be helpful, and an adjustable, raised seat attached to an ordinary toilet makes all the difference in the world. Raised seats add between 4 and 6 inches of height to a conventional toilet. They're usually adjustable in 1-inch increments. Prices for elevated seats range from $25 for a one-piece plastic molded seat to $75 or $100 for a deluxe model with a contoured seat, padded armrests, guardrails, and a splashboard.

Any toilet that's used by an elderly person should have a padded seat, because aged skin has lost its elasticity, its lubricating oils, and its underlying adipose tissue—the fat padding that is the body's built-in cushion. Consequently, sitting

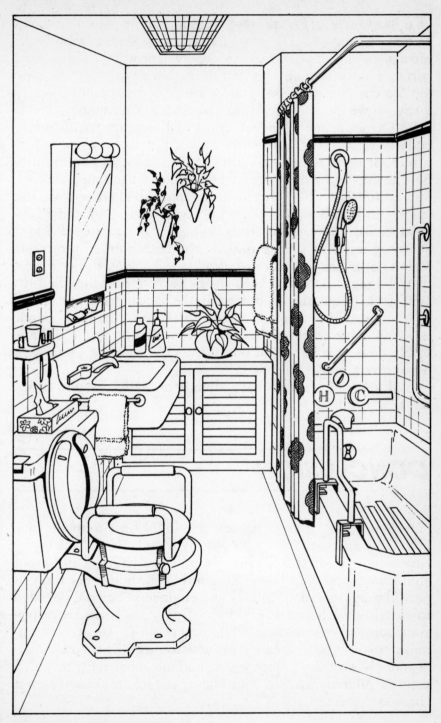

Figure 8-4. Model bathroom.

on a hard surface, for whatever reason, can be painful and can also be chafing and irritating to dry, fragile skin. Our buttocks are a portable, all-purpose cushion which protects us from hard surfaces and sharp objects, but in the later years the covering for the cushion dries out and cracks, and the padding wears away, so we have to substitute store-bought cushions.

The general principles we employed in other rooms apply equally well to the bathroom: no scatter rugs, unsteady furniture, or loose wires, and shiny chrome kept to a minimum. Set the maximum on the hot water heater for the sink, shower, and bathtub at 120° Fahrenheit. Lever-shaped faucets are the easiest to use, but whichever ones you have, they should be color-coded, textured, or simply labeled hot and cold. Light switches are best placed outside the bathroom so that your friend never has to enter a dark room. To be on the safe side, install a night-light and keep the hallway approaches well lit. Don't hide frequently used items in the back of medicine chests or in cabinets below the sink. And make sure the toilet paper is within easy reach of the toilet—it would be tragic to have to blame a broken hip on out-of-the-way toilet paper! Figure 8-4 shows a model bathroom.

Bathtubs and showers have already been discussed in Chapter 5, "Bathing."

CONCLUSION

It doesn't take a lot of money or a lot of time to make your home safe and secure for your elderly friend. Think back to the time when you first had children and you had to child-proof your home. You didn't need to rebuild your home, nor did you need the services of architects and engineers. You only needed to carefully watch your children at play and then rearrange your home to ensure their safety and comfort. The same commonsense approach is called for now to meet the special needs of your elderly friend. Once you've had the opportunity to watch your friend move around your house, you'll know exactly what changes are necessary.

9 Bowel Care

Bowel movements are like relatives and the rain: They cause problems when they come too often and when they don't come enough. Regularity, that cherished American ideal, is nothing more than someone's usual and customary bowel movement pattern. If you're the type of person who has had one bowel movement every twelve hours twenty-eight minutes and seventeen seconds for the last fifty years, then for you regularity is one bowel movement every twelve hours twenty-eight minutes and seventeen seconds. But if you're the type of person who's never been regular, then for you regularity is your usual shifting, unpredictable pattern. It's all individual; there is no good or bad, no ideal for which to strive. There are no magical colors, quantities, or textures that signify good health, nor are there evil ones that signal impending doom. The only time for concern is when your normal pattern is interrupted.

Bowel movement patterns usually don't change. When they do, it means that something is wrong and needs to be fixed. Most of the time, 99.9 percent of the time, the repair work can be done at home. We'll discuss that now, but first a warning: If any change in bowel movement pattern, whether constipation or diarrhea, lasts more than a week, call a doctor. Though it's rare, a change that persists can signal the onset of serious disease and must be investigated by a doctor.

The big joke about old people, in hospitals as well as nightclubs, is their preoccupation with bowel movements. The high drama of life and death often surrounds their missed bowel movements, and future bowel movements are awaited with the same nervous expectation that surrounds waiting for a kidnapper's next call. History is important in absolving the elderly of these excesses. Someone who is 65 or 75 years old today was old enough in the 1920s and 1930s to grow up with Carter's Little Liver Pills and the prevailing wisdom of that time that a daily bowel movement, perhaps even a purgative, was the foundation on which healthy lives were built. It is difficult to disabuse someone of ideas and habits learned fifty years ago. A relaxed approach to bowel movements is a recent innovation. Probably the young people of today will grow old with a more flexible approach to bowel movements than the present older generation has.

Survival instincts are also responsible for the elderly's preoccupation with their bowel movements, as well as with other aspects of their body. People don't jump in one quantum leap from a vigorous youth to a frail old age. A lot of life is packed in between. As friends and relatives pass on, there are fewer and fewer people left to help when problems arise. Survival becomes a matter of self involvement. When you're alone, fending for yourself, you are naturally concerned about the details of your world, and you can easily become preoccupied with subtle changes in your day-to-day life. Normal, self-protective instincts can imperceptibly give way, over the years, to excessive, hypochondriacal concerns about bodily functions. When older people start worrying about missed bowel movements, remember their early training and remember that subtle changes in their bodily functions naturally assume greater significance to them later in life.

CAUSES OF CONSTIPATION

✗ Decreased Physical Activity

There is always a good reason for an increase or decrease in the frequency or quality of bowel movements or the quantity of stool. For example, a decrease in physical activity will decrease the number of bowel movements, as will loss of fluid, either from not drinking or sweating too much in the summertime.

The gut is like an automated conveyer belt taking food through the processing department and then disposing of the wastes. A decrease in physical activity slows down the conveyer belt, and a decrease in amount of fluid produces dry, hard stools that interfere with waste removal. The bowels respond quickly to activity. One day of bed rest is enough to slow them down and diminish the number of movements. Likewise, as soon as you're out of bed moving around, the bowels respond, and movements will increase in number within hours.

✗ Diet Changes

Since your diet is ultimately responsible for your bowel movements it's not surprising that changes in your diet alter your bowel movements. Conservation of mass applies to food intake and bowel movements as well as to atomic physics, and simply cutting back on food consumption reduces stool production. An elderly person who stops eating or who reduces his or her usual intake because of poor teeth, depression, or any number of other reasons will have fewer and smaller bowel movements.

Roughage, the natural fiber found in green vegetables and fruits, can absorb and store moisture (just like the rice and potato pieces kept in saltshakers and tobacco tins to prevent caking or drying). Since roughage can't be digested, it simply holds onto water in the gut, keeping the stools soft, moist, and bulky—which makes waste removal easy. Reducing the roughage in your diet can lead to hard, dry, small, and infrequent stools. The same thing is true of fluids, which also add bulk to stools. See Chapter 2, "Nutrition," for a complete discussion of food and nutrition.

When you eat is almost as important as *what* you eat. The gastrocolic reflex is a reflex that empties the bowels after a meal. Food in the gut stimulates the emptying contractions in the colon. The reflex is not terribly powerful, and we can and usually do overcome it consciously or by habit. But for elderly people with troubling constipation, it is best for bathroom visits to be scheduled after meals, to take advantage of the reflex.

✗ MEDICATIONS

Medications are notorious constipation producers. The following list shows a variety of well-known culprits. These drugs slow down the conveyer belt so that food takes longer to pass through the gut. Consequently, bowel movements become less frequent and stools dry out during their leisurely trip. Antihistamines, antacids, and iron supplements are common offenders, often repeat offenders because they can be bought without a prescription. Antihistamines are found in many cold preparations, antacids in upset stomach remedies, and iron supplements in multivitamins. A careful drug inventory must be taken whenever the bowels slow down.

DRUGS THAT CONSTIPATE

X

Antacids containing aluminum or calcium (Gelusil, Maalox)

Anticholinergic compounds (Donnatol, Lomotil, Probanthine)

Antihistamines (Benadryl, Pyribenzamine, Dramamine)

Antiparkinsonism drugs (Sinemet, levodopa)

Diuretics

Iron salts

Narcotic analgesics (codeine, Darvocet, Demerol, Percodan)

Phenothizines (Mellaril, Phenergan)

Tricyclic antidepressants (Elavil, Sinequan)

Sedatives and hypnotics (Dalmane, Doriden, Seconal)

X EMOTIONAL CONFLICTS

Changes in physical activity, diet, and medication account for most instances of constipation. Emotions can be responsible as well. Our bodies are always expressing our inner feelings—when we feel good we stand up straight, when we are depressed we hunch over. Bodily functions such as eating, urinating, and defecating are also sensitive to our psyches and respond, sometimes dramatically, to changes in our emotional lives. The mind-body connection is true for everyone, but it is dramatic with elderly people. Some elderly people react to stress by avoiding the bathroom and becoming constipated, while others develop diarrhea. When you are looking for the cause of constipation in your elderly friend or relative, there is nothing better than a relaxed and open talk to uncover emotional problems, worries, or depressing thoughts. As you care for an elderly person over time, you will learn the language of his or her body and come to know the significance of changes in bodily functions. You will know what constipation (or diarrhea) means for the special person you're looking after, and you'll be able to respond quickly and confidently to changes.

✕ AWKWARD SOCIAL SETTINGS

Awkward social situations are another cause of constipation. An elderly person who has difficulty getting up from a chair, walking, or maneuvering in a cramped bathroom will often ignore the body's urge to evacuate in situations where the physical difficulties would be embarrassing or attract attention.

✕ PAIN AND DISCOMFORT

Pain, tremor, and weakness can all contribute to the slow, labored motions that force an elderly person to ignore bodily needs rather than expose the infirmities of old age to excessive attention. But continuing to ignore the signals and urges for evacuation will lead, in time, to constipation. For elimination of this cause of constipation, elderly people must learn to respect the wisdom of their bodies and society must be sensitized to the needs and abilities of elderly people, so that slow, awkward actions are accepted and do not attract attention.

If bowel movements are painful or uncomfortable, an elderly person is likely to avoid them; but missed bowel movements constipate future ones, making it necessary to strain next time. This leads to more discomfort and an endless, vicious cycle.

Dry skin, rashes, and hemorrhoids can all interfere with bowel movements. Bowel movements are uncomfortable and unpleasant when the skin in the groin and perineum is dry and cracked. The same is true when there are rashes and skin infections in these areas. More commonly, hemorrhoids, which are engorged veins around the anus, interfere with bowel movements because of pain. They can come and go unnoticed for years, or they can itch and burn and sometimes stain underwear from oozing or bleeding. Sometimes they can be so painful and tender that having a bowel movement becomes impossible. If your friend or relative becomes constipated, you have to look at his or her backside and anus. While your friend is still in bed, have him or her roll onto one side, spread the cheeks, and look.

(There's no need to probe internally with your fingers. Leave that for the doctor, if the need arises.) If the skin is dry, you should apply petrolatum or some other moisturizing cream twice a day (see Chapter 6, "Grooming"). If there is a rash, an infection, or a bulging hemorrhoid, call the doctor. Your calls to the doctor will be rare if you make it a practice to watch and observe the elderly person in your care. Most problems are not serious medical problems that need the attention of a trained professional. Observation, understanding, and horse sense go a long way themselves.

⊁ ARCHITECTURAL BARRIERS

An elderly person will avoid the bathroom if it's difficult to get to or difficult to use. Like fire exits in the movies, bathrooms should have easy access, free and unencumbered pathways. Likewise, an uncomfortable toilet or one that's difficult to negotiate can make evacuation a difficult, painful experience that will be avoided, and in time this will lead to constipation. Assistive devices, architectural modifications, and principles of safe seating are discussed in detail in Chapter 8, "The Environment." The important thing is to make sure that lack of comfort, accessibility, or safety is never the reason an elderly person skips a bowel movement. They are problems that are so easy to remedy.

MEDICATIONS FOR CONSTIPATION

What if, in spite of all your efforts at preventive medicine and healthy living, your elderly charge continues to get constipated? He or she is up walking around, eating nutritious meals, drinking lots of fluids, and not taking constipating medicine; the bathroom is easy to get to, the toilet is comfortable, and there are no upsetting emotional experiences or embarrassing social situations. And yet constipation recurs regularly. You could give a Fleet enema; follow it up with a tap-water enema; mix up a batch of milk of magnesia, Colace, Pericolace, magnesium citrate, cascara, senna, castor oil, or phenolphthalein (or any combination from the over 700 brands of medicines for treating constipation on the market today); insert a Dulcolax suppository; leave the room and wait for an explosion. There are better approaches.

The next line of defense against recurrent constipation, after diet and exercise, is medical, and consists of laxatives and enemas. Some elderly people simply have sluggish bowels: Usually as a result of years of laxative abuse they have a slow conveyer belt that can't be speeded up. Other people, because of old habits or simple orneriness, refuse to drink enough fluid or eat enough fiber. And sometimes, even the best-intentioned people are too ill to get out of bed and move around. In these cases a little outside help is useful.

Just remember that you don't need the military might and explosive power of the Royal Air Force to nudge along a bowel movement.

Laxatives come as pills, syrups, and suppositories. They fall into four main categories: stimulant cathartics, saline cathartics, bulking agents, and stool softeners (see the following list). But any individual laxative may have a combination of properties, and all laxatives have some degree of stool-softening action. The softeners do just what their name suggests: They soften the stool and make its removal easier. These drugs lower the surface tension of the feces, allowing more water to be incorporated into the stool, which makes it softer.

✗ LAXATIVES

Saline cathartics	Magnesium salts, phosphate preparations, milk of magnesia
Stimulant cathartics	Aloe, cascara, phenolphthalein, castor oil, Dulcolax, Perdiem, Pericolace
Bulking agents	Bran, psyllium, Metamucil, Perdiem
Stool softeners	Colace, Pericolace

But stool softeners are useful only if the stool is hard and you want it softened. Obviously, they are useless if the stool is already soft—which is often the case with elderly people. Medicine is 98 percent common sense. Look at the stool: If it's soft, toughen it up, don't soften it further. Use of bulking agents is one way to firm up the stool. They are undigestible and they attract and absorb water, swelling up like rice and adding bulk to the stool. There are many on the market, but ideally a person's diet should provide all the bulk necessary with fiber from fruits, grains, and vegetables. See Chapter 2 for information on nutrition and diet.

Saline cathartics contain high concentrations of salts and pull water from the body into the intestines. Milk of magnesia is the best example. These agents can be irritating to the bowel, and they can upset the body's delicate electrolyte balance. They may be helpful occasionally, but they are not recommended for long-term use.

Stimulant cathartics irritate the inner lining of the bowel and the underlying nerves. This in turn stimulates and strengthens the muscular contractions that push the stool along. After ingestion of a stimulant cathartic, the natural activity in the gut is speeded up, and wave after wave of contractions empties the bowels. Castor oil is a favorite stimulant, as is the old-time black and white (senna and cascara). The problem with these laxatives is that people are apt to abuse them.

Uppers and downers like cocaine and heroin usually come to mind when talking about drug abuse, but stimulant laxatives are abused drugs as well. A full 30 percent of people over age 65 depend on them for their bowel movements! Nature isn't even given a chance. The danger is that continued use damages the nervous system's wiring in the intestines, interfering with spontaneous bowel movements. The bowel becomes lazy, unable to initiate its own evacuation, and simply waits for the next stimulant fix. An occasional purgative can be helpful, but avoid creating a habit. These laxatives shouldn't be used routinely to treat chronic constipation.

When someone isn't able to swallow a pill or liquid, a suppository may be the answer, though many people object to suppositories because of modesty or because they have trouble keeping them in. The mildest suppositories contain hyperosmotic agents such as glycerin that pull water into the stool.

But the stronger and more common suppositories contain stimulant cathartics, and everything we've said about stimulants applies to these suppositories as well.

Enemas are the best defense against recurrent constipation. They are also the last defense and should be started only after diet changes, counseling, and physical activity programs have been ineffective. After all else fails, an enema is the simplest and most effective way to empty a sluggish bowel.

Soapsuds enemas, which were once the rage (as much as enemas could be the rage), are out. We now know that soap can irritate the lining of the colon and create more problems than it solves. Don't use ice cold water to refresh the bowels in hot weather, and stay away from the hot water tap in the winter. This might sound silly to you, but there is a lot of wild thinking about the bowels. With enemas, as with so much else in life, the simplest is the best. A tap-water enema, the water either tepid or at room temperature, given as a last resort will clear the most indolent and lethargic bowels of accumulated stool. The following lists the steps for giving a safe and helpful enema. Elderly people can be taught to administer their own enemas. While tap-water enemas are relatively safe (as long as the amount of water is kept to a minimum), administering them can be inconvenient. Disposable enema kits such as a Fleet Enema, eliminate the fuss and bother of giving an enema; there are no bags to fill and no tubing to clean. The only problem is that many kits contain sodium salts which can be absorbed in the colon and upset the body's delicate electrolyte balance. Elderly people on sodium restricted diets should not use these enemas, but for everyone else they are superb.

GIVING AN ENEMA

1. Relax and reassure your friend or relative. Explain the procedure; insure privacy during the procedure; arrange for bedding protection; and make ready a bedpan, bedside commode, or bathroom toilet.
2. Make sure the enema bag tubing is clamped, and fill the enema bag with 1 to 2 pints of warm tap water, about 105° Fahrenheit. Un-

clamp the tubing and let the water run through it, warming it and displacing the air. Reclamp.

3. Lubricate the last 2 inches of the tubing.
4. Position your friend or relative in bed on his or her left or right side, whichever is more comfortable.
5. Point the lubricated end of the tubing toward the navel, and with a slight twisting motion insert it 2 to 3 inches into the rectum.
6. Raise the enema bag slowly, but no higher than 2 feet above the mattress. Unclamp the tubing.
7. Clamp the tubing and remove it when your friend or relative has a strong desire to defecate.
8. Help your friend or relative onto a bedpan, bedside commode, or bathroom toilet, and explain that the enema solution must be retained for at least five minutes.
9. Wash thoroughly and dry all the equipment.

To review, the prerequisites for normal bowel movements—which are different for each individual and have more to do with personal history than with national standards—are good nutrition with adequate dietary fiber, physical activity, attentiveness to the body's urges, elimination of architectural barriers, and opportunities for emotional release. When the bowels are unresponsive to these preventive health measures, or when it is impossible to implement the measures (e.g., when someone is confined to bed), a tap-water enema is recommended. Stimulant cathartics should be reserved for occasional use during especially sluggish times.

IMPACTION

Besides promoting a more comfortable, trouble-free life, regular bowel movements prevent the complications of untreated constipation, the most important of which is impaction and its associated fecal incontinence. Continued constipation leads to one of two things, depending on the type of stool. If the stool is hard, it actually plugs the bowel, preventing the disposal of further waste, and the bowel slowly backs up with feces. Eventually, there is so much stool that some starts leaking out around the plug. Alternatively, when the stool is soft and mushy (usually the result of a poor diet that is low in fiber and high in processed food), it accumulates in the lower end of the bowel, stretching the opening so that the anal sphincter (the valve that controls emptying) can't close properly; every time there is an increase in pressure—from coughing or sneezing, for example—feces get pushed out. Of course, the hard stool needs fluid and stool softeners, while the soft stool doesn't. Impaction can lead to more than just incontinence. It can also cause abdominal distention and obstruction of the entire gut. For these reasons, a physician or skilled nurse must be consulted to begin treating the impaction. This ordinarily begins with digging out the impaction, which is uncomfortable for the patient and requires the gentle and skilled hands of a professional. The best treatment, as in everything else in medicine, is prevention.

INCONTINENCE

Fecal incontinence is the inability to control the bowels, causing frequent soiling of undergarments and bedclothes. It is a subject that embarrasses people and one that is usually avoided or denied. The so-called accidents are allegedly the most common reason elderly people are placed in nursing homes. This is supposed to be the one absolutely unapproachable, untreatable, irreversible problem that makes living comfortably at home impossible and nursing home placement unavoidable. But infants are incontinent, soiling everything in sight, and no one puts them away in nursing homes. It's just as difficult to clean up after an infant as after an elderly person, but incontinence is expected in infancy and not understood afterward. Incontinence is not difficult to manage, and while it can't always be stopped, it can always be handled at home easily and safely with a minimum of effort. The key is to be prepared and unembarrassed. Embarrassment is certainly no reason to ship someone off to a nursing home.

— Incontinence is not diarrhea. *Incontinence* does not mean frequent bowel movements—it means uncontrolled bowel movements. And there are two broad categories: Either you're aware of an impending movement but can't or won't stop it, or you're not aware until it's too late. Obviously, being aware makes it all the more embarrassing and difficult to cope with.

Senility is the biggest cause of incontinence without awareness. Senility is not synonymous with old age, nor is it the final resting place after life's journey. It is not caused by retirement, and you don't catch it in Florida. Real, irreversible, unchangeable senility is either a disease itself or it is caused by another disease. As we stressed in Chapter 4, "Understanding the Elderly," senility is not the normal, expected outcome of old age. When it is the result of another disease, it can be cured if the underlying disease can be cured. When it is a disease itself, like Alzheimer's disease, it is, at the present time, uncurable. While no one knows what causes Alzheimer's disease, and no one can cure it, there are still lots of things that can be done to improve life for its victims. Most of these were mentioned in Chapter 4, but we will discuss the bowel program now.

Seepage around an impaction is the most common cause of incontinence in elderly, immobilized people. If an impaction is identified—by a skilled nurse or physician—and removed, the preventive program we have already described, including diet, activity, and laxatives, must be instituted at once to avoid further trouble.

Drugs can cause incontinence also. Many neurological diseases can affect the innervation of the bowels and lead to incontinence. Cancer of the bowels, infections, and poor circulation to the bowels can produce incontinence as well. Therefore, once again the refrain, see your doctor. Incontinence, like constipation and diarrhea, is a change in bowel habits and thus deserves immediate medical attention. Once the cause is determined and you know that there is no tumor or other disease, then you can manage the situation without worry, and do a better job than a stranger in a nursing home or hospital. Remember, this book is not meant to turn you into a doctor. When a diagnosis is needed, a doctor with access to a hospital and state-of-the-art medical equipment is essential. But once a diagnosis is made, you can start doing what you do better than anyone else—take care of the person you know and love, using the basics and relying on common sense.

In elderly people, incontinence often produces well-formed stools rather than mushy stools or seepage, but at inappropriate times. Your overall strategy, then, should be to take control of the bowel movements and make sure that there are no unexpected ones. The first step—which should be familiar by now—involves proper diet and activity. With this foundation in place and well-formed stools being produced, the next step is to gain control of the bowels using suppositories. Enemas are not helpful for senile people or people with incontinence from neurological disease, because they can't hold the enema in long enough for it to do any good. But a suppository is easily kept in place and quickly produces a bowel movement, thus preventing accidents. Suppositories can be given at any time of the day, but a regular schedule must be established. Try a mild suppository first, such as a glycerin suppository; if it doesn't work, go to something stronger, such as a Dulcolax suppository. It takes about half an hour for a suppository like Dulcolax to stimulate a bowel movement.

You and the person you're taking care of must decide on the best time for bowel movements. Often, the morning is a convenient time: The suppository can be inserted while the person is still in bed, and a bedpan, bedside commode, or bathroom toilet can be readied for the evacuation. You will have to experiment for the right schedule. Some people need daily suppositories, but usually three times a week is sufficient.

If there are accidents in spite of these measures, absorbent undergarments or incontinent pants, also called diapers, must be used to protect the skin, the clothing, and the house. Incontinent pants are embarrassing, there's no way around that, but sometimes, very rarely, their use is unavoidable. When they are used, they must be changed as soon as they get wet—which means that they must be checked frequently, at least every two or three hours. Bear in mind that though your friend or relative may need incontinent pants today, he or she may not need them forever. Incontinence often waxes and wanes, and from time to time the pants should be discarded to see if your friend or relative has regained control or to see if suppositories can do a more effective job. Incontinent pants can be expensive. The disposable types are the most expensive, often going as high as $30 for fifty. If pants are changed six to seven times a day, that comes to $30 a week for diapers alone. Marsupial pants, the standard form of incontinent pants, are cheaper. They consist of a plastic cover that has a leakproof pouch for disposable liners. The cover is reusable and goes for about $10, while the liners run about $10 for fifty. Washable, reusable cloth diapers, with or without a plastic cover, are also available. For even greater economy, you can make incontinent pants using old linen for the cover and old towels or store-bought underpads (fifty for $7 or $8) for the liners. Incontinent pants, liners, and underpads can be found in any medical supply house. Check with your insurance company to see what, if anything, is covered. Medicare does not cover any absorbent undergarments.

Caring for an incontinent person is seldom physically demanding. The difficulties that people encounter are psychological and emotional. All of us are accustomed to thinking of bodily functions as private activities, and we associate loss of control with loss of personal dignity. The key to helping your friend live comfortably, despite his or her loss of control, is to come to grips with your own feelings about incontinence. Then you will be free to relate to your friend with respect and dignity, accidents and embarrassing moments notwithstanding.

DIARRHEA

Diarrhea is usually the result of a virus upsetting the intestines and requires only rest, patience, and clear liquids. The danger of diarrhea in the elderly, as well as in little children, is dehydration. You can lose tremendous quantities of fluids in diarrheal stools over the course of a couple of days. This loss, coupled with no food intake, can lead to severe fluid losses, electrolyte imbalance, and dehydration. A condition that is initially only unpleasant can become life-threatening if ignored or untreated. When the intestines are in high gear, rejecting all food and secreting their own fluids, the only commonsense thing to do is leave them alone; let them rest and recover. This means no solid food during a bout of diarrhea—but lots of fluids to offset the losses—and a slow, careful resumption of a normal diet when the diarrhea abates. After a period of diarrhea, the intestines are overworked and irritated and can handle only easily digestible food in small quantities. Anything more substantial would only further irritate the gut, creating diarrhea anew. The following is a suggested diet plan for dealing with diarrhea. Keep away from fatty foods, stimulants such as coffee and tea, and depressants such as alcohol during a bout of diarrhea. The length of time each step in the plan is followed depends on the severity of the diarrhea. For example, for a mild case you can skip the clear liquid step and go directly to full liquids. On the other hand, during a severe case your elderly friend or relative might have to stay with clear liquids for a couple of days. Advance from step to step as the diarrhea clears. But don't forget that diarrhea that lasts for more than three or four days constitutes a genuine change in bowel habits and could signify a serious underlying disease. Therefore, persistent diarrhea deserves a doctor's attention. There are lots of antidiarrheal medicines, but they are usually prescription drugs which can't be purchased without a doctor's consent and they should be used only for occasional, symptomatic treatment. Even nonprescription drugs such as Kaopectate should be used only symptomatically. There are no drugs that are designed for chronic, long-term use. But apples are. Do you remember the expression, "An apple a day keeps the doctor away"? Apples contain pectin, a complex carbohydrate used in almost all antidiarrheal medications. It's not clear how pectin works—probably by absorbing water and protecting the bowel lining—but it does work, and it makes the old-fashioned folk medicine understandable in today's language.

DIET PLAN FOR DIARRHEA

STEP 1   Clear liquids (anything you can see through): gelatin; sherbet; consommé; clear juices such as apple, grape, and cranberry

STEP 2   Full liquids: ice cream, cus-
                          tards, puddings, pulp juices
                          such as orange and grape-
                          fruit

STEP 3   Bland diet: toast, boiled
                          chicken, stewed meats, soft
                          vegetables

STEP 4   Regular diet: foods included
                          in the seven dietary goals
                          (See Chapter 2)

A FINAL NOTE

One final word before leaving our discussion of bowel function. In all your bowel crusades, whether against constipation,
incontinence, or diarrhea, common sense must direct the action. It's easy to lose confidence when taking care of an elderly
person with many medical problems. Bowel problems can be
especially troublesome, time-consuming, and frightening. But
as long as you're concerned and caring, basic, unadulterated
common sense will show you the way. Trust yourself. If things
get out of hand, you can always ask for help. But concern, basic
knowledge, and common sense will take you far on your own.

10 Bladder Problems

Urinary incontinence, or leakage of urine, is a more common problem in the elderly than fecal incontinence, and is unfortunately responsible for tens of thousands of nursing home placements a year. Urinary retention (the inability to urinate), as well as frequent urination, urgency, pain, and infection, are also troublesome problems for the elderly. But usually they can all be handled at home, once a diagnosis is made and a management plan is chosen. The best plan depends on the person with the problem.

Frequency of urination is common in elderly people. Most of the time it is caused by medication, such as a diuretic (water pill) taken to control high blood pressure. But it can also indicate an infection of the bladder, diabetes, or some other serious medical condition, so if it is recent, have a doctor check it out. In the meantime you should make sure that it doesn't create more discomfort than necessary. You can do this by being aware of the problem and making a commode available at all times. Frequency at nighttime, or nocturia, is a dangerous setup for either an accidental loss of urine or a fall in the hallway, because it's so easy to ignore the urge to urinate when you're lying sleepily in a warm bed and the bathroom is a long, cold walk away. A portable commode by the bedside is a good idea. It's lightweight and it can be emptied in the morning. You can buy one in any medical supply house and in most drugstores.

Incontinence can range from occasional slight losses of urine to frequent, drenching accidents. Incontinence robs a person of more than bladder control; it also takes away personal dignity and autonomy. Many elderly people will hide their accidents and not admit them to anyone while they withdraw from social contacts to avoid their feelings of shame and embarrassment. The stereotype of an incontinent person is based on untreated incontinence: a wet, foul-smelling person uncontrollably drenching furniture, clothing, and carpets with urine. But incontinence is treatable, and there is no reason for anyone to be wet, to be dirty, or to smell because of lost bladder control. Incontinence is embarrassing, but it is not the end of the world. We all came into the world incontinent and it didn't stop anyone from loving us or taking care of us. There's no reason that it should in the twilight of our lives either. Incontinence is easily, safely, and hygienically manageable at home.

THE ENVIRONMENT

The first thing to do when you want to help a person who has wetting accidents is to determine whether incontinence is responsible. An arthritic woman with stiff joints who has pain standing up, more pain walking, and even more squeezing through a crowded hallway and cluttered bathroom is not incontinent when she has accidents because she can't get to the toilet in time! We've already talked about how to create a safe and comfortable home environment in Chapter 8, but it's important to emphasize again that the bathroom and toilet in your home must be easily accessible to your elderly friend. What seems like a perfectly easy route to the bathroom for you might be a long, tortuous march over obstacle-laden terrain for your friend. And what seems like a luxuriously comfortable toilet seat for you might be a dangerously low, imprisoning seat for your friend.

INCONTINENCE

How can you help with real incontinence—an uncontrollable loss of urine that has nothing to do with bathroom accessibility? The first thing is to find the cause of the incontinence, and this can only be done in conjunction with a physician. Once the cause is found, the management and day-to-day care is up to you. Incontinence is not normal; it is not an expected, un-

avoidable aspect of old age. It is a sign that something, some-
where, is wrong. Very often that something can be cleared up
in a short time and the incontinence made to disappear. For
example, an infection in the urinary tract might be irritating
the bladder, causing urine to be pushed out. Such infection is
particularly prevalent in women. Once the infection is discov-
ered, treated, and eradicated, the incontinence will disapppear.

Medications are another common source of reversible incontinence. Some medications, such as the diuretics people take
for high blood pressure, make you urinate more frequently.
Other medicines, such as the decongestants taken for colds, can
hold back the urine until so much of it accumulates in the
bladder that it starts to leak out under its own pressure. The
bladder is just an elastic sac with muscles in the walls to push
the urine out and a valve at the bottom to hold the urine in.
Anything that interferes with the function of the muscles or the
valves can cause incontinence. Many women who have had lots
of children have weak valves (because the supporting structures
in the groin have stretched), and they often lose their urine
under stress. When they cough, sneeze, laugh, or cry, the pressures on the bladder increase and the weak valve can't hold
back the urine. This is called *stress incontinence*, and it's easy
to correct.

Neurological diseases such as strokes or multiple sclerosis
indirectly affect the nerves in the bladder wall muscles, often
making them so irritable that urine gets pushed out sponta-
neously and without warning. Diabetes also affects the nerves,
often destroying them so that they can't stimulate the muscles
and the bladder simply fills and fills until urine spills over on
its own.

In men with prostate disease, the prostate can grow so large
that it blocks the flow of urine and causes either an absolute
retention of stagnant urine or a dribbling overflow whenever
the amount gets so great that it overcomes the "stuck" valve.
In women with fibroid disease, the same type of problem can
develop when the fibroids enlarge. And constipation can lead
to dribbling-overflow incontinence in both men and women:
The rectum bulges so far forward that the urine outlet valve
gets blocked and the urine dribbles through whenever it can.
As we'll see, all of these so-called organic causes of incontinence
can be dealt with easily enough.

The most troubling sort of incontinence is that brought on by an altered mental state. Depression in the elderly can have many faces. With one person a loss of energy might be all that is seen, while with another person it might be a loss of memory. And it is not uncommon for depression to mimic dementia in the elderly. Certainly depression can lead to incontinence. The loss of interest in life, the hopelessness and the social withdrawal that are common in depression, can lead by degrees to a loss of interest in self and neglect of bodily functions and self-care. And memory loss—so common in old-age depression—further complicates the picture.

Sometimes an elderly person feels so powerless that incontinence becomes an expression of anger. Sometimes it is even a form of manipulation. But when an elderly person becomes incontinent for these reasons, it is not premeditated willfulness.

Elderly people usually manage well with stressful situations, but they can occasionally decompensate with childlike behavior. The technical term for this is *regression*. You can often see it in hospitals, where elderly people are not just stressed beyond their limit—they're also treated as children, further encouraging their regression. Senility can lead to incontinence, not because it affects the bladder, but because a senile person often acts like a child with no control over bodily functions. The person's inhibitions are released, and he or she allows urination and defecation to occur whenever the need arises, without thinking of the consequences.

SIMPLE SOLUTIONS

Fecal incontinence is usually easy to control with a bowel program that trains the bowels to evacuate on schedule. But there are no such programs for urinary incontinence, which is, therefore, a much more difficult problem to manage. You may hear people say that incontinent people should have their fluid intake restricted. You can try cutting back by one or two glasses of water or juice at nighttime, but that's all. Don't overdo it. The list of troubles created by ingestion of too little fluid is endless. For one thing, the bacteria that infect the urine don't like deep, running water; they do much better in the shallows, thriving on small, infrequent amounts of stagnant urine. Don't try to stop incontinence by eliminating the need to urinate! Generally the more a person drinks, the better off he or she is.

It's also helpful to encourage incontinent people, especially women with stress incontinence, to consciously contract their pelvic floor muscles to hold back the urine. They do this by pretending to stop a bowel movement and tightening the ring of muscles around the anus. A good exercise is trying to start and stop the flow of urine three times during each urination. The pelvic floor muscles can also be exercised anytime by contracting them for six seconds in sets of four or five repetitions.

Timed voidings is another approach to bladder control. The person with the incontinence problem tries to keep voidings to a fixed schedule, with the hope of staying dry and continent in between. If he or she is successful, the interval is extended. Half-hourly or hourly voidings are not uncommon initially, but the long-range goal is to make the continent interval as long as possible—three or four hours at least. Bladder drills call for holding the urine for increasingly longer periods of time, and they are sometimes helpful for women with stress incontinence.

Timed voidings, bladder training, and pelvic floor exercises are helpful for some people. But for others, especially the senile and neurologically impaired, more drastic measures are needed.

A good deal of incontinence can be treated successfully with special medication that a urologist can prescribe. Some types of incontinence can be corrected by surgery: When a large prostate in a man causes incontinence, it can be removed, and when a weak pelvic floor in a woman causes incontinence, it can be strengthened. It is only when incontinence persists despite these measures that special undergarments should be used. These undergarments can range from absorbent pads to diapers.

For mild or infrequent wetting, absorbent pads placed in the crotch of the underwear will do. The pads must be changed at least every four hours, because the skin should always remain dry. Wet skin is a setup for skin breakdown, ulceration, and infection. Also, to eliminate odor, urine should be cleaned up immediately. Marsupial pants—the incontinent pants with a built-in pouch for disposable absorbent pads—are helpful in managing the more severe forms of incontinence. See Chapter 9, "Bowel Care," for additional information.

A catheter is a final option, but it is a dangerous one. People with permanent catheters always have medical problems (infections, stones, etc.). Sometimes, though, the benefits outweigh the risks. Catheters are much safer for men than they are for women, because they can be fitted over the penis and attached via a plastic tube to a collecting bag fastened around the leg or bed rail. These are the so-called condom or Texas catheters, and they are safe because nothing enters the body. A woman doesn't have this option; when she needs a catheter, the tubing must go directly into her bladder. Thus a passageway for bacteria is established, and infections are inevitable. One way to minimize the risk of permanent catheterization is to insert the catheter on a schedule to drain the bladder—like assisted timed voidings. But this can become a nuisance if someone has to be catheterized frequently. It is practical only when catheterization is needed once every four or more hours. Inserting a catheter, draining the urine, and taking care of a permanent catheter are skills that are best learned by practice. Should the need for a catheter arise, a doctor or nurse will instruct you and your friend or relative in the proper techniques.

Absorbent, cloth, bed-linen protectors with waterproof backing are useful, especially when nocturnal incontinence is a problem. They are usually available from diaper or linen services. Disposable absorbent pads can also be helpful. Double-layered launderable sheets are a new product from Australia. Urine drains through to the bottom layer where it is absorbed, while the top layer which is in contact with the body stays dry. Plastic covers for frequently used chairs and sofas will help keep the furniture and house clean and dry when accidents occur.

Elderly people's senses of smell, touch, and temperature are often reduced, and they may not know that they are wet and smell, so you'll have to check frequently. Understand that accidents are unavoidable. Never reprimand your friend for having one—it is unpleasant enough for him or her already.

There are thousands upon thousands of incontinent people in America. Most have adjusted to the problem and continue to live normal, healthy lives. And many have devised their own clever ways of dealing with unexpected problems. A new organization called Help for Incontinent People (HIP) has been established in South Carolina (P.O. Box 544, Union, SC 29379), and a recent newsletter carried a letter from an incontinent person that described using a portable hair dryer to control accidental but expected moisture in undergarments. In the same issue, a man wrote in describing how to tape plastic sandwich bags to the abdomen to collect dribbling urine. Where there's a will, there's a way.

11 *Warning Signs of Illness*

When it comes to health and illness, elderly people are different from younger people in several respects. For one thing, when they get sick, they're sicker. And they stay sick longer and recover more slowly. Small insults to the body or mild infections that would go unnoticed in a young person can destroy an elderly person, whose reserves and capacities for stress are markedly reduced. For this reason, it is important for you in caring for an elderly person to learn to recognize illness when it begins. Prevention is always the best medicine, and second to this is early detection. Here, too, the elderly are different. Their symptoms are often vague, unusual, and nonspecific— even when serious, life-threatening disease is present. Their bodies don't always show the dramatic changes we're used to in young people. Pneumonias can rip through the lungs without producing coughs or fevers. Heart attacks can do their damage silently without chest pain.

Still, the mind and body are an exquisitely delicate, finely tuned, and fragile system, and in elderly people especially, the mind is often the showplace for bodily changes. Normal physiological responses to organ and tissue damage are slowed, blunted, and sometimes even totally destroyed with advancing years, but the mind remains forever alive, fragile, and sensitive to change. It is often the first and sometimes the only area to reflect changes in the body proper. For example, since pneumonia in an elderly person doesn't always have the usual signs of cough and fever that we expect in young people, the first sign of it is apt to be confusion from the reduced supply of oxygen to the brain—so a disease of the lungs shows up as a change in the mind. This is not unusual and, in fact, is more often the case than not.

PHYSICAL CHANGES

Even though you can't count on the typical signs and symptoms of illness showing up in sick elderly people, you must be able to recognize them when they occur. The point isn't that they're unimportant, only that they're unreliable. A persistent cough or a high fever is a warning sign at any age.

You'll be able to notice physical changes, whether they're subtle or dramatic, only if you can compare them with a normal state of affairs. As soon as your friend or relative moves in, observe his or her normal functioning and get acquainted with his or her baseline state of health. Skin color, temperature, and pulse are easy to monitor and are three of the most sensitive indicators of health status.

Always check the eyes: Are they bright? Are they bloodshot? Is there a glassy, dull film over them? Any yellow tint? Make a note of your friend's or relative's skin color. Pale skin is a reflection of poor health. It can represent anemia or inadequate nutrition, as well as more serious conditions. The skin can be yellow, gray and ashen, red and flushed, or blue and cyanotic, depending on the underlying state of health. The color of the skin is one of the first, most reliable, and dramatic signs of illness.

The pulse, which is best taken over the radial artery in the wrist, is another source of useful information. Feel for the pulse with the tip of your index finger (Figure 11-1) and count the beats for one minute: That's the pulse, beats per minute. Any change in pulse is a warning, and a rapid, slow, or irregular pulse is abnormal. The temperature is also a good marker of illness. Proper technique is critical for getting an accurate reading. For oral temperature measurements, shake the thermometer down two or three times to collect the mercury in a continuous line at the bottom of the tube, then place it under the tongue, close the person's mouth, and keep it closed for three minutes. You can't get a reliable reading in less than three minutes. And make sure there's no hot or cold food remaining in the mouth. For rectal temperatures, be sure to lubricate the thermometer, keep it in for two to three minutes,

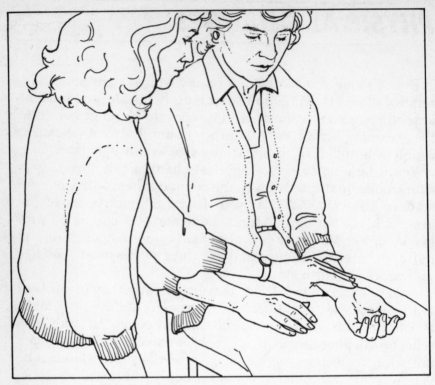

Figure 11-1. Taking a pulse.

but don't push it in too far, and don't leave your "patient" unattended—there's nothing more embarrassing or dangerous than a migrating thermometer. When possible, use an oral thermometer. An oral temperature over 100° Fahrenheit (37.8° Centigrade) or a rectal temperature over 101° Fahrenheit (38.4° Centigrade) is a sign of illness. A consistent, low-grade oral temperature, even one as low as 99.6° Fahrenheit, can also signal the presence of illness.

Take your friend's pulse and temperature at the same time every day for a week after he or she moves in. Then you'll have a record of his or her normal functioning and you'll be in a better position to evaluate changes when they occur. Look at his or her skin every day, making mental notes of any color changes, and check his or her temperature and pulse once a week.

The physical changes associated with cancer are no different from the changes seen with other diseases. But there is a special element of fear when cancer is suspected. You, as the care giver, must appreciate the early warning signs and symptoms of the common cancers that affect elderly people. The list that follows summarizes the most obvious changes. (Adapted from "Age Page, Cancer Facts for People Over 50," National Institutes of Health, U.S. Department of Health and Human Services, 1983.) Contact the family doctor if your friend or relative has even one of these signs or symptoms. And remember that a regular medical checkup, at least annually, is the surest way to safeguard your friend's or relative's health.

X WARNING SIGNS OF CANCER

BREAST	Change in breast shape; lump in the breast; discharge from the nipple; pain or tenderness
COLON and RECTUM	Changes in bowel habits; bleeding from the rectum; black, tarry stools; bright red blood in the stool; pain on defecation
LUNG	Persistent cough; shortness of breath; coughing up of blood
PROSTATE	Painful urination; difficulty in urinating; frequent urination; urgency of urination
UTERUS, OVARY, and CERVIX	Bleeding after menopause; vaginal discharge; pain during intercourse; enlargement of the abdomen
SKIN	A sore that doesn't heal; change in shape, size, or color of a wart or mole; new mole develops

COMPLAINTS: VAGUE AND NONSPECIFIC

There is a great temptation to dismiss the vague complaints of old people as unpleasant but unavoidable aspects of old age—as if complaining were part of old age in the same way that rebellion is part of adolescence. But nothing could be further from the truth. Complaining is not the final stage of life. The long journey, filled with challenges and sacrifices along the way, does not lead inexorably to a land of frustrated, annoyed, and carping retirees. We have more to look forward to than that. But the myth is widespread, probably because illness in an elderly person is seldom well-defined and localized. Pneumonia, for example, isn't confined to the lungs, and heart attacks are not limited to the heart. The vagueness of the complaints and the nonspecific nature of the symptoms make it difficult for us to diagnose the problem. There are no easy answers—and the frustration is ours. Yet one truth stands out: Change is a sign that something is wrong.

Someone who complains at age 35 is usually still complaining at age 85, and it's difficult to know when something is seriously wrong. But a tight-lipped stoic who starts complaining late in life, vaguely and nonspecifically, is usually in real trouble. Someone who has a painful knee might have injured his or her knee or hip, or perhaps arthritis has flared up. But the painful knee might also reflect anxiety, depression, or sadness. Perhaps a good friend has moved away or there has recently been a fight at home. Just as bodily injuries affect the mind, so emotional problems can masquerade as physical ailments. This doesn't mean that someone whose pain is an expression of emotional conflict is lying. The pain is real and is further evidence that the mind influences the body. A person's pain threshold or sensitivity to discomfort depends on his or her emotional state. Chronic aches and pains that are usually overlooked can flare up during emotionally charged times. On the opposite side of the coin are stories of soldiers with mortar and saber wounds fighting for hours during the heat of battle, oblivious to their wounds. The emotional response to injury and the body's response to stress must never be overlooked. The same soldier who fought on the battlefield without complaints with what would ordinarily be an agonizing wound, can also be found at an unpleasant job, crying like a baby over an apparently trivial injury. The same person, called a hero in one instance and a malingerer in another, is simply demonstrating the power of the mind over the body in both cases.

The mind and body are a coordinated and integrated system that over the years becomes more and more sensitive to outside influences. As its sensitivity increases, its reactivity generalizes and its responses become widespread and long-lasting, so that a single, localized disturbance has repercussions everywhere. It is not usually possible to confine a disease to one organ or body part; the entire body becomes involved. And this multiple-organ involvement, as much as the vagueness and nonspecific nature of medical complaints, characterizes illness in the elderly.

MENTAL AND BEHAVIORAL CHANGES

The question is, how do you know when something is seriously wrong when the whole body is involved, the complaints are vague, and the emotions are charged? After all, a mild cold virus could get all your muscles aching, make you complain that something is wrong, frustrate and upset you, and be gone in twenty-four hours. The answer is that something is seriously wrong when there is a persistent change. Recognizing change is the key to understanding the problems of elderly people. A change in daily life that lasts for more than a couple of days is significant (everyone, no matter how old, is entitled to one bad day).

There are also special warning signs of illness in the elderly. Any mental deterioration is a red flag. Memory loss, confusion, agitation, mood change, and so on are serious changes that deserve attention. They don't occur without a reason. Any kind of progressive deterioration is serious and is a warning as strong as a high fever in the young. Signs as subtle as loss of motivation, diminished initiative and drive, and loss of social skills are all as valid and significant as actual physical changes. Weight loss, loss of appetite, sleeplessness, and drowsiness can signify depression or actual physical illness. Increasing frailty, especially unsteadiness and a tendency to fall, must be appreciated and not dismissed as part of old age. An elderly person who becomes more immobile, who retreats to bed and does less during the day, is asking for help. Any sign of incontinence, bowel or bladder, is a sign of illness. A change in the type, character, or number of complaints—more aches and pains, for example—is also a warning. All of these alterations should be reported to the family doctor. Some may be nothing more than the ups and downs of a normal life, others may be due to medication and may disappear with a change in dosage, while others may actually signal a treatable disease. Drugs such as steroids, tranquilizers, barbiturates, analgesics, and even diuretics and arthritis medications can influence an elderly person's mental outlook and behavior.

In looking after an elderly person you must be alert to the physical signs of disease as well as to the emotional and behavioral changes. Illness can announce itself in thousands of ways, boldly and dramatically with a high fever and productive cough, or timidly and uncertainly, hiding behind subtle changes in behavior. Whatever disguise illness takes, whatever sign the body uses to warn of its presence, the actual danger signal, the common denominator of all warning signs, is change. Change in the physical constitution, especially the temperature, pulse, and color of the skin, are signs of a clear and present danger. And changes in the pattern of daily life, especially increased immobility, incontinence, and mental impairment, are signs every bit as compelling.

Since you know the elderly person you're looking after, you are sensitive to changes and are able to pick up subtle shifts and alterations easily. This is why you can take care of someone at home so much better than a nurse or other professional could possibly do in a hospital or nursing home—you know the person intimately. No additional training, high-tech equipment, or professional skills are needed. Once again, common sense and caring carry the day and actually allow you to do a better job than the professionals in institutions.

12 Caring for the Bedridden

You need a plan of action for the times when your elderly friend or relative is too ill or too weak to get out of bed. Should an illness suddenly appear, your friend's or relative's doctor will recommend either hospitalization or home treatment. If home treatment is chosen, you'll be delivering most of the care yourself, getting instructions from the doctor and perhaps from a visiting nurse as well. Once the immediate illness passes, it's important that your friend or relative convalesce and regain his or her former strength and vitality as quickly as possible. He or she can do this during a brief stay in a nursing home, at a rehabilitation center, or at home. Elderly people are as resilient as they are vulnerable, and they usually quickly recover even from the most overwhelming illnesses and return to their former lives with renewed vigor. But some illnesses leave permanent scars in their wake, and for those elderly who are afflicted, life is never again the same. Some are left bedridden indefinitely, while others, never regaining their former strength, are forced to modify their lifestyles and limit their day-to-day activities.

Your elderly friend's or relative's future health, physical functioning, and well-being are shaped, in large measure, during the period of convalescence and rehabilitation. You wear many hats during the day as you attend to the different needs of your bedridden friend or relative. You have to become a social director, of sorts, to make certain that he or she is mentally and emotionally stimulated while in bed. You'll be arranging for friends to drop over for visits and for the children to stop in during the day. It's also a good idea to install a television or radio in the room and to encourage interests and hobbies that can be pursued in bed, such as reading and knitting. You'll be spending a lot of time in the room occupied with nursing chores, but it's a good idea to set aside an additional ten to twenty minutes a day for leisure time—for sitting quietly with your friend or relative, talking about the day's events, or simply bringing him or her up to date on the latest family developments.

It's all too easy for a bedridden person to lose hope and become discouraged when progress is slow, but you can help prevent this "giving up" attitude by fostering a positive and determined outlook. The most potent elixir we have is made from cheerfulness, hopefulness, and a caring heart. Without confidence and motivation, the important work of rebuilding strength, endurance, and physical function goes undone. When there are permanent physical impairments, the psychological adjustment and acceptance of a limited lifestyle also begin during this period. Throughout the convalescent and rehabilitation period, care must be taken to avoid the unnecessary, easily preventable complications of bed rest, such as bed sores, muscle wasting, and joint contractures.

Caring for someone who is confined to bed takes a long-term commitment, patience, a sense of humor, special nursing skills, and an ability to organize the day's activities. Everyone reading this book has the necessary commitment, patience, and sense of humor. The nursing skills are simple and easy to learn. The problem area is organization. There is a strong, natural temptation to devote all one's free time to caring for a bedridden person. But the temptation must be resisted, because in the long run it is counterproductive. You can't sustain such devotion without eventually tiring out and compromising your abilities to provide the best care. And when you're overtired and frustrated, you can't even enjoy the pleasure of helping someone have a better life.

The actual time involved in the physical care of someone in bed is minimal: a couple of minutes to turn the person, ten minutes to make the bed while it is occupied, half an hour to give a bed bath. But if you are without a plan, the various caregiving activities can interfere and overlap with one another, making some activities unnecessary and others redundant, and in the confusion creating unrealistic and overwhelming demands on your time. Poor scheduling simply multiplies your time commitments, and thus drains your energy and exhausts your emotions. To protect your sanity and your effectiveness, organize your day's activities, making sure to include free time and leisure for yourself.

THE ROOM

The room in which an elderly bedridden person lives should be clean and cheerful. A bright, motivated outlook thrives in warm, nurturing surroundings, while dirt and clutter are fertile ground for depression. A lot of equipment is used in caring for a bedridden person, and it's easy to create a mess by leaving tape, pitchers of water, medicines, and the like lying around. Keep the room neat and orderly by setting aside space for all the supplies and returning them to their proper places after they're used. Plants and flowers liven up a room and freshen the air. They also provide moisture during the winter months when the heating system dries the air out. Pictures and wall hangings, even finger paintings by a grandchild, are comforting and reassuring. It's easy for an elderly person who is confined to a bed to lose track of time, but a large calendar and desk clock will emphasize and reinforce the passage of time; they will keep a bedridden person oriented and involved in day-to-day family life. A clock radio with an alarm set to the elderly person's favorite station can get each day off to a bright and early start.

Try to provide a room that has a lot of windows and a good exposure, so that your elderly friend or relative, though confined to one room, can still look out the window and enjoy the changing world, the sunrises and sunsets. Since old, familiar objects make a room warm and cozy, use your friend's or relative's favorite belongings as furnishings. But keep the room uncluttered, with easy access to the bed. If you can, put the head of the bed where the person in it will have a clear view of the window. Five feet of empty space on either side and at the foot of the bed will let you turn most wheelchairs without knocking into walls and furniture. It's best to plan for a wheelchair ahead of time, rather than find out later, when one is needed, that the room is too small. Many elderly people who will eventually recover completely require a wheelchair sometime during their convalescence.

Choose a room that's near the action, not one that's off the beaten path. The room becomes a bedridden person's home, and if it's nearby and inviting, the family will visit more readily, stopping by en route to another room, looking in or saying hello from the doorway, calling out from the hall—casually, unobtrusively, keeping the person in bed involved with the family. Also, it's a lot easier to clean a room that's in the middle of the house than one that's far removed; it's also easier to prepare and deliver a hot meal to a nearby room, and in the event of a medical emergency, the closer the room the better.

Try to get a telephone for the room, and keep it within easy reach of the bed. A social life and news from the outside are as important to bedridden people as to the rest of us. A buzzer system (Figure 12-1) that connects the room with the rest of the house protects a bedridden person who needs help, but who can't reach anyone by calling out. You could be busy in the kitchen, absorbed with television, or asleep in the bedroom and not hear your friend's calling for help. A buzzer system will let him or her reach you anytime. It takes about half an hour to install a system, and you can buy all the parts at a local hardware store for about $10. If your electrical wiring know-how is rusty, have someone at the hardware store or a local high-school engineering whiz help you.

For a bedridden person, life revolves around the bed. A safe, comfortable bed is a safe, comfortable world. A hospital bed is perfect but not essential; you can adjust an ordinary bed to meet most of a bedridden person's needs. The major advantage of a hospital bed is that it allows you, the care giver, to minister

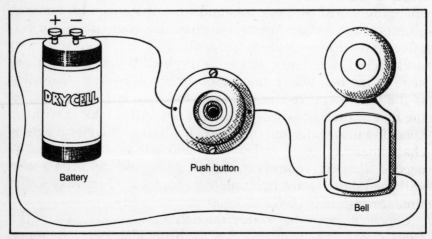

Figure 12-1. Home buzzer system.

to the needs of your loved one easily. An ordinary bed is at a good height for getting into and out of, but it's too low for good "patient" care. A hospital bed raises to 30 inches, at least, which is a comfortable height at which to change the sheets and to feed, turn, and bathe the person in bed without straining your back. Side rails are used in hospitals to protect people from rolling out of bed, but more often than not elderly or confused people will try to climb over the rails and injure themselves in the process. Side rails are useful when you change the sheets with someone in the bed; as you work on one side of the bed, the person in bed rolls to the other side and holds onto the rail. It isn't necessary to have a hospital bed to enjoy the covenience of side rails, however. They can be purchased for regular beds at most medical supply houses.

Another useful aspect of a hospital bed is the articulated design which lets you raise and lower the head and foot sections independently. But you can easily accomplish the same thing with an ordinary bed by using a foam wedge pillow, a foam slant, or a pile of ordinary pillows.

Hospital beds and mattresses are sold separately. Most mattresses are covered with odor-retardant, water-repellent material, but if the one you have isn't, you should buy a separate cover. The mattress should be firm and provide good support—after all, it's being used twenty-four hours a day. A foam egg-crate mattress placed under the top sheet helps distribute the body weight and prevents bedsores. A 3-inch-high foam mattress costs about $20 for a twin-size bed and goes up for a full-, queen-, and king-size bed. A single mattress suffices for someone who can move around easily in bed alone, but two together, providing 6 inches of cushioned support, are better for a very weak or frail individual. The combination of a firm, solid mattress on the bottom and a soft, yielding one on top is comfortable and highly protective.

Sears has a good line of hospital beds and mattresses with prices ranging from $400 to $1100. You can buy a hospital bed outright, buy one on an installment plan, or rent one for short periods of time. Medicare covers 80 percent of the cost of renting or purchasing (under the Durable Medical Equipment category) as long as a physician requests the bed.

There are two accessories that make life in bed more manageable: an overhead trapeze bar and an over-bed table. The

trapeze bar lets a bedridden person sit up and exercise independently, and thus prevents the muscle wasting that happens
so easily in with bed rest. Over-bed tables come with drawers,
vanities, and adjustable tops. They return a measure of freedom
and control to the bedridden person by providing an individual
work space and a grooming and eating area. The cost for one
is about $100. Of course a bed tray serves pretty much the same
purpose and is cheaper, about $30. Figure 12-2 shows a model
room for a bedridden person.

PRESSURE AND POSITION

If you've ever spent several days in bed with the flu, you
probably remember how weak and unsteady you were when
you finally got out of bed. Bed rest is a double-edged sword
that old age only sharpens. An elderly person who takes to bed
to fight off or recover from an illness faces the dangers of bed
rest, and these are compounded for anyone who is confined to
bed indefinitely because of a chronic condition. Muscles atrophy, bones weaken, and joints stiffen. Bowel function slows,
the heart and lungs lose their reserve, and the mind dulls. And
the chances of bedsores and joint contractures developing increase every day.

There is a great temptation to put pillows under a bedridden
person's knees in the mistaken belief that this will prevent
stiffness, but pillows bend the knees and hips, which stiffen
more readily in this position. Knees and hips kept bent for long
periods of time become frozen into that position, which certainly makes it harder for the person to stand up and walk.
Another temptation is to pull the top sheet tight, but this also
pulls the feet down. If they become stuck in this position, your
friend or relative, when he or she eventually gets out of bed,
will be forced to walk on the toes. The correct position for bed
rest is lying with the knees straight, the ankles bent, and the
toes pointing up to the ceiling. The arms should remain loose,
slightly bent at the elbows, and kept away from the body—
never tightly pressed against the body. The hands have to remain in a useful working position. This can be accomplished

Figure 12-2. Model room for a bedridden person.

by grasping a rolled-up towel. The head rests best on one or two pillows, rather than propped up against a dozen. The top of the shoulders, the neck, and the head should all rest on the pillows.

Some positions, like the bent-knee position, are deforming in themselves, but maintenance of any position for too long is unhealthy. The weight of the body squeezes the skin against the bed, creating pressure on the skin and collapsing the blood vessels underneath. The collapsed blood vessels deprive the skin of its blood supply, and, since blood nourishes the skin, when the supply is shut off for too long, the skin dies. The dead skin sloughs and a decubitus (lying down) ulcer—bedsore, or pressure sore—is formed.

You can get an idea of how effectively pressure reduces the blood supply by watching your fingers turn pale as you tightly grasp an empty glass. Any time the skin is subjected to constant pressure, it is at risk for developing a bedsore. In fact, unrelieved pressure is the only cause of bedsores. Ordinarily, when we lie in bed we continually shift our weight so pressures don't build up. Even during sleep we unconsciously change positions, shifting and redistributing our weight. But when someone is too weak to move, is paralyzed, or has no sensation, the shifting and turning do not occur, and eventually the skin breaks down. In these circumstances you have to be especially vigilant: You have to guard the skin and do the turning yourself. To avoid bedsores, pressures against the skin, especially against skin sandwiched between boney prominences and the bed surface, must be relieved every two hours, so you have to plan for a two hourly turning schedule during the day. At night, to safeguard your sleep and the sleep of your elderly friend or relative, the schedule can be relaxed to every four hours. Of course, whatever schedule you choose, 6 inches of foam on top of a firm mattress is mandatory. And remember, it's better to lose sleep than for your friend to develop a bedsore.

There are three basic positions for a bedridden person: back lying, left-side lying, and right-side lying. Stomach lying is also possible, but it's a much more difficult position to assume. You can alternate the basic positions along with varying degrees of the side-lying positions. When a person lies on his or her side, there is a tendency for the legs to cross and for the knees or ankles to rub together. You can head off any pressure buildups in these areas by putting a pillow between the legs. Placing pillows under the feet and legs also protects the heels in the back-lying position. Pillows spread the body weight over a large area so that pressures can't build up in one spot and damage the skin. Choose pillows that are soft, with a lot of give to them. Avoid the fat, overstuffed ones, and also avoid stiff, irritating pillowcases.

There's no need to twist, shove, or pull a bedridden person into a comfortable position every two to four hours. If you use a draw sheet, each move will be simple and effortless. Fold an ordinary top sheet in half, top to bottom, and drape it across the fitted bottom sheet so it covers the area from above the upper back to below the buttocks and extends over both sides of the bed. This is a draw sheet. A bedridden person lying on top of one can be easily moved into any position. Look at the woman in Figure 12-3 who is being turned in bed. To turn her onto her right side, raise the bed to its highest position, put the left bed rail down, and, standing on the left, roll up the draw sheet like a blanket roll. Grab the roll with both hands, palms up, and pull it toward yourself, sliding the woman to the left at the same time. Keep your back straight, your knees slightly bent, and one foot in front of the other and pull with your arms. Now, put the left bed rail up, move to the right side, and put the right bed rail down. Reach across to the far side of the bed and again pull the draw sheet on the left side toward yourself: This time the woman will "roll" onto her right side. Put the bed rail up, and she'll be able to steady herself by holding onto it. While she's in this position, take the opportunity to check her back for any reddened area or skin breakdown. Also, rub her back each time she's turned. Put a pillow against her back to prevent her from rolling over, and one under her head and another between her knees to prevent pressure buildup. Make sure that the right arm is not caught underneath the body; bent at the elbow and no higher than the shoulder is the safest and most comfortable position. The left arm falls naturally over the body, with the hand resting on the bed or a pillow or holding onto the bed rail (Figure 12-4).

To turn her onto her back from the right side-lying position, simply remove the pillows from against her back and gently roll her onto her back. Use the draw sheet to center her in bed. Make sure her body is aligned and put one pillow under her

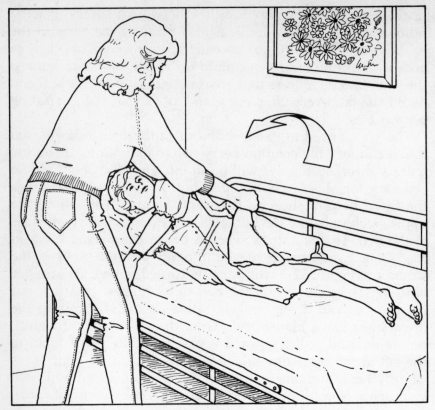

Figure 12-3. Turning someone in bed.

head and others under the lower legs to raise the heels off the
bed when necessary—but none under the knees. If there is a
tendency for the ankles to bend down, pointing the toes away
from the ceiling, a padded footboard will limit the motion. A
footboard is nothing more than a board wedged between the
mattress and bed frame at the foot of the bed. It's positioned
so that it's perpendicular to the bed. A footboard will also
prevent a bedridden person from sliding down in bed and will
keep the top sheet from pulling the toes down.

Figure 12-4. Woman lying on her side.

THE BED BATH

The bed bath is reserved for those people who are too sick or too weak to get out of bed and bathe themselves. Don't think that a bed bath should be saved exclusively for the bedridden. There may be days when a normally independent person is simply unable to perform personal hygiene for himself or herself. Perhaps he or she has a cold or the flu or has just returned from a stay in the hospital. Whatever the reason, your energy and proficiency may be called upon to provide the cleanliness and comfort that your elderly friend or relative is unable to provide for himself or herself.

Giving a bed bath is not a difficult task, though at first it may seem overwhelming. Here on a bed in front of you lies a grown human being whom you must wash, and you don't know where to begin. Before you start with the physical work, take out a pencil and paper. The first steps simply involve planning and organization.

Make a list of the things you will need. The following lists the items most often used when a bath is given in bed. You may wish to add to or delete from this list.

✝ BED BATH SUPPLIES

ESSENTIALS

1. Washbasin filled with warm water
2. Mild soap
3. Moisturizing lotion
4. Washcloth
5. Two towels
6. Fresh linens for a bed change (three sheets and a pillowcase)
7. Clean pajamas
8. Toothbrush and toothpaste
9. Hairbrush and comb
10. Bath blanket (lightweight cotton blanket)

ADDITIONAL ITEMS

1. Razor
2. Shaving cream
3. After-shave lotion
4. Perfume
5. Makeup

Place everything on an uncluttered table within easy reach of the bed. If possible, the table should be waist high, so that frequent bending is unnecessary. Remember your back. If you use improper body mechanics, many of the tasks you perform for a bedridden person could cause strain on your back and turn you into a bedridden person. Concentrate on using the strong muscles of your legs and arms, rather than the weak ones in your back, and always bend at the knees.

If your elderly friend or relative has a hospital bed, raise the entire bed to a height that is a comfortable working position for you. When you are doing work like this, it will become obvious how much easier a hospital bed can make everything for you. If your friend is in a regular bed, the best way for you to save your back is to give the bath while sitting on the edge of the bed.

The first time you bathe someone, you'll be doing a lot of assessing. There is probably a good deal that your friend can do alone. The face, hands, upper body, and genital area are easy to reach, and many people prefer to wash these areas by themselves. As you continue to help, you will discover the likes, dislikes, and personal preferences that have been acquired over a lifetime.

Oral hygiene should always be included with the bed bath. Many things can make your friend feel better, and on the top of the list is a thorough cleansing of the mouth. If your friend is awake and alert but unable to get out of bed, put the articles he or she will need within easy reach and encourage him or her to use them frequently. If, on the other hand, you are caring for someone who is unable to cleanse his or her mouth alone, you will be responsible for providing this important aspect of personal hygiene.

If your friend is unresponsive and helpless, your job will require more time and energy. Usually, when someone is bedridden and unresponsive, he or she is not able to eat and drink normally. Because of the decreased fluid intake, the mouth becomes very dry and often a thick coating forms on the tongue. Your friend may not even be able to open his or her mouth upon request. In that case, you'll have to open the mouth. A tongue blade is probably the best device to use. Just insert the tongue blade carefully between the upper and lower teeth or gums and gently pry the mouth open. Don't use a lot of force. Once the tongue blade is between the teeth or gums, the mouth often opens automatically.

Oral hygiene begins with cleansing the mucous membranes. This can be done with a large cotton-tipped applicator, which is available at medical supply stores. Moisten it lightly in warm water and gently cleanse the mucous membranes and tongue. If the coating on the tongue and membranes is thick, a solution of half water and half hydrogen peroxide will do the trick.

If your friend's or relative's mouth has a tendency to close, keep the tongue blade in place. Never use your fingers to hold the mouth open: A human bite is painful and dangerous.

Your friend's or relative's head should be turned to the side when you introduce any fluid into the mouth, because a potentially dangerous situation can arise if fluid slips from the mouth to the lungs. Always use as little fluid as possible. When using a cotton-tipped applicator, make certain it is moist and not wet.

Once the mouth surfaces are clean, you can begin to clean the teeth by using your friend's or relative's regular toothbrush. If the bristles are stiff, soften them by running hot tap water over them. It is best to use only a small amount of toothpaste, because thorough rinsing is difficult. Clean all surfaces of the teeth well, and then clean the tongue—also with the toothbrush. A final "rinse" can be done with cotton applicators moistened with water or moist gauze wrapped over a tongue blade; even a cool, moist washcloth can be used to rid the mouth of toothpaste. Whatever method you choose, you need simply wipe all the surfaces clean. As a final touch, moisten all mucous membranes with a cotton-tipped applicator or gauze on a tongue blade and apply petrolatum jelly or some other emollient to the lips to keep them moist.

It is not unreasonable to cleanse the mouth of an unresponsive person every hour. If your friend or relative is awake and alert, encourage him or her to rinse the mouth frequently with warm water—this is the next best thing to brushing. If your friend has dentures, they should be removed and cleaned every three or four hours while he or she is awake. To clean dentures, simply scrub them with a denture brush, toothpaste, and cool water. If the dentures are kept clean, a bedridden person will be more likely to wear them.

Once the oral hygiene is taken care of, you're ready for the bed bath. Assuming that you'll be giving a complete bed bath with no assistance, the following procedure will save steps and conserve your energy. Try giving the bath this way the first time, and then alter the steps to fit your needs. Regardless of how you choose to give the bath, keep in mind your friend's safety, warmth, comfort, and modesty. Also remember that all of your movements should preserve your back.

Wash one side of the person at a time; for discussion's sake, we'll start with the left side. Have the bed at a good height, the right side rail in the up position, and a basin filled with warm, fresh water. Cover the patient with a bath blanket and undress him or her from underneath the cover. Wash the face, ears, neck, and hands. When washing the eyes, use a soapless damp cloth and wash from the inner to the outer eye. If the facial skin is dry, as elderly people's often is, soap is necessary only every other day. Simply wiping the face with a warm washcloth is enough on the days that you aren't using soap.

When you're not giving a shampoo and you won't be changing the bed immediately after the bath, you can keep the linen dry by tucking a couple of clean towels under the left side of the body. Use long, firm strokes to wash the left arm, upper torso, abdomen, leg, and foot. Rinse your washcloth, wipe off the soap, and dry the area thoroughly. Next, roll your friend to the side-lying position, so that he or she is now on the right side. Your friend can grab onto the side rail. Wash the left buttock and as much of the back as possible. Roll your friend onto the back, raise the side rail on the left side of the bed, and move around to the right side, putting the right side rail in the down position. Now wash the right side of the body just as you did the left, then wash and thoroughly dry the genital area. Change your water. With the right side of the body cleansed, roll your friend to the side-lying position so that he or she is now on the left side. Wash the right shoulder, back, and buttock, and dry thoroughly. Keep your friend comfortable in this side-lying position by propping or cushioning him or her with pillows.

Now it's time for the back rub. A vital aspect of routine care for a bedridden person, a back rub improves circulation and helps to relax the entire body. If your friend has a tendency to lie on the back more than on the side, look carefully for any reddened areas and rub these especially well. A back rub is most soothing when a balm or lotion is used. A good moisturizing lotion, such as KERI LOTION or Lubriderm, moisturizes the skin and soothes the body at the same time. Take the chill out of the moisturizer by placing the closed bottle into a basin of warm water; the lotion will warm up in five minutes. If your elderly friend is feverish or if the weather is hot and sticky, he or she may prefer use of rubbing alcohol to lotion. Don't use alcohol often, however, because it is too drying for the skin.

When giving a back rub, use firm pressure and go from the sides of the back to the center, and from the bottom of the spine upward. Always include the entire back, from the buttocks to the neck.

After the back rub is finished, your friend can be returned to the back-lying position. A wonderful way to end the bath is to fill your basin once more with fresh, warm water and immerse the feet directly into the basin. This is very soothing to someone who spends the whole day in bed. While the feet are soaking, your relaxed and refreshed "patient" can comb his or her hair. A clean towel or pillowcase can be put down to collect any fallen hairs.

After the feet are soaked, thoroughly dry them, without forgetting the area between the toes. Your friend will be totally relaxed by now and may very well choose to take a nap.

If your friend or relative needs a shampoo, now is a good time for it. Washing the hair is important, but it can be messy. A shampoo every other week is usually enough. Prepare the bed by covering the top half of it liberally with absorbent, plastic-backed pads, like Chux. Alternatively, you can use an inflatable shampoo basin or a plastic rinse tray ($10 to $20 in most pharmacies and medical supply houses). Now proceed as you would to wash your own hair. Wet your friend's hair, but don't flood the bed. Apply a small amount of shampoo and work it into a lather. Rub the scalp vigorously with the tips of your fingers—not your fingernails. If the hair is not too dirty, one washing will be enough, but if it is dirty or oily, a second washing will be necessary. If your friend has long hair that tangles, work a small amount of instant conditioner into the hair, then rinse well. Towel dry the hair, then gently comb it out. A wide-tooth comb will prevent the hair from tearing and pulling out as you comb out knots.

If you prefer, shampooing can be done before the bath or as a separate activity anytime during the day—the choice is up to you and your friend. Regardless of when the shampoo takes place, your friend's hair should be dried immediately afterward. This can best be accomplished with a blow dryer, which you can pick up in most department stores and better pharmacies for about $15. Always keep the heat setting at medium to avoid burning the skin.

After you've given your friend or relative a bed bath or shampoo, it's a good time to change the bed linens. If you've never made an occupied bed, it can seem like an insurmountable problem. It's actually quite simple and shouldn't take you more than five or ten minutes after you've gotten the hang of it. Look at Figure 12-5 and go over the following steps.

MAKING AN OCCUPIED BED

1. Collect and have ready all the necessary linens: top sheet, bottom sheet, draw sheet, pillowcases.
2. Working on one side at a time, roll your friend or relative as far as you can to the opposite

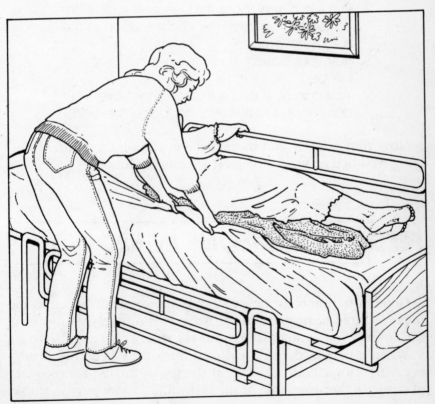

Figure 12-5. Making an occupied bed.

side of the bed. (If you have a hospital bed, make sure that the side rail on the opposite side of the bed is up.)

3. Tuck the soiled bottom linens toward the center of the bed. Continue to tuck them well under your "patient."
4. Now you can put down the fresh bottom sheet and draw sheet on the side nearest you.
5. Place the side rail closest to you in the up position and have your patient roll toward you. Let him or her know he or she will be rolling over a small hump of linens. (If yours is not a hospital bed, place two chairs on the side of the bed to protect your friend from falling out.)
6. Go around to the other side of the bed and remove the soiled linens.
7. Pull the clean linens through and tuck them under the mattress. The under portion of the bed is now made.
8. Roll your patient back toward the center of the bed.
9. You can now place the top sheet over your patient and tuck it into the foot of the bed.

Now that your friend or relative is completely bathed and lying in a bed of fresh linens, it is time for lunch.

FEEDING SOMEONE IN BED

Good nutrition must never stop. When someone becomes too incapacitated to prepare his or her meals or simply to walk to the dining room, you must assume the role of chef and dietitian.

When a person doesn't feel well, mealtime becomes drudgery. Nutritious food, which is at the top of the list for recovery of strength, becomes one of the last things a sick person thinks about.

Family meal preparation should, if possible, center around the likes and dislikes of the ill person. If you serve food he or she likes, there is a greater chance that he or she will eat it. And this means that you can prepare just one meal for the whole household.

Your friend or relative may be feeling weak and tired, but he or she must not be allowed to develop a lazy attitude about eating. Eating has a better chance of remaining an important and significant part of your friend's life if he or she is able to sit in a chair and eat. Meals should be eaten in bed only as a last resort.

When mealtime arrives, provide your friend with soap and a basin of water and suggest that he or she wash the hands and comb the hair. In the meantime, you can ready a chair by covering the cushion with an underpad and clean sheet and cushioning the back with a pillow. Have a blanket ready in case he or she gets chilly. Position a table that is the appropriate height in front of the chair. When you assist your friend out of bed, use the techniques discussed later in this chapter.

If your friend is returning from the hospital, consult the dietitian at the hospital before discharge. He or she can be contacted through the head nurse. The dietitian is a valuable source of information who can make life much easier for you by offering tips on good nutrition and meal preparation specific to your friend's needs.

Common sense is the key to menu planning, especially when chewing or swallowing is a problem. Serve foods that are soft, such as poached chicken and beef stew. Always cut food in bite-size pieces. If your friend or relative still has trouble, pureeing in the blender is the next step. Pureeing should be a last resort, however, since pureed foods can be humiliating because of their similarity to baby food. Straws are always good to have on hand, because drinking from a cup can be difficult for some people.

Your elderly friend or relative should be fed by you only if he or she is physically unable to feed himself or herself. If it becomes necessary to feed your friend, allow him or her to retain as much control as possible.

For example, if the plate contains roast beef, peas, and potatoes, let your friend decide in which order he or she would like to eat the different foods. Don't hurry him or her; allow your friend to eat at his or her own pace. This can be time-consuming, so it's a good idea to have several members of the family help out.

BEDPANS AND URINALS

When someone is bedridden, all of life's activities, including urinating and having bowel movements, must be performed in bed. It's not unusual for the person providing the care to be uneasy about bowel and bladder care. Remember that the person in bed is also uneasy, and that the cause of everyone's uneasiness and embarrassment is lack of privacy. It usually isn't long before a bedridden person is strong enough to use a bedpan or urinal alone. In the meantime, being sensitive to the person's need for privacy will ease the burden for everyone.

Men use a urinal for voiding and a bedpan for moving their bowels, while women use a bedpan for both. Urinals come in one size, they're made of plastic, and they look like flower vases except that they have handles. They cost about $5. Bedpans are made of metal or plastic and they come in two sizes: a normal size and a small size. The small bedpan is called a *fracture bedpan*, and it is wedge-shaped in the front so that it can be moved in and out of position without moving the bedridden person—an important consideration in the case of fractures or immobility. Metal bedpans get cold easily, so if you're going to use one, remember to warm it up first by running warm water over it. Plastic bedpans are just as durable, they're less noisy when handled, they don't change temperature, and they're cheaper. A normal plastic bedpan costs about $5 and a fracture bedpan a couple of dollars more.

Most men can use a urinal by themselves; occasionally you'll have to raise the head of the bed or add a pillow to make the bed position more comfortable. Sitting on the edge of the bed with legs hanging over the side is convenient if the person in bed can get into a sitting position. Keep the urinal close to the bed so your friend can use it by himself without calling for help. This is especially important during the night.

It's not as easy to use a bedpan as a urinal. If your friend has trouble moving, a fracture bedpan requires the least movement. If he or she can move easily, you should encourage as much independence as possible. Sitting and squatting are the most natural positions for evacuation of the bowels, because they let the abdominal muscles and gravity aid the evacuation. Therefore when a bedridden person uses the bedpan, you'll have to adjust him or her to approximate the sitting position as closely as possible. If he or she can sit on the edge of the bed, that's ideal. Otherwise, raise the head of the bed (or add a pillow) and bend the person's knees. If your friend has the strength and mobility to use the bedpan alone, simply place it within easy reach, provide toilet paper, and leave the room to guarantee privacy. If there is an overhead trapeze, he or she can use it to raise himself or herself up onto the bedpan. Sometimes you'll have to help by slipping your hand under the buttocks to push up to make room for the bedpan. If your friend is too weak to lift himself or herself, you'll have to turn him or her onto the side, place the bedpan against the buttocks, and, as you're holding it in place, turn him or her back onto the bedpan. When the bowel movement is completed, turn your friend back to the side, wipe the buttocks area, and remove the bedpan. Cover it with a towel as you carry it to the bathroom, and empty the contents in the toilet. Be sure to provide your friend or relative with a basin of water, a washcloth, and a towel to clean his or her hands and groin area.

If your friend or relative can get out of bed but is too weak to walk to the bathroom, a bedside commode is an essential piece of equipment. Prices range from $50 to $100, depending on the construction and the manufacturer, and with a doctor's order it is covered by Medicare. A bedside commode is a metal frame chair with a removable plastic seat and pail. The pail comes with a lid and can be boiled for cleaning purposes. A bedside commode can vastly enhance a frail elderly person's independence and privacy.

When your friend or relative has regained enough strength to leave the bedside area, it's time for him or her to try using the bathroom. Generally, after a long stay in bed, a person will need help walking even short distances. Your assistance may be enough, but more likely than not a walker will be required for stability, safety, and security. Walkers range in price from

$40 to $70, and like other durable medical equipment they are covered by Medicare. Most have adjustable heights ranging from about 30 to 40 inches, depths about 19 or 20 inches, and widths about 24 inches. The most common problem with walkers is that they're too wide to get through many bathroom doors. If the person using one is strong enough, he or she can angle the walker and walk sideways through the door. Otherwise, you can take the door off its hinges and save about another 2 inches of space. Of course you'll have to put up a curtain in its place to ensure privacy. Another 1½ inches can usually be saved by removing the door molding.

Sometimes when hip and knee strength are severely limited, an elevated toilet seat makes sitting down and getting up easier. (These seats are discussed in Chapter 8, "The Environment.") You can also position a bedside commode (without the pail) over the toilet seat and accomplish the same thing.

Chapter 5, "Bathing," and Chapter 8, "The Environment," describe other additions to the bathroom, such as grab bars and safety rails, that can make life easier and safer for your elderly friend or relative.

RECUPERATION

A person who has been bedridden for a long time will ordinarily regain strength and endurance slowly. One day the person may sit up in bed for the first time, and the next day he or she may move unassisted to the edge of the bed. Recuperation is a slow, natural process through which the body heals itself. It takes time, it's different for each person, and it progresses in stages. From sitting on the edge of the bed, the recuperating person advances to sitting in a chair, and then to standing alone and taking a few steps. Before long the few steps turn into a walk, and eventually, without anyone's noticing or being aware of dramatic changes, the person is participating again in his or her former activities. Nonetheless, while your friend or relative is in bed you have to guard against complications such as joint contractures and muscle atrophy. And during the first few days out of bed, he or she will depend on you for assistance in walking and in transferring to and from the bed. By comforting and encouraging your friend or relative during this period, you can help nature with its recovery work, and sometimes even speed up the natural processes. The transition from being bedridden to resuming a normal lifestyle is emotionally difficult, and people often become discouraged by their weakness, the slow progress, and memories of their former selves. Nature will do its work as long as hope stays alive. You'll have to encourage, comfort, cajole, challenge, stimulate, or do whatever else it takes to keep hope alive and motivation high.

RANGE-OF-MOTION EXERCISES

While your friend or relative is still in bed, you can initiate a program of exercises. Range-of-motion exercises are the simplest ones that will keep the joints limber and prevent contractures. To stay loose and mobile, joints have to move— if they don't, they stiffen up. Ordinarily, a normal day's activities will bend and stretch all our joints through a wide enough range of motion to keep them in shape. Normal walking bends the ankles and prevents the extended ankle contractures (the toe-walking position) that are so common in bed-bound people; sitting down and standing up move the hips and knees through their ranges of motion, preventing contractures in these joints. Range-of-motion exercises are meant for people who are too weak to participate in a full day of activity and whose joints might stiffen up because of inactivity. The exercises are nothing more than the ordinary movements of the joints from one end of their range of motion to the other. The ankles, knees, and hips are most likely to stiffen in bed, but range of motion exercises should be given to the shoulders, elbows, wrists, fingers, and thumbs as well. All the joints should be moved through their normal range of motion —"ranged"—five to ten times once or twice a day (Figure 12-6).

If your friend or relative is too weak to exercise alone, you'll have to do the ranging. Choose a joint and support the extremities above and below it with your hands. Then gently, slowly, and steadily move the part farthest from the body through a complete range of motion, making certain not to cause any pain or force any motion. Never make any sudden moves, and always listen to your friend if he or she complains of pain or fatigue. For example, when ranging the knee, lift and support

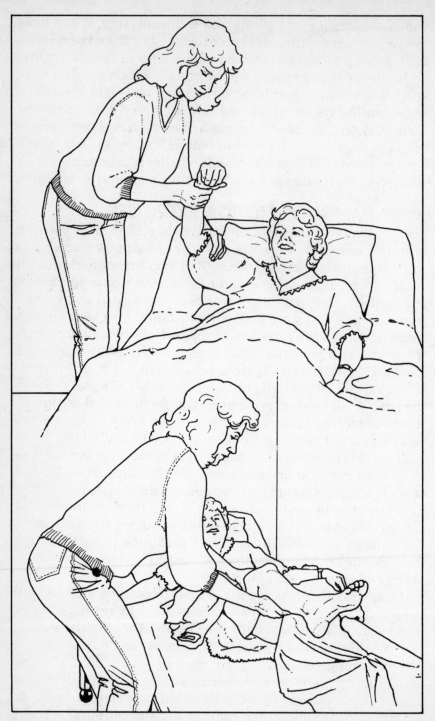

Figure 12-6. Range-of-motion exercises.

the thigh with one hand; with the other hand on the calf, slowly bend and straighten the leg five to ten times. Ranging all the joints should take you no more than ten minutes. As soon as your friend is strong enough, he or she should try exercising alone. Initially, the joints and extremities should be supported by the bed to eliminate the extra burden of gravity. Later, when more strength has returned, the joints and extremities can be raised in the air without your assistance and exercised against gravity. As additional strength returns, more resistance can be added, either by the addition of weights to the extremities or by manual resistance of their movements. When you range a bedridden person's joints, only you get stronger; but as soon as the bedridden person takes an active part in the exercise, he or she also gains strength.

Once your friend is strong enough to exercise alone in bed, it's time for him or her to get out of bed. This is a major step in the recovery process, especially for someone who has been bedridden for a long time. Since the capacity of the heart and lungs declines with bed rest just as readily as the strength of muscles declines, you'll have to make sure that your friend isn't overtaxed when first getting out of bed. If there is any difficulty breathing, chest pain, sweating, nausea, skin pallor, or dizziness, stop whatever is going on and help him or her back to bed. If the pulse is irregular or has increased more than 20 beats per minute over the lying-in-bed pulse, stop the activity, help your friend back to bed, and call your physician for further advice. Irregular pulses are abnormal, and you shouldn't continue activities that produce them. Pulse increases over 20 beats per minute indicate that a considerable effort is being made to perform the activity; they're not dangerous, but it's best to be on the safe side and cut back to less strenuous activities. Eventually, as strength and endurance increase, the same activity will produce smaller pulse increases and become easier to perform.

SITTING UP

The first step in getting out of bed is sitting up on the edge of the bed. Practice getting out of bed yourself, and then you'll be able to better help your friend or relative. If you're going to sit up on the right side of the bed, flatten the bed and roll onto your right side as close to the edge of the bed as possible. Place your right arm with its elbow bent underneath your body, and as you push up on your elbow, swing your feet off the bed so they drop to the floor. Keep pushing with your elbow and then your hand, until you're sitting up straight. When people have trouble sitting up alone, the best bet is to push and support them from the side and also help them swing their legs off the bed. If your friend is too weak even to begin the maneuver, roll the head of the bed up or prop him or her up with pillows. If you're standing on the right side of the bed, put your left arm around your friend's shoulder and with your right arm reach across his or her legs and grasp the left knee. Then, in one motion, lift up and rotate him or her into a sitting position (Figure 12-7). If there's any complaint of dizziness in this position, wait a couple of minutes to see if the feeling disappears. If it doesn't, help the person back to the lying position. If the pulse increases by more than 20 beats per minute and stays elevated for several minutes, it's also time for the person to lie down again.

Figure 12-7. From lying to sitting position.

Let's assume that when your friend sits up on the edge of the bed, there's no dizziness or rapid pulse change. The next area of concern is balance: can he or she sit unassisted without toppling over? Often it takes a while to regain enough balance and coordination to be able to sit without listing to the side or falling backward or off the bed. You can stand at the side of the bed and provide support. If you oversee the sitting routine two or three times a day, before long your friend or relative will be able to sit alone without swaying or falling.

SITTING IN A CHAIR

As soon as strength, endurance, and balance are recovered to the point where your friend or relative can go from a back-lying position to a sitting position alone without getting dizzy or unsteady, it's time for him or her to leave the security of the bed and shift to a chair. Provide a chair with armrests, and move the chair as close to the bed as possible, placing it on your friend's stronger side. Sometimes a person favors one side over the other, or, especially after a stroke, one side is stronger than the other. Make sure your friend is wearing slippers or shoes, and a sweater if there is a chill in the air.

If your friend has enough strength to stand up alone, he or she should start from the sitting position, then lean forward gently at the hips and straighten up while pushing off with the hands against the bed. Next, your friend should take short steps until he or she is standing with the back to the front of the chair and the calves touching the front of the seat. Then, holding onto the armrests, your friend should bend slightly at the hips and slowly lower himself or herself into the chair.

If your friend doesn't have the strength for all of this, you can help him or her up. Stand in front of your friend, keeping your feet about a shoulder's width apart; now bend your knees, straighten your back, and place your hands under his or her armpits, close to the body. Ask your friend to lean forward at the hips and to rock back and forth to gather momentum. On the count of three, he or she should try to stand while at the same time you push up in the armpits. Keep your back straight throughout all this activity—it won't help anyone to have you laid up in bed for a few weeks nursing a strained back. Your friend or relative can hold onto you for support while getting up and while standing. Once standing, he or she can shuffle or take short turning steps to back into the chair and then, holding onto you or the armrests, slowly lower himself or herself into the chair.

When a person is out of shape, it takes a lot of effort to sit for a long time. Initially, a person who has been bedridden for a long time should sit for only fifteen to twenty minutes at a time in the morning, the afternoon, and the evening. The sitting time can be increased gradually—a doubling of the time every two or three days is usually well tolerated. The goal is for the person to spend at least half the day out of bed.

WALKING

Once it's easy for your friend to sit up for long periods, it's time for him or her to stand up and try walking again. After weeks and months of beds and chairs, a person will usually need a walker or cane to get started. A walker with four legs and two side bars to hold onto is the most stable walking aid and offers the greatest security. There are three types of walkers. The standard walker has rubber tips on its legs and is picked up and moved forward with each step; it is the stablest type. The gliding walker has metal plates on its legs and is pushed along the floor; it's the best type for someone with poor balance who might fall during the brief, unsupported moments when a standard walker is lifted off the floor. A rolling walker has wheels on its legs, which make moving around effortless but which don't give much support. A rolling walker is dangerous, because it can roll away or take you for a ride, but if it's your friend's or relative's choice, make sure, at least, that it has locks that can be activated by pushing down on the walker.

Whichever walker you choose, get a folding model so it can be easily transported in a car or conveniently stored at home. Walkers are durable medical equipment and are covered by Medicare. Most walkers are about 2 feet wide and 3 feet high, but the height is adjustable, usually in 1-inch increments. The walker should be adjusted so that when it's being used, there is a slight bend in the elbows. If it's too high or too low, the person using it will quickly become fatigued.

Following the steps given here, practice standing, walking, turning, and sitting with a walker yourself. Once you've learned how, you'll be in a better position to teach your friend or relative. Of course, when he or she begins using a walker you should be nearby, to provide security, encouragement, information, and physical support.

To stand up with a walker, slide forward to the edge of the chair, put one hand on the walker, the other on the armrest of the chair (to distribute the weight), bend slightly at the waist, push up into a standing position, and grasp the walker with both hands. Now move the walker forward slightly and follow it with the foot of the weaker or more painful side. Next, lean on the walker and, pushing with your arms, lift yourself and move your "good" side forward. Keep repeating this sequence, and before you know it you'll be zipping right along with the walker.

Turning with a walker can be precarious. Never pivot on one foot with a walker and never let your feet get too close together. Always turn toward your stronger side—moving the walker first, then the weaker or painful side, and finally the good side (the same sequence used for walking in a straight line)—until you've completely turned around.

When you're ready to sit down, find a sturdy chair and turn with the walker until your back is in front of the chair. Move the walker back toward you, then step backwards with your good side, followed by your weaker or painful side. Continue moving backward in this sequence until the back of your legs touch the edge of the chair. Then reach back with one hand and grasp an armrest, steady yourself, reach back for the remaining armrest with your other hand, lean forward slightly at the hips, and lower yourself slowly into the chair.

When the walker becomes too easy, a cane is the next step. Some people are able to progress from using a walker directly to independent ambulation, but most people need a cane during the transition. There are three basic types of canes: walk cane, quad cane, and regular cane (Figure 12-8). The walk cane comes with rubber or glider tips, and, because of its wide base of support, it is the stablest type of cane. Like all canes, it is carried in the hand opposite the painful or weak side; if pain and weakness are not problems but balance is, the cane should be carried on the easiest, most comfortable side.

Like a walk cane, a quad cane has four legs, but it has a

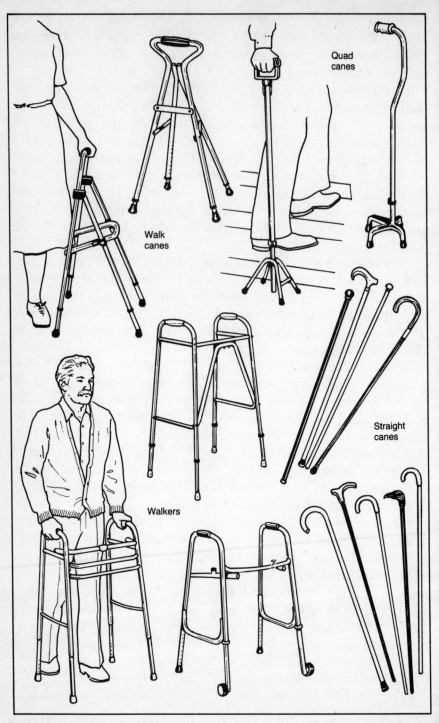

Figure 12-8. Walking aids.

shorter grasping area and only one long vertical support. In terms of stability, it is intermediate between a walk cane and a regular cane.

A regular cane is simply a long stick, though in smart shops you can find them twisted into any shape, carved out of any material, and painted in any color. In times past, the cane was a symbol of power and affluence, and in the early 1800s, a gold-headed cane came to represent the medical profession—no self-respecting physician appeared in public without a cane. Today, sadly, the cane has fallen into disrepute and people avoid its use. Still, for anyone who has the strength to walk but is unsteady or unsure, and especially for anyone with a painful hip or knee, a cane is the simplest, safest, and easiest to use walking aid. In fact, no harm would be done, and a lot of good would be accomplished, if canes came back into style and more people used them as a matter of course.

Like anything else, a cane should fit the user. With the cane held 6 inches ahead and slightly to the outside of the good foot, your friend's or relative's elbow should be bent about 30 degrees. In this position the arm muscles can be used to their best advantage, and weight-bearing will be most efficient.

There are three basic ways to walk with a cane: (1) Move the cane forward, then move the "bad" leg up to it, and, while pushing down on the cane, step up even with it with the "good" leg. (2) With additional strength, you can step past the cane with the last step. Move the cane forward, then move the bad leg up to it, and, while pushing down on the cane, step past it with the good leg. (3) With even more strength, you can combine the first two movements. Move the cane and bad leg forward at the same time, and then, while pushing down on the cane, step past it with the good leg.

Your friend or relative might need a cane indefinitely, for balance and support, for pain relief, or as a security blanket. But even if he or she doesn't need one, in the words of Dr. Walter Blount, past president of the American Academy of Orthopedic Surgeons, "Don't throw away the cane." Canes do no harm—they can only help. Today canes are avoided as symbols of infirmity the same way hearing aids were avoided a decade ago. But this attitude is wrong and unfair. Both the cane and the hearing aid make people more independent, not less; they open up the world and make more of it accessible, and they make possible experiences that would otherwise be missed. We'd probably have many more elderly people walking longer distances with healthier hips and knees and fewer falls if canes came back into style and people started using them not only for health reasons, but also to be well dressed and fashionable.

SUMMING UP

Being confined to a bed for most or all of the day is certainly no fun. Boredom is commonplace, and depression and lethargy make matters worse. Lying in bed for hours on end can also make someone feel tired and sloppy.

The last thing you want is for your friend or relative to become lazy, apathetic, or poorly motivated. The road to recovery can be difficult, and it is best traveled with energy and optimism. You, as a care giver, can play a major role in the mental and emotional well-being of your friend or relative by taking a down-to-earth, commonsense approach to his or her care.

We have mentioned a few of the things you can do to prevent your bedridden friend from slipping into the doldrums. Think of the little things that make you happy. Chances are they'll do the same for someone else. And, remember, the best thing that you, the care giver, can do for your elderly friend or relative is to be pleasant and optimistic. Happiness is often contagious.

13 Community Resources

From time to time you're going to need help caring for your friend or relative at home. Asking for help is neither a sign of defeat nor an act of surrender—it is a realistic effort to get the best possible care for your loved one. And it isn't a matter of how committed you are, or how much free time you have, or how skilled you are in providing care. Nobody can be an expert in all subjects at all times, and there will undoubtedly be days when you'll need additional information or assistance with unfamiliar tasks.

More important than your storehouse of information and your technical skills is your ability to cope with the emotional burden of caring for a frail or ill friend or relative. In spite of the good work that you're doing and the knowledge that your presence and concern are helping another person to a better life, you're still going to tire, and often become frustrated from the constant demands of care giving. Don't ever fall into the trap of believing that you can never leave your friend or relative alone or in the hands of another person. The only way you're going to remain effective over the long haul is to get away for short periods of time. A rest from the constant demands of care giving will renew you and make you a better provider. Develop your own interests: schedule time away from the house; indulge yourself; and get help whenever you're tired, troubled, or confused. Do whatever it takes to stay relaxed and confident.

Every community has a variety of resources for home health care, and it's best for you to learn about them before the need arises. There are services and supplies available to satisfy practically every human need. In a community well endowed with home care services, a motivated family can find whatever help it needs to keep a loved one at home. If you're away during the day and your friend or relative gets lonely, companions can visit for a few hours. If you get sick and can't shop, clean house, or prepare meals, homemakers and home health aides can take up the slack. Meals can be delivered to the door, and therapists can oversee an activities program. And for medical problems, ambulances and car services will deliver patients to doctors' offices as well as to hospitals, skilled nurses will make house calls, and medical alert systems can be installed for emergencies.

Services have been invented to help with every activity needed for independent living at home. If you can think of an activity that you might need help with someday, there is probably a town in America in which that help is provided today. Of course, not every service is available in every town. In cities resources abound, and the problem is making your way through the red tape and organizational maze of services, while in rural areas resources are scarce, and the problem is piecing together the appropriate help from a few sources. But in rural areas community spirit is strong and neighbors will often help one another, making the formal support systems of cities unnecessary. And the Red Cross, YMCAs, local churches, and civic and fraternal organizations are always helpful.

Sometimes organized home care services appear to be part of a secret, underground world. When you don't need home care services, you scarcely know they exist, and most people have no idea how to plug into the network of services, but when you need help and finally make contact with the home care world, you realize that there exists a vast and elaborate network of helping services, apparently hidden from the rest of society. The problems for most people are finding and financing the right services. Public agencies, private organizations, and volunteer groups all provide help, but availability is patchy and eligibility requirements are confusing and variable. For publicly funded services and services covered by Medicare, the regulations governing how much of which service for how long and for whom will be covered can be bewildering for even the most seasoned bureaucrat.

The following is a list of services that can be found in most communities. Rarely will all be available in one community, but there will always be something to get you started. Unfortunately, there's no central agency or board that coordinates and evaluates all home care services. There is often duplication of services, as well as uneven quality of services. You'll simply have to investigate your own town's resources and put together what you need from the existing services.

COMMUNITY RESOURCES

Information and referral
Medical services
Nursing services
Health-related services

    Podiatry
    Dentistry
    Optometry, optician services
    Pharmacy

Therapy services
    Physical therapy
    Occupational therapy
    Speech therapy

Social services
    Medical social services
    Legal advice
    Mental health services
    Telephone reassurance
    Friendly visiting services

Transportation
Personal and household assistance
Monitoring and protective services
    Monitoring systems
    Escort services

Medical supplies
Specialized services
    Pulmonary rehabilitation
    Intravenous therapy
    Laboratory testing

Meal services

Outlets for work and leisure activities
Respite care
Hospice care

INFORMATION AND REFERRAL

When you need outside help but you aren't sure where to go for it or even what to ask for, a local information and referral service is your best bet. It will either answer your questions itself or refer you to someone who can. Information and referral services deal with information: They collect, classify, and file it so that it's on hand when you need it. And if they don't have the information, they'll know where to get it.

The public library is the oldest information and referral service. A visit to the local library and a chat with the librarian can introduce you to all the hidden resources of your community. The key to unlocking any bureaucracy, organization, or network is asking the right questions and getting the right answers—and librarians are expert at this.

The telephone book is another good resource. Today most phone books have a special section called "Guide to Human Services" that's printed on colored paper and located in the back of the book. This guide lists all the local service agencies, grouping them according to the problems they handle. In addition to entries for particular problems such as transportation or housing, there's usually a separate entry for general information and referral. Take a few minutes to leaf through your phone book and get acquainted with the vast array of available services. If your phone book doesn't have a special human services guide, call the local office of a national service organization and explain your problem. People in the helping professions like to help, and even if they can't handle your particular problem, they may be able to direct you to the right place. The following is a list of national organizations that could be helpful to you directly or with referrals. Appendix D, "National Resources," is a more complete list that provides addresses for the national offices. Sears, Roebuck and Co. recently issued free state directories of information and referral services as part of their catalog of supplies for people with physical disabilities. This is a valuable resource for elderly people as well.

NATIONAL SERVICE ORGANIZATIONS

Administration on Aging
American Cancer Society
American Red Cross
Arthritis Foundation
Disabled American Veterans
Easter Seal Society
Goodwill Industries
March of Dimes
Multiple Sclerosis Society
National Association of the Deaf
National Federation of the Blind
Social Security Administration
United Way
Visiting Nurses Association
YMCA, YWCA/YMHA, YWHA

MEDICAL SERVICES

Every person over age 40 should have a personal physician who knows about his or her general well-being and keeps track of his or her medical history. A specialist who looks after a particular problem can also be a personal physician, but more often than not a general practitioner or family doctor fills that role. A personal physician becomes even more important in the later years of life, because someone has to keep track of all the problems, treatments, and medications. Elderly people often have multiple medical problems and consequently often have many specialists. A listing of the most common specialists follows. Find out which hospitals your friend's or relative's physicians use and keep the emergency room phone numbers and the physicians' phone numbers in a handy location. Physicians are usually affiliated with only a few hospitals, and they can't take care of their patients at other hospitals. It would be unfortunate if, during an emergency, your friend or relative were taken to a hospital where his or her physician didn't practice.

MEDICAL SPECIALISTS

Cardiologist and cardiac surgeon. A cardiologist specializes in diseases of the heart, and a cardiac surgeon operates on the heart. Cardiac surgeons are responsible for the well-known cardiac bypass operations.

Dermatologist and plastic surgeon. A dermatologist specializes in diseases of the skin, and a plastic surgeon operates on the skin. Plastic surgeons are well known for their cosmetic surgery, ranging from face lifts to breast and buttocks reconstruction. They're also experts in burn care.

Endocrinologist and general surgeon. An endocrinologist specializes in diseases of the endocrine glands, such as diabetes and hypothyroidism. A general surgeon operates on the glands.

Gastroenterologist and general surgeon. A gastroenterologist specializes in disorders of the digestive system. A general surgeon operates on the digestive tract.

Gynecologist. A gynecologist specializes in diseases of the female reproductive system and also operates on the reproductive organs.

Neurologist and neurosurgeon. A neurologist specializes in disorders of the nervous system, such as Parkinson's disease and multiple sclerosis. A neurosurgeon operates on the nervous system.

Oncologist. An oncologist specializes in cancer, and surgeons from different specialties operate, depending on which organ is involved.

Ophthalmologist. An ophthalmologist specializes in diseases of the eye and also operates
on the eye.

Physiatrist. A physiatrist specializes in physical
medicine and rehabilitation and works toward improving physical well-being and
functional capacity.

Psychiatrist. A psychiatrist specializes in mental
and emotional problems and works toward
improving emotional well-being.

Radiation oncologist. A radiation oncologist directs the use of radiation therapy for cancer
treatment.

Rheumatologist and orthopedic surgeon. A
rheumatologist specializes in diseases of the
joints. An orthopedic surgeon operates on joints
and bones.

Urologist. A urologist specializes in disorders of
the urinary tract and male reproductive system, and also operates on the urinary tract
and reproductive system.

NURSING SERVICES

If you need the assistance of a nurse, there are many options
available. Your local Nursing Bureau or Nursing Registry, whose
address and phone number can be found in the yellow pages,
will send a nurse to your home upon a simple phone request.
If a nurse is required after a hospital stay, the private duty
Nursing Registry at the hospital will arrange for a nurse to
accompany the patient home. But for insurance companies to
pay for nursing expenses, a physician's order for skilled nursing
care is required. Skilled nursing is important when there are
actual technical procedures to be performed, such as changing
an indwelling bladder catheter, or when your friend's or relative's medical condition is so precarious that frequent monitoring of his or her clinical condition is required. Both registered

nurses (R.N.s) and licensed practical nurses (L.P.N.s) provide skilled nursing care, but when clinical judgment and assessment skills are important, registered nurses are preferred. L.P.N.s go through a one-year practical nursing program, usually at a community hospital or college, while R.N.s either go through a two- or three-year program and receive a nursing diploma, or, what is more common nowadays, go to a four-year college and receive a Bachelor of Science degree in nursing. All nurses are licensed by the state in which they practice. Having more training and education, registered nurses are better able to assess difficult and changing situations and to make the appropriate interventions. They're also good teachers, and they can tell you about the diseases your friend or relative has and teach you how to perform simple procedures such as giving injections and bandaging wounds.

Hospitalization is a difficult experience for both the patient and the family, and a registered nurse can ease the patient's return home. If your friend or relative is still in a delicate condition at the time of discharge or if skilled procedures will be required, such as suctioning a tracheostomy or irrigating a wound, an R.N. can perform the procedures, assess the situation, and teach you what to look for, what to do, and how to do it. If your friend is not seriously ill, registered nurses are usually not needed for more than a few days. As soon as the transition from hospital to home is complete and your friend is medically stable, an L.P.N. can assist with the remaining procedures, monitor vital signs, and check to see that you know what to do when the nurses aren't around.

Historically, home health care in America grew out of the pioneering efforts of nurses at the turn of the century. The first Visiting Nurse Association was established by Lillian Wald in 1893 as part of the Henry Street Settlement House in New York City, and it quickly became a model for home care services throughout the country. From the very beginning, visiting nurses saw themselves as care givers and educators, and they brought both medical care and education to the homes of the sick and the disabled. Training in self-care, disease prevention, and health maintenance was as important as, and sometimes more important than, the actual treatment of an illness. And the family was as much a recipient of the training as the patient.

Today, nurses are just as eager to teach the family as to treat the patient, and there are times when the teaching is more important than the treating. Nurses with a special interest in diabetes can advise family members about proper diet, exercise, and hygiene, and also teach them how to use insulin. Specialized "ostomy" nurses can instruct a family in the care and maintenance of a colostomy or ileostomy. Nurses can teach families just about anything: from cleaning and bandaging a wound to administering injections to taking care of feeding tubes, intravenous lines, and bladder catheters.

With a doctor's order, skilled nursing care is covered by Medicare: eighty percent with an ordinary Medicare policy and 100 percent with the 65 Special. Fees vary from one part of the country to another, from one community to another, and even from one agency to another. If a registered nurse visits for only an hour or two a day, the hourly fee can range from $20 to $50; L.P.N.s charge a few dollars less. Visiting Nurse Associations and other nonprofit groups will usually send a nurse for a single one- or two-hour visit each day, but the for-profit, private home care agencies will also arrange for shift work if it is requested, just like in the hospital. Shift work, usually in eight-hour blocks of time—seven to three, three to eleven, eleven to seven—turns out to be much less expensive, with R.N.s charging from $12 to $15 an hour. Holiday, weekend, evening, and night work can be more expensive. Nursing care in eight-hour blocks is thought of as a luxury and is ordinarily not covered by Medicare.

HEALTH-RELATED SERVICES

PODIATRY

Podiatrists are trained and licensed to diagnose and treat disorders of the feet—everything above the ankles is off limits. They can prescribe medicine and perform surgery, and their services are reimbursed by Medicare. Elderly people with diabetes should have podiatrists perform all routine foot care, including toenail trimming. Many podiatrists make house calls.

DENTISTRY

A dentist diagnoses and treats diseases of the teeth and gums. Since the mouth is so small, it may surprise you that dentists, like doctors, specialize: An endodontist specializes in root canal work, a periodontist specializes in gum disease, and a dental surgeon performs surgery. There are also paraprofessionals helping the dentist. Dental hygienists clean and polish teeth, take x-rays, and teach basic dental care, and dental assistants assist the dentist while he or she works and also help in the laboratory and with processing x-rays. Dental services (with the exception of surgery on the facial bones) are not covered by Medicare. Some dentists will make house calls and begin simple treatments at home.

OPTOMETRY, OPTICIAN SERVICES

Optometrists examine and test eyes and prescribe, supply, and adjust eyeglasses and contact lenses. In some states they can use drugs to treat eye disease, but they are not physicians. They receive postgraduate training in a school of optometry, not a school of medicine. Opticians, on the other hand, learn their trade on the job, receiving little in the way of formal training. Opticians supply and adjust the eyeglasses and contact lenses that ophthalmologists (the medical specialists) and optometrists prescribe. Medicare pays for only a limited number of services performed by an optometrist, and it doesn't pay for any of an optician's services.

PHARMACY

Your local drugstore could be a citadel of learning, a veritable Fort Knox of medical information. Pharmacists are professionals who train in schools of pharmacy, and many of them know more about the day-to-day handling of drugs than anyone else. If you want to know when, how, or where to take a medicine, or how one medicine interacts with another one or with food or drink, ask a pharmacist. They're a valuable community resource not to be forgotten.

THERAPY SERVICES

PHYSICAL THERAPY

Physical therapists help with problems of movement. They develop and supervise exercise programs to strengthen muscles and stretch joints, and they are expert in the use of heat, ice, water, and other physical treatments for pain relief. A physical therapist will be most helpful in the first days after a debilitating illness, when your friend or relative will have the greatest difficulty getting out of bed, sitting in a chair, and starting to walk. A therapist will be able to assist with all these activities and develop an exercise program to ensure further progress. Most important, a therapist will be able to help you supervise and assist with the same activities. All home care professionals have two jobs: to help the patient and to teach the family. The goal is always independence. Registered physical therapists get a BS degree in physical therapy or a BS or BA degree in some other subject with a certification in physical therapy. A physical therapist's assistant trains at the associate level in a community college, and a physical therapy aide gets on-the-job training. There is no national registration for physical therapists, but registered therapists and assistants are licensed by the states. As long as physical therapy is requested by a physician, Medicare will foot the bill.

OCCUPATIONAL THERAPY

Occupational therapists help with activities of daily living such as bathing, dressing, and preparing meals. They are expert in teaching self-care skills and leisure-time activities, and they're especially helpful with fine motor activities such as using keys, tying shoelaces, opening drawers, and sewing. Occupational therapists also know how to splint joints to prevent deformities. Registered occupational therapists go to four-year colleges (some go on for master's and Doctoral degrees as well), while certified occupational therapists go to two-year community colleges, and occupational therapy aides get on-the-job training. Registered occupational therapists are registered, and certified occupational therapists are certified through national examinations, and some states also have licensing requirements. Medicare covers occupational therapy services if they are ordered by a doctor and if skilled nursing care, physical therapy, or speech therapy is also required.

SPEECH THERAPY

Speech therapists help with communication disorders. They're highly trained professionals, having both a bachelor's and a master's degree. Speech therapists are most helpful to elderly people who have had strokes and problems communicating, but they can also help with problems such as swallowing and eating dysfunctions. Speech therapists can help get the family started on a comprehensive rehabilitation program immediately after a hospitalization. Again, the services are covered by Medicare as long as they're requested by a physician.

SOCIAL SERVICES

MEDICAL SOCIAL SERVICES

Medical social services are provided by social workers who act as information and referral sources, but in addition to finding the resources to meet your needs, they can also coordinate and supervise the services. Social workers know a lot about the costs of home care. They'll be able to help you through the tangle of insurance forms and regulations and to let you know about the federal, state, and local assistance you're entitled to and what your own insurance policy covers. Social workers can also provide general counseling and emotional support. Most home health care agencies and Visiting Nurse Associations have social workers on staff to help identify your particular needs and arrange for the appropriate services. The Social Service departments in most hospitals are gold mines of help and information for people ready to be discharged.

LEGAL ADVICE

Legal problems may turn up for your elderly friend for which you are not prepared—problems such as making out a will, social security or pension claims, probate and estate planning, and so forth. If you don't know a good lawyer, the local

Bar Association is a good resource that will recommend one, and if you have only a limited income, the local branch of the Legal Aid Society will take your case and even go to court for you for only a minimal charge.

MENTAL HEALTH SERVICES

Anyone can help a person with mental and emotional problems simply by being a good listener and a good friend. But there are professionals who know how to get a person to talk freely about painful feelings and how to lead a person gently through an emotional conflict to a comforting resolution. Psychiatrists, who are medical doctors, clinical psychologists, who have a Ph.D. or a master's degree, and some social workers are trained to counsel people with emotional problems. Psychiatrists are the only ones who prescribe medicines, and they're also the only ones whose services are reimbursed by Medicare—except, when a clinical psychologist works with a physician, psychiatrist, or other doctor, Medicare will pick up the psychologist's bill as well.

Don't get the idea that emotional help is only for your elderly friend or relative. Caring for an elderly person can be burdensome, and even the most well-meaning, well-intentioned, and compassionate people can become, from time to time, emotionally fatigued and need the support and reassurance of outsiders—if only for blowing off steam and letting out frustrations. Don't hesitate to ask for help if you feel pressured, angry, guilty, or unhappy. Both you and your friend or relative will benefit and feel better afterward.

Don't feel that you must see a professional every time you need help, however. Mutual help groups and support groups are being formed every day in communities across the country. Families caring for an elderly friend or relative have felt the need to share their experiences, frustrations, conflicts, and victories with one another, and they have informally organized local support groups. Meeting weekly in each other's homes or in public buildings such as churches and synagogues, these groups offer members the opportunity to exchange information, solve problems, share experiences, and ventilate frustrations. In addition to providing emotional support, they also help with practical, day-to-day matters, such as finding the best medical supply house in town, or the most reliable transportation service, or the most responsible health care agency.

To set up a support group, you might call a few neighbors who are also taking care of an elderly friend or relative and invite them to your home for an informal gathering. To get additional information and to learn about the experiences of others, there is the National Support Center For Families of the Aging (P.O. Box 245, Swarthmore, PA 19081) and the National Self-Help Clearinghouse (33 West 42nd Street, Room 1227, New York, NY 10036).

TELEPHONE REASSURANCE

Telephone reassurance is proof that the good neighbors who have always been part of the American landscape are still alive serving their communities. If you have to leave town for a few days and want someone to check on your friend or relative in your absence, a volunteer from a telephone reassurance project will call each day at a predetermined time; if there's no answer, a neighbor, police officer or fire fighter will check up in person. In some areas teenagers do the calling, and in other areas elderly people themselves check up on one another. Churches, synagogues, hospital auxiliaries, business clubs, and other volunteer organizations throughout the country have established telephone projects. There are also telephone clubs and "Dial a Listener" services in some parts of the country for elderly people who are shut in and simply want to talk with someone.

FRIENDLY VISITING SERVICES

Friendly visiting services are another proof that the good-neighbor spirit is alive and well. If you're going out of town for an extended period of time, volunteers will visit your friend or relative on a regular basis, usually once or twice a week. They'll talk, write letters, read aloud, play cards, or just plain listen. Often young people—high school and college students—"adopt" grandparents, visit regularly, and even help with errands. The only qualifications a visitor or companion needs are a sense of responsibility; reliability; and a friendly, caring nature. Visiting services are offered by a variety of volunteer agencies and organizations, including some unions who offer them as benefits for their retired members.

TRANSPORTATION

What if your friend or relative has a doctor's appointment when you're out of town, or simply wants to meet a friend for lunch when you plan to be across town having lunch yourself? Transportation projects abound. Many communities, having sensed that a lack of transportation was preventing their elderly citizens from enjoying and participating in community affairs, have organized transportation services. Cars, buses, and station wagons, some even equipped for handicapped and wheelchair-bound people, have been appropriated for the elderly for day trips, outings, shopping tours, and door-to-door doctor and hospital visits. When necessary, the drivers also double as escorts or bodyguards. While most transportation services run by volunteer groups such as the Red Cross or the YMCA are free, most ambulance services are private and costly. Whenever possible, leave the ambulances for true medical emergencies and use your community's version of a transportation system for the elderly—"Dial a Ride," "Dial a Bus," or the like—for ordinary activities.

PERSONAL AND HOUSEHOLD ASSISTANCE

Personal and household assistance is the type of simple, mundane help that is often overlooked or taken for granted, but without which all the expensive, high-tech medical interventions in the world would be useless. A well-maintained home and good personal care are the prerequisites for a healthy lifestyle, as well as the foundation on which all help depends. If you plan to be away from home, even for a short time, and your friend or relative is unable to care for himself or herself in your absence, outside assistance must be arranged.

Homemaker–home health aides provide most of the personal and household assistance. Aides are not required to have formal

training or to be licensed or certified, but the National Home
Caring Council recommends sixty hours of training in personal
care, basic nursing, and home safety and management. Aides
are known as home health aides, nursing assistants, or atten-
dants when they help with personal care activities such as
feeding, bathing, toileting, and dressing. When they help with
light housekeeping—food shopping, meal preparation, dusting,
vacuuming, ironing—they're known as homemakers. Heavier
housekeeping—seasonal cleaning, attic and basement cleaning, home repairs, yard work and the like—is done by house-
keepers or chore workers.

Many communities have separate homemaker–home health
aide agencies, but just as many have comprehensive home care
agencies that offer homemaker–home health aide services as
part of a total home care package. Publicly funded home care
agencies (e.g., county home care and family services), nonprofit
agencies (e.g., the Visiting Nurse Association), and private, for-
profit agencies (e.g., UpJohn Health Care Service, Inc.) all em-
ploy homemaker–home health aides. The issue is not whether
an agency is publicly sponsored, nonprofit, or for-profit, but
whether it supervises the aides it employs. Aides are not ex-
tensively trained, but since they care for frail elderly people,
they're often in situations that call for quick action, clinical
judgment, and decision making. It's important that you have
confidence in the aide in whose care you leave your friend or
relative, and, for this reason, supervision by a registered nurse
or social worker is important and helpful. If there's a choice
between an agency that supervises its aides and one that doesn't,
choose the one that supervises—it's guaranteeing the quality
of its services.

Medicare will pay for a part-time home health aide, as long
as a skilled nurse or therapist (physical therapist or speech
therapist) is also involved on the case and the patient is home
bound and under the care of a physician. While Medicare was
invented as insurance against acute medical illnesses, and was
never intended to cover the costs of chronic care, on an inter-
mittent basis it can ease the financial burdens of caring for a
friend or relative at home. Most nonprofit agencies mainly provide Medicare-reimbursable services, but the private agencies
will be able to help you with nonreimbursable services such
as a homemaker, a chore worker, or a home health aide for an

extended period of time. Costs vary throughout the country, but as a rule a home health aide will cost $8 or $9 an hour and a homemaker slightly less.

MONITORING AND PROTECTIVE SERVICES

MONITORING SYSTEMS

What happens if your friend or relative gets too ill to call for help while you're away? If friends and neighbors stop by or call regularly, help is readily available; otherwise, your friend could be seriously ill for days without anyone's knowing about it. Thanks to new communications technology, elderly people can now call for help electronically. Systems with names such as Lifeline, Helpline, and Alert One link elderly people at home with hospital emergency rooms and community emergency centers. The systems consist of three parts: a wireless, hand-held transmitter the size of a television remote-control tuner; a digital transmitter attached to the telephone that can pick up signals from the hand-held transmitter up to 150 or 200 feet away; and a large emergency-room or emergency-center receiver. When a button on the hand-held transmitter is pushed, an electronic signal is forwarded to the digital transmitter and then carried over the telephone lines (even if the telephone is off the hook) to the emergency headquarters receiver. As soon as headquarters receives a signal, the person signaling for help is identified and called back immediately. If there is no answer, designated friends or relatives are called; and if they can't be reached, the fire department or local police are asked to make an emergency visit. Most of the systems have automatic timers that activate the call-for-help signal every twelve or twenty-four hours. If a person is OK, he or she simply resets the timer every twelve or twenty-four hours; otherwise it automatically goes off at headquarters and help is immediately dispatched. This means that the person will never be left unconscious or too weak to call for help for more than twelve hours. Some systems incorporate additional protective features such as burglar alarm capabilities and household temperature monitoring. Regardless of the number of protective features, there's usually a one-time entry fee for the system, about $100, and then a monthly rental and maintenance charge between $10 and $20. Since electronic protective devices are so new, there is as yet no insurance coverage for them, though there is mounting pressure to have them covered.

You don't need sophisticated electronic equipment for all types of protective monitoring. For example, people in many parts of rural Maine use a blue light system: Every household has a blue light in a window, and when someone needs help he or she turns on the light; anyone traveling by, friend or stranger, is alerted and summons help. Telephone reassurance programs also provide monitoring service as well as emotional support.

ESCORT SERVICES

When your friend or relative wants to get out of the house but you're involved elsewhere, escort services can be helpful. Even the most able-bodied elderly people are sometimes scared to go out alone: Traffic can be heavy and crossing the streets dangerous; neighborhood vandals can make leisurely walking hazardous; and in the winter ice can make sidewalks treacherous. A volunteer or a paid worker will escort your friend and provide physical assistance, emotional support, and protection.

MEDICAL SUPPLIES

The corner drugstore is your best bet for common, inexpensive medical items such as a thermometer, an enema bag, gauze pads, and cotton balls. For durable medical equipment and uncommon items—urinary catheters, for example—you'll have to go to a medical supply house. Check the yellow pages or ask one of your information and referral sources for a list of local dealers. Most supply houses have catalogs, so if you know what you want you can order by telephone and have the supplies delivered. Otherwise, you can visit the store, inspect the equipment, and pick out what you want. (See Appendix E, "Special Supplies.")

Durable medical equipment can be expensive, and insurance companies strictly define such equipment. For example, Medicare defines *durable medical equipment* as equipment that serves a medical need, that can be used repeatedly, and that is useless to anyone without an illness or injury. Medicare also requires a physician to fill out a Certificate of Medical Necessity, indicating the patient's diagnosis, prognosis, and status, as well as estimating how long the equipment will be needed. Once the physician fills out the form and the patient files a Form HCFA-1490S, "Patient's Request for Medicare Payment," Medicare will reimburse (after a deductible is met) 80 percent of the equipment cost. Inexpensive equipment can be bought outright or rented at the patient's discretion, but Medicare will cover the rental fees only until the purchase price is reached. For expensive equipment, Medicare reviews the situation and makes recommendations to the patient, based on its new rent/purchase guidelines, to buy or rent. Again, Medicare pays the rental charges only until the purchase price is reached. If purchase of the equipment is recommended, purchase must be made at one time in one lump sum. While Medicare pays 80 percent of the cost, you'll have to pay 20 percent, and a 20 percent co-payment on a pricey item can be a lot of money to shell out at one time. For this reason, many people prefer to rent the equipment. Also, once you buy the equipment, you're responsible for all repairs and maintenance, but if you're renting, the company will keep the equipment in shape and do the repair work for nothing. Some items that you might think are durable medical equipment turn out not to be. For example, shower stools and bathroom safety bars are considered more in the line of luxury items and are nonreimbursable. So check first before you put in your order—you might be able to improvise the equipment you can't afford.

Surprisingly, there is no licensing board for medical supply houses, nor is there any national accrediting body. Since well-maintained, properly working durable medical equipment could be vital to the continued health and well-being of your friend or relative, you should check out the local supply houses carefully. At the very least, make sure the one you use is bonded, which means that it has its own liability insurance against dangerous equipment malfunctions. (Equipment manufacturers also have insurance.) Insurance doesn't guarantee high quality and dependability, but it does show common sense, at least. The durable medical equipment business is thriving, in the billions of dollars today, and there is, predictably, considerable competition. Ask questions and shop around. Nonprofit home care agencies such as the Visiting Nurses Associations are often unbiased and objective, and you can ask one of them for recommendations. When you talk to a sales representative, have a list of questions in front of you so you won't get flustered by what can be a confusing sales pitch. Use the following list as a model. Delete or add questions as you like, but never hesitate to ask what's on your mind. It's your money, your time, and your family's comfort.

QUESTIONS FOR THE MEDICAL EQUIPMENT SUPPLIER

1. Do you have the equipment?
2. What is the cost?
3. What is the rental fee?
4. Should I rent or buy the equipment?
5. How much will Medicare pay?
6. How long will Medicare pay?
7. How do I bill Medicare?

SPECIALIZED SERVICES

PULMONARY REHABILITATION

Caring for a person with a long-standing, debilitating lung disease, such as asthma, emphysema, or bronchitis, at home requires the support of a broad range of services that are usually pulled together in a pulmonary rehabilitation program. Often complicated equipment that must be kept working around the clock—a liquid oxygen system, an oxygen concentrator, a suction machine, even an artificial breathing machine—is installed in the home. Equipment failure must be serviced immediately, at any time of day or night—oxygen is not something you can do without for very long. Respiratory therapists visit regularly and are on call for emergencies as well. They service the equipment and provide inhalation therapy. Physical therapists oversee the person's exercise and teach the person proper breathing techniques and energy-saving work habits. Laboratory technicians are often called into the home to draw blood, do an electrocardiogram, and perform other specialized diagnostic tests. Nurses oversee medications, check physical signs and symptoms, and coordinate the day-to-day operation of the pulmonary rehabilitation program, reporting clinical changes directly to the physician in charge. Most home health care agencies offer comprehensive pulmonary programs and will either have the necessary durable medical equipment or know where to get it for you. Medicare covers most aspects of at-home pulmonary rehabilitation.

INTRAVENOUS THERAPY

Recently, Medicare introduced a new prospective payment system that pays hospitals flat fees based on patients' diagnoses (there are 476 diagnostic-related groups, DRGs, to choose from) rather than on cost of services or days of treatment. Consequently, hospitals are discharging patients earlier, and treatments that were once the exclusive property of hospitals, including intravenous therapy and hyperalimentation, are now provided at home. Blood, intravenous antibiotics, and intravenous feedings can all be administered at home. Many hospitals now have their own home care departments to provide these services; otherwise they can arrange for them through local home care agencies. All acute, medically necessary treatments are reimbursed under Medicare. Over the next few years, more and more acute care will be given at home, as hospitals become concentrations of specialists and high-tech megabuck equipment, treating only the most critically ill and diagnosing, stabilizing, and quickly discharging the rest of us.

LABORATORY TESTING

If your friend needs laboratory tests but is too ill to go to a hospital or a physician's office, laboratory personnel can come to your house. A nurse or laboratory technician will obtain blood and urine samples, do an electrocardiogram, and even arrange for a portable x-ray if necessary. The specimens and x-rays will be delivered to the hospital laboratory or to an independent laboratory. The results will be sent directly to the physician, who will then notify you and your friend.

MEAL SERVICES

Good nutrition is always important and should never stop. But there will be times when you'll be out of town or will simply want to treat yourself to a night away from the kitchen. There are a number of easy, inexpensive ways to guarantee nutritious meals for your friend. First of all, don't underestimate your friend's abilities. He or she may not be able to shop but may be able to cook, as long as there's food at home. You can prepare the ingredients for each meal beforehand, pack them together, label the packages ("dinner for Monday night"), and store them in the refrigerator or freezer. Your neighbors may be willing to help as well—perhaps with shopping, preparing the ingredients, cooking, or serving the meals.

If your friend or relative can't cook and if neighbors are unavailable, many services will deliver hot meals to the house. Ask one of the home health care agencies or the social service department of your local hospital about home-delivered meals. Prices vary from one part of the country to another, but $3 to $4 a meal is average. The quality of the meals also varies from one service to another, so you might want to order only one or two meals initially to see if they're nutritious and if your friend or relative likes them. Private services will deliver as many meals as you like, seven days a week, for as long as you like.

Meals on Wheels is the best-known home-delivered meal service; it has a sliding fee scale, there's often a waiting list, and preference is given to the needy. A hot noon meal and a cold evening meal are delivered five days a week. Meals on Wheels programs are usually organized by religious or civic groups.

The one problem with home-delivered meals is that your friend or relative eats alone and misses the pleasures of social contact at mealtimes. For this reason, group meal and congregate dining projects are flourishing everywhere. Hot meals are served in easily accessible public places such as school cafeterias, senior centers, and churches. Meals can even be prepared at one location and served at another. For example, friends can arrange for meals to be delivered to one another's homes where they can dine together.

OUTLETS FOR WORK AND LEISURE ACTIVITIES

No matter how close and caring your family is, life at home may not be enough to satisfy the social needs of your elderly friend or relative. Opportunities for a social life outside the home are important. Elderly people enjoy each other's company and benefit from seeing one another and talking over problems together. It's comforting for people at the same stage in life and with similar experiences to share their thoughts, hopes, and memories. And when work and community involvement are undertaken, a sense of dignity and personal worth is encouraged.

Senior citizen centers come in all shapes and sizes. When professionally staffed, they are called multipurpose centers, and when volunteers are primarily involved, they're called clubs. Whatever they're called, they offer elderly people a rich assortment of leisure activities. Most are open year-round, five days a week, and offer elderly people the chance to get together informally to talk, play cards, or take part in any of many supervised programs, which range from ceramics classes to exercise classes to lectures on health. Senior citizen centers are sponsored by religious, fraternal, and civic organizations and they're usually free, although sometimes there's a nominal charge.

When health care professionals such as physical therapists and nurses are involved, medical services, as well as the social and recreational ones, are provided and the center is called a geriatric day care center, which is actually a cross between a senior citizens center and a day hospital. If you're going to be away for any length of time and your elderly friend or relative needs medical attention, but not around-the-clock care, a day care center is a perfect way to provide the appropriate care. Centers are usually open from nine in the morning to five at night, and the costs, which are not covered by Medicare, range from $10 to $20 a day and include transportation and one hot meal.

While senior citizen centers are the most common resource for leisure time activities for elderly people, don't overlook the ordinary community resources that are available to people of all ages. Local libraries often sponsor book clubs and discussion groups for the elderly; bookmobiles deliver books to the home bound, including large-print and talking books for the visually impaired. Museums, community colleges, high schools, and trade schools also offer special programs for the elderly.

When an elderly person wants to combine work with social and cultural activities, the opportunities are limitless. Three national programs with local branches across the country deserve special mention: Retired Senior Volunteer Program (RSVP), Service Corps of Retired Executives (SCORE), and Foster Grandparents Program. The RSVP program promotes volunteer work in almost every community institution, from schools and libraries to hospitals and courts. SCORE is more restrictive, appealing primarily to retired executives and offering them opportunities to use their years of experience and expertise as consultants to struggling businesses and as teachers and lecturers to high school, college, and civic groups. Foster Grandparents is a beautiful project that enriches the lives of everyone it touches. Elderly people are given the chance to help with the care of young children living in infant homes, hospitals, and special schools. Both the child and the "grandparent" enjoy and benefit from the trust and loving relationship that develops.

On a local level, schools and libraries hire elderly people as part-time aides, museums hire them as guides, and there are always handyman and babysitting jobs advertised on community bulletin boards. Even private industry is getting into the act. Firms are recruiting retired executives to lead training programs, and other retired employees to guide visitors through the plants and showrooms. And the American Association of

Retired Persons (AARP) has its own free employment agency, Mature Power.

For activists, there are the Gray Panthers, the National Council of Senior Citizens, and the American Association of Retired Persons (you don't have to be retired, just over age 50). These three national groups—and there are more on a local level—organize the elderly as an influential voting bloc, they lobby for programs important to the elderly, they act as watchdogs on Capitol Hill on behalf of the elderly, and they fight ageism whenever and wherever it rears its ugly head.

The American Association of Retired Persons, with more than 19 million members, is involved in more than lobbying and legislative activities. It also sponsors educational programs, funds research, publishes books and pamphlets, organizes volunteer projects, and provides special membership services and discounts, such as a mail-order pharmacy, a group health insurance program, an investment program, a motoring plan, and a travel service.

RESPITE CARE

Respite care is a new concept for Americans. It is popular in Europe as a support service for families of the elderly and disabled, but while it is gaining in popularity here for families of disabled children, it is still relatively unknown to families of elderly people. Respite care is the temporary care of an elderly or disabled person for the express purpose of providing relief for the family from the burden of constant 24-hour-a-day care. Respite care lets families take a break from a few hours to several months. A night out, a weekend off, a vacation away, all become possibilities. And if you live alone with your friend or relative and become ill, respite care is available until you recover. Respite care can be provided in your home or outside your home. In-home services cover the full spectrum of home care, including nursing, homemaker–home health aide care, and chore services. When the needs are not great, companions alone may be sufficient. Out-of-home respite care is varied. An elderly person can be looked after in a nursing home on a temporary basis, or a free-standing facility, even a hotel, can be the setting for respite care. Cooperatives are another idea: Cooperating families, using their own homes, provide respite care for one another. And foster families is yet another model in which a family "adopts" an elderly person, giving the biological family time off. Costs for respite care vary with the level of care, but since most projects are funded by the government, the costs are reasonable and often based on a sliding scale. Of course, you can always organize your own cooperative with other families, provide a needed service, and reap the psychological and emotional rewards of starting such a project.

HOSPICE CARE

Hospice care is more than an extended home care program. It is a philosophy and a way of dying. Hospice care is provided in homes, hospitals, and free-standing facilities. The goals are always the same: to let terminally ill patients live comfortably with their families until they die, and to let their families live comfortably afterward. Hospice programs are not alternatives to medical treatment. On the contrary, they rely heavily on physicians, and their objectives are to alleviate suffering and relieve patient symptoms, as well as provide emotional support to the patient and family. A primary concern of all hospice programs is the relief of pain—no one should suffer needlessly from untreated pain in this day and age. When hospice care is provided in homes, a physician and nurse are usually on call 24 hours a day and the full range of home care services are available 7 days a week. Hospital-based hospice care and free-standing hospice facilities try to foster as warm and homelike an environment as possible: Patients decorate their rooms with furniture brought from home, a communal kitchen is available for meal preparation, and there are around-the-clock visiting hours. Hospice services are partially covered by Medicare and by most private insurance companies. For additional information about hospice programs around the country, contact The National Hospice Organization, 1901 North Fort Myer Drive, Arlington, VA 22209.

HOSPITALIZATION: A WORD OF CAUTION

If your friend or relative is hospitalized, you should start planning for his or her discharge immediately. In fact, a meeting with a discharge planner or a social worker from the hospital's social service office on the day of admission, or earlier, is a good idea. You'll want to know the estimated length of hospitalization and how long a recovery period is anticipated. To prepare for your friend's or relative's homecoming, you'll have to know, far in advance, which home care services will be needed. Go down the list of community resources on page 191 and check off the services you'll need. What about special equipment—a hospital bed, for instance? Or modifications in the house, like installation of safety bars? You don't want to be caught on the day of discharge with no equipment at home and none of the services mobilized. Since hospitals are discharging patients earlier and more disabled than ever before, and since the number of elderly people is growing every day, the demand for home care is quickly outstripping the supply. Today, to guarantee a smooth and trouble-free return home for your friend, you must begin planning for his or her discharge at the time of admission.

14 Epilogue

In the preceding pages we've tried to convince you that it's only right and just for you to take care of an elderly friend or relative. We've tried to allay your fears by showing you that it takes only common sense, a few facts, and a lot of love to do a good job. Now it's time for a word of caution. Don't neglect your own life or your family's life for the sake of your new tenant. If you didn't love and want to take care of your friend or relative, you wouldn't have invited him or her to live with you. Now that he or she is with you, you have to protect yourself and your family from your own good intentions and willingness to help.

If you aren't careful, before long you will have given up your independence and sacrificed important relationships in the day-to-day routine of caring for your friend or relative. You can care for someone completely without sacrificing your life in the process, but you must be aware of the pitfalls.

A separate entrance to the house or an in-law apartment for your new family member would be ideal. A separate telephone with its own number is also a good idea. Of course, separate entrances, in-law apartments, and telephones are luxuries, but the idea is clear: You can take care of a loved one, but you and your family still have a separate life which must be preserved. If you give up your home life and expect or demand limitless sacrifice from your spouse and children, the good deed and kind works you have undertaken will only breed resentment.

If your elderly parent is a guest in your home, he or she will have to realize that while you'll always be his or her child, you and your spouse are still adults, and you both have your own ideas about family life and child rearing. There will be times when your friend or relative interferes with your family or makes unreasonable demands, and you'll have to put your foot down and reinforce the fact that it is your family and your home. Don't feel bad or guilty about this. Do it gently, firmly, and with love.

Caring for an elderly friend or relative is a noble and charitable deed. It is also a great responsibility. Not only must you care for an elderly person, which is difficult and challenging in itself, but you must also look after your family in its new role as care giver. Set aside time when the family can talk about frustrations and difficulties without guilt or embarrassment. Talking is the simplest way of venting anger, easing frustration, and preventing resentment. Also, set aside time for your family to be alone. Most group outings will include your friend or relative, but make sure some are reserved exclusively for your family. And encourage your friend or relative to do the same thing, to plan outings alone without you and the rest of the family.

As long as you are careful and respectful of each person's independence and special feelings, there will be no problems. You can only be complimented and honored for what you are doing. It would be a better world with stronger values and a more spiritual sense, if more people followed your lead and appreciated their connection and recognized their responsibility to their aged friends and relatives. We thank you for your commitment and wish you good luck.

Appendix A

In Case of Emergency

You need two types of emergency medical plans—one for when your friend or relative gets acutely ill, and the other for when you get ill.

WHEN YOUR FRIEND OR RELATIVE IS SICK

1. Call your friend's or relative's doctor and report the situation. Always keep the doctor's telephone number displayed in a prominent location (on the refrigerator, above the telephone, etc.).

2. If the doctor can't be reached, call the emergency phone number, 911, and ask for help.

3. Call and tell a friend or family member what has happened and that you're going to the hospital.

4. Take important phone numbers and change for phone calls with you. You'll want the doctor's phone number and the numbers of friends and family members who should be notified during emergencies and who could also give you advice and support over the phone.

5. Bring your friend's or relative's insurance cards and social security number with you.

6. Bring along enough money to get something to eat. You may be at the hospital a long time.

7. If you ride along in the ambulance, arrange for a ride back home once the situation at the hospital is under control.

8. If your friend or relative is admitted to the hospital, before you leave make certain that the nurses have your phone number and know how to reach you.

9. Write down your friend's or relative's room number, visiting hours, the hospital telephone number, the name of the doctor in charge, and the name of the head nurse. Leave word that you are to be notified—at any time, day or night—if there are any serious changes.

10. Go home and try to rest. Pray, hope for the best, and realize that your loved one is in good hands and that you are doing everything that is humanly possible.

WHEN YOU ARE SICK

1. Before any emergency occurs, find someone who agrees to look after your friend or relative in your absence. During an emergency, either this person will move into your home or your friend or relative will move out.

2. Draw up a power of attorney and keep it in a safe but accessible place.

3. Keep your will and trusts updated and keep them and other important papers and keys to safe deposit boxes in secure, accessible places that are known to at least one friend or family member.

4. When you're feeling sick, call your doctor, or ask your friend or relative to call, and explain the situation.

5. If your doctor can't be reached, call the emergency medical number, 911, and ask for help.

6. In the event you go to a hospital, call the person who has agreed to look after your friend or relative and explain what is happening and where you are going.

7. Take your insurance cards, driver's license, and social security number with you to the hospital.

8. Leave enough cash and checks with your friend or relative to cover expenses for one week.

9. Leave the name of the hospital and the name of your doctor at home.

10. If you are admitted to the hospital, give the doctor and nurse the name and number of your friend or relative as well as the name and number of the prearranged guardian. If you have the strength, call home and let everyone know how things are; otherwise, ask your nurse to make the call.

Appendix B

Common Medical
✗ Problems

ARTHRITIS

Arthritis affects more than 30 million Americans. It is not a single disease, but a group of more than a hundred conditions. The two most common forms, and the two that most frequently affect the elderly, are osteoarthritis and rheumatoid arthritis. Osteoarthritis is a degenerative disease of the joints that is caused by wear and tear, and usually affects weight-bearing joints such as the hips and back. Rheumatoid arthritis is an inflammation of the joint linings that is caused by immune reactions within the body, and can affect any joint in the body as well as other organs. Treatment of arthritis consists of physical therapy, occupational therapy, drugs, and in severe cases, surgery. The goal is always to maintain free motion at the joint, reduce pain and stiffness, and prevent permanent destruction. Aspirin is the first-line drug. Anti-inflammatory drugs like Motrin, steroids, gold, and other more potent medicines are used when aspirin fails to bring the desired relief.

DIABETES

Approximately 10 million Americans suffer from diabetes. Elderly people are especially hard hit—one out of every six people over age 65 is affected. When we eat, sugars and starches are broken down to glucose, which circulates in the bloodstream as one of the body's chief energy sources. In diabetes, the control mechanisms that regulate the amount of glucose in the bloodstream break down, and glucose levels can rise to alarmingly high levels, damaging almost every organ in the body as they rise. Type I diabetes, the most serious form of the disease, usually starts in childhood or adolescence and requires insulin throughout life for its treatment. Type II diabetes is more common among the elderly and seldom requires insulin; instead oral medicine, diet, and exercise are relied upon for treatment. While diabetes is primarily a disease of glucose metabolism, all parts of the body are affected in some way sooner or later. Of particular importance to the elderly are the feet. Diabetes often damages the nerves to the feet, blunting sensation there, and also reduces the blood supply to the area. Add to this a poor healing response and a generally lowered resistance to infection, and the feet become danger zones for uncontrollable infections. If your friend or relative has diabetes, be sure to check his or her feet at least once a day. Beware of any sores, blisters, breaks, bruises, callouses, tears, cuts, or even simple reddened areas. Report them to your doctor at once; don't wait for an infection to set in.

Because of their difficulty fighting infections, diabetics must be attentive to the skin on all parts of the body, not just the feet. Skin should always be clean and dry. Teeth and gums must be checked as well, to avoid infections in the mouth.

PARKINSON'S DISEASE

Parkinson's disease affects 1 to 2 percent of the elderly population. It is a disorder of the brain that creates problems in movement, posture, balance, and walking. Its cause is unknown and there is no cure, but there are several drugs that control the signs and symptoms. People with Parkinson's disease will often be expressionless, they'll have a tremor at rest, their posture will be stiff, they'll move slowly, their balance will be poor, and when they walk they'll shuffle and not swing their arms. They can be depressed, demented, and incontinent and have trouble speaking and swallowing. Treatment consists of physical therapy, occupational therapy, and drugs. Common drugs are Symmetrel, Sinemet, Parlodel, Larodopa, Artane, and Cogentin. These all have serious side effects and their use should be carefully monitored by a physician.

PROSTATE PROBLEMS

Benign prostatic hypertrophy, which is a benign enlargement of the prostate, is probably universal in men over age 65. The prostate is a gland the size of a walnut that sits next to the bladder and surrounds the urethra, the tube through which urine exits the body. When the gland enlarges, it obstructs the urethra and creates urination problems. A frequent urge to urinate is common, as is dribbling after urination. If the enlargement is too great, the obstruction is total and the flow of urine is completely shut off. Treatment consists of surgical removal of the part of the prostate that is causing the obstruction.

Prostate cancer is the third leading cause of death in elderly men. Approximately 75,000 new cases are diagnosed each year. The symptoms are the same as those of benign prostatic hypertrophy, and both conditions can be detected by a rectal exam, which is why yearly checkups are mandatory for older men. A variety of treatments are available, including surgical removal of the entire gland, partial removal of the gland, hormone therapy, and radiation therapy.

STROKE

Strokes affect more than half a million Americans each year. Although a stroke can occur at any age, the majority of stroke victims are elderly people. A stroke, also known as a cerebral vascular accident, or CVA in medical parlance, is a sudden interruption of the blood supply to the brain. Since blood provides oxygen and nutrients to the brain, any interruption in its supply will damage brain cells. Most commonly, either a clot forms in one of the blood vessels, preventing blood from reaching part of the brain, or one of the vessels breaks and blood escapes. The result is a sudden onset of paralysis, disturbed sensation, and sometimes an inability to speak and think clearly. The paralysis usually affects one whole side of the body, though it's not uncommon for one extremity, arm or leg, to be most involved. Even when there isn't a trace of movement following a stroke, a lot of muscle power can eventually return. In fact, it isn't possible to know the extent of a person's impairment for certain until six months down the road. When an active, vigorous person, whatever his or her age, suffers a stroke, an intensive rehabilitation program should be instituted as early as possible.

The two most common underlying causes of blood clots and broken blood vessels are atherosclerosis and high blood pressure. Therefore, efforts to prevent strokes must be directed at controlling these conditions, through diet, exercise, relaxation, and drugs.

Appendix C

The ABCs of Medicare Insurance

Medicare is a federal health insurance program designed to make health care affordable and available to all elderly and certain chronically disabled people. It is divided into two parts. Part A is hospital insurance and Part B is medical insurance. Part A is automatically available without a premium to anyone who is eligible for social security; otherwise, it can be purchased for $214 a month. Part B is optional, and premiums are about $15 a month, regardless of Social Security status—still one of the best buys around.

Medicare Part A helps pay for hospital care, medically necessary skilled nursing care, home care, and hospice care. Medicare bases its coverage on benefit periods and sets a limit on the number of reimbursable days within each period. For hospital care, a benefit period starts the day you enter a hospital and ends when you've been out of a hospital for sixty consecutive days. Part A will help defray the cost of the first ninety days of care during each benefit period. If your hospitalization exceeds the ninety-day limit, you can draw on an additional sixty lifetime reserve days. As soon as you've been out of the hospital for sixty days, a new benefit period starts and you're entitled to another ninety days. Once you've used a reserve day, it's gone forever.

Even within the ninety-day limit you can accumulate substantial out-of-pocket costs, because Medicare pays only for certain services; you are responsible for the rest. The following list summarizes the major services covered by Medicare as well as some of the obvious noncovered ones. (From *Your Medicare*

Handbook, U.S. Department of Health and Human Services, Health Care Financing Administration.)

MEDICARE COVERAGE OF HOSPITAL SERVICES

COVERED SERVICES

1. A semiprivate room (2–4 beds in a room)
2. All meals, including special diets
3. Regular nursing services
4. Costs of special care units, such as intensive care unit, coronary care unit, etc.
5. Drugs furnished by the hospital
6. Blood transfusions furnished by the hospital
7. Laboratory tests included in the hospital bill
8. X-ray and other radiology services, including radiation therapy, billed by the hospital
9. Medical supplies, such as casts, surgical dressings, and splints
10. Use of appliances, such as a wheelchair
11. Operating and recovery room costs, including hospital costs for anesthetic services
12. Rehabilitation services, such as physical therapy, occupational therapy, and speech pathology services

SOME SERVICES NOT COVERED

1. Personal convenience items, such as television, radio, or telephone
2. Private duty nurses
3. Any extra charges for a private room unless it is determined to be medically necessary

Your hospital bill can continue to rise, even leave the earth's atmosphere, because of Medicare deductibles. A deductible is the money you must pay before Medicare kicks in. It's a one-time cost of $490 for the first sixty days, and then $123 a day for the next thirty days. Once you're into reserve days, the deductible is $246 a day. If you use up your reserve days (after 150 days in the hospital), your Medicare benefits are over, and you're responsible for the entire hospital bill. The limit on the number of covered days, noncovered services, and deductibles are three good reasons to purchase Medicare supplemental insurance, so called Medi-Gap insurance. Most commercial insurance companies as well as Blue Cross/Blue Shield sell supplemental insurance policies. Contact your insurance agent and look through several types of policies. An excellent resource, with lots of shopping tips, is the pamphlet *Health Insurance: How to Evaluate and Select Health Insurance* by Michael A. Rooney and the Staff of the People's Medical Society (free to members of The People's Medical Society, 14 East Minor Street, Emmaus, PA 18049; additional copies are $4.95).

Medicare Part B helps pay for doctors' services, outpatient hospital care, physical therapy and speech therapy, home health care, hospice care, and a variety of services and supplies not covered by Part A (including laboratory tests, ambulances, medical supplies, vaccines, prosthetic devices, and durable medical equipment). Once again there are covered and noncovered services, which are summarized in the following list. (From *Your Medicare Handbook*, U.S. Department of Health and Human Services, Health Care Financing Administration.)

MEDICARE COVERAGE OF DOCTORS' SERVICES

COVERED SERVICES

1. Medical and surgical services, including anesthetic
2. Diagnostic tests and procedures that are part of your treatment
3. Radiology and pathology services by doctors while you are a hospital inpatient
4. Other services which are ordinarily furnished in the doctor's office and included in the bill, such as:

- X-rays you receive as part of your treatment
- Services of your doctor's office nurse
- Drugs that cannot be self-administered
- Transfusions of blood and blood components
- Medical supplies
- Physical therapy and speech pathology services

SOME SERVICES NOT COVERED

1. Routine physical examinations and tests directly related to such examinations
2. Routine foot care
3. Vision or hearing examinations for prescribing or fitting eyeglasses or hearing aids
4. Immunizations (except pneumococcal vaccinations or immunizations required because of an injury or immediate risk of infection)
5. Cosmetic surgery unless it is needed because of accidental injury or to improve the functioning of a malformed part of the body

Also there is a yearly deductible of $75. Unlike Part A, Part B does not have a limit on the number of treatment days, but its reimbursement policy can leave you holding a large part of the bill anyway. Instead of reimbursing all or part of a doctor's bill, Medicare Part B determines a reasonable charge for the service and reimburses 80 percent of it. The problem is that what is reasonable to Medicare is often unreasonable to your doctor, and the charges Medicare approves are usually quite a bit lower than your doctor's charges. Not only must you pay the difference between your doctor's bill and the approved charges, you must also pay 20 percent of the approved charges. For example,

If your doctor charges: $100

and

Medicare approves: $50

$$You\ owe:\ \$100\ -\ \$50\ =\ \$50$$
$$plus\ 20\%\ of\ \$50\ =\ \$10$$

Total: $60

You can imagine how quickly your medical expenses can add up—another reason to make sure you have supplemental insurance coverage.

There are two methods that Medicare uses to pay its share of your doctor's bill. With the first method, it pays 80 percent of the approved charges directly to you and you use the money to pay your doctor's bill. With the second method, your doctor signs up to be a Medicare participating physician, agreeing to accept directly from Medicare 80 percent of the approved charges, and you pay the remaining 20 percent. In exchange for getting his or her money directly from Medicare, your doctor agrees not to bill you for any difference between the actual charge and Medicare's approved charge.

All Medicare insurance claims must be submitted on Form 1490S, "A Patient's Request for Medicare Payment." If your doctor is a participating physician, he or she will submit the claim. Otherwise you submit the claim along with itemized bills for the services. If you disagree with a Medicare decision on the amount of reimbursement or even on whether a service is covered, you can ask for a review. If you're still not satisfied after the review, you can request a formal hearing.

The rules and regulations governing Medicare insurance are complex. This section is meant only as a beginning. Several volumes the size of this entire book would be needed to explain fully all the subtleties and intricacies. If you want more information, Your Medicare Handbook is a good place to start. This pamphlet is published by the U.S. Department of Health and Human Services, Health Care Financing Administration—the same office that runs the Medicare program. It should be required reading for anyone who is involved with Medicare insurance. For your own copy, write to the Superintendent of Documents, U.S. Government Printing Office, Washington, DC 20402 (price $1.75, GPO Stock number 017-060-00172-1).

Appendix D

National Resources

The following is a sampling of national agencies, associations, councils, congresses, clearinghouses, federations, foundations, and organizations that specialize in the needs of elderly and disabled people. The list is by no means complete, but it will lead you to additional resources, and the national groups will direct you to their state and local counterparts.

Adaptive Environments
Massachusetts College of Art
621 Huntington Avenue and
  Evans Way
Boston, Massachusetts 02115-5801   (617) 739-0088

Administration on Aging
330 Independence Avenue, S.W.
Washington, D.C. 20201   (202) 245-2158

Alexander Graham Bell Association
  for the Deaf
3417 Volta Place, N.W.
Washington, D.C. 20007   (202) 337-5220

Alzheimer's Disease and Related
  Disorders Association
Suite 600, 70 East Lake Street
Chicago, Illinois 60601-5997   (312) 853-3060

American Academy of Physical
  Medicine and Rehabilitation
Suite 1300, 122 South Michigan
  Avenue
Chicago, Illinois 60603-6107   (312) 922-9366

American Association of Homes for
the Aging
Suite 400, 1129 20th Street, N.W.
Washington, D.C. 20036   (202) 296-5960

American Association of Retired
Persons
1909 K Street, N.W.
Washington, D.C. 20049   (202) 872-4700

American Cancer Society
90 Park Avenue
New York, New York 10016   (212) 599-8200

American Council of the Blind
Suite 1100
1010 Vermont Avenue, N.W.   (202) 393-3666
Washington, D.C. 20005   1-800-424-8666

American Diabetes Association
National Service Center
1660 Duke Street   (703) 549-1500
Alexandria, Virginia 22314   1-800-232-3472

American Dietetic Association
10th Floor
430 North Michigan Avenue
Chicago, Illinois 60611   (312) 280-5000

American Digestive Disease Society
7720 Wisconsin Avenue
Bethesda, Maryland 20814   (301) 652-9293

American Foundation for the Blind
15 West 16th Street
New York, New York 10011   (212) 620-2000

American Geriatrics Society
Suite 400, 770 Lexington Avenue
New York, New York 10021   (212) 308-1414

American Health Care Association
1200 15th Street, N.W.
Washington, D.C. 20005   (202) 833-3050

American Heart Association
7320 Greenville Avenue
Dallas, Texas 75231   (214) 750-5300

American Hospital Association
840 North Lake Shore Drive
Chicago, Illinois 60611   (312) 280-6000

American Humane Association
P.O. Box 2788
Denver, Colorado 80201   (303) 695-0811

American Liver Foundation
998 Pompton Avenue
Cedar Grove, New Jersey 07009   (201) 857-2626

American Lung Association
1740 Broadway
New York, New York 10019   (212) 315-8700

American Medical Association
535 North Dearborn Street
Chicago, Illinois 60610   (312) 645-5000

American Nurses Association
2420 Persing Road
Kansas City, Missouri 64108   (816) 474-5720

American Occupational Therapy
   Association
1383 Piccard Drive
Rockville, Maryland 20850   (301) 948-9626

American Parkinson's Disease
   Foundation
116 John Street
New York, New York 10038   (212) 732-9550

American Physical Therapy
   Association
200 South Service Road of Long
   Island Expressway
Roslyn Heights, New York 11577   (516) 484-0095

American Printing House for the
Blind
P.O. Box 6085
Louisville, Kentucky 40206   (502) 895-2405

American Psychiatric Association
1400 K Street, N.W.
Washington, D.C. 20005   (202) 682-6000

American Psychological Association
Division of Adult Development and
Aging
1200 17th Street, N.W.
Washington, D.C. 20036   (202) 955-7610

American Red Cross
431 18th Street, N.W.
Washington, D.C. 20006   (202) 639-3000

American Speech and Hearing
Association
10801 Rockville Pike
Bethesda, Maryland 20852   (301) 897-5700

Amputee's Service Association
P.O. Box A3819
Chicago, Illinois 60611   (312) 274-2044

Arthritis Foundation
115 East 18th Street
New York, New York 10003   (212) 477-8700

Association for the Education of the
Visually Handicapped
Suite 320
206 North Washington Street
Alexandria, Virginia 22314   (703) 836-6060

Association for the Severely
Handicapped
7010 Roosevelt Way, N.E.
Seattle, Washington 98115   (206) 523-8446

Better Hearing Institute
Suite 700, 11430 K Street, N.W.   (202) 541-4558
Washington, D.C. 20005   1-800-424-8546

Braille Institute of America
741 North Vermont Avenue
Los Angeles, California 90029   (213) 663-1111

Cancer Care
1180 6th Avenue
New York, New York 10036   (212) 221-3300

Center for Science in the Public
  Interest
1501 16th Street, N.W.
Washington, D.C. 20036   (202) 332-9110

Concern for Dying
250 West 57th Street
New York, New York 10107   (212) 246-6962

Consumer Information Center
Pueblo, Colorado 81009   (303) 948-3334

Continental Association of Funeral
  & Memorial Societies
Suite 530, 2001 S Street, N.W.
Washington, D.C. 20009   (202) 745-0634

Disabled American Veterans
National Headquarters
Room 1026, 550 Main Street
Cincinnati, Ohio 45202   (513) 684-2676

Elder Craftsmen
135 East 65th Street
New York, New York 10021   (212) 861-5260

Emphysema Anonymous
P.O. Box 3324
Seminal, Florida 33542   (813) 334-4226

Epilepsy Foundation of America
Suite 406, 4351 Garden City Drive
Landover, Maryland 20785   (301) 459-3700

Family Service Association of
  America
254 West 31st Street
New York, New York 10001   (212) 967-2740

Federation of the Handicapped, Inc.
211 West 14th Street
New York, New York 10011   (212) 206-4200

Gerontological Society of America
Suite 300, 1411 K Street, N.W.
Washington, D.C. 20005   (202) 393-1411

Gray Panthers
Suite 601, 311 South Juniper Street
Philadelphia, Pennsylvania 19107   (215) 545-6555

International Senior Citizens
   Association
1010 South Flower Street
Los Angeles, California 90015   (213) 748-0510

Leukemia Society of America
Public Education and Information
205 Lexington Avenue
New York, New York 10016   (212) 679-1939

Library of Congress
Division for the Blind and
   Physically Handicapped
1291 Taylor Street, N.W.
Washington, D.C. 20542   (202) 287-5100

Mental Health Association
1021 Prince Street
Arlington, Virginia 22314-2971   (703) 684-7722

Multiple Sclerosis Society
205 East 42nd Street
New York, New York 10017   (212) 986-3240

Myasthenia Gravis Foundation
61 Gramercy Park North
New York, New York 10010   (212) 533-7005

National Amputation Foundation
12-45 150th Street
Whitestone, New York 11357   (718) 767-8400

National Association of Area
  Agencies on Aging
Suite 208 W
600 Maryland Avenue, S.W.
Washington, D.C. 20024   (202) 484-7520

National Association for the Deaf
814 Thayer Avenue
Silver Spring, Maryland 20910   (301) 587-6282

National Association of Hearing and
  Speech Action
10801 Rockville Pike   (301) 897-5700
Rockville, Maryland 20852   1-800-638-8255

National Association for Mental
  Health
1021 Prince Street
Alexandria, Virginia 22314   (703) 684-7722

National Association of Social
  Workers
7981 Eastern Avenue
Silverspring, Maryland 20910   (202) 565-0333

National Association for the
  Visually Handicapped
22 West 21st Street
New York, New York 10010   (212) 889-3141

National Cancer Institute
Office of Cancer Communications
Building 31, Room 10A18
9000 Rockville Pike
Bethesda, Maryland 20892   (301) 496-5583

National Congress of Organizations
  of the Physically Handicapped
1291 Taylor Street
Washington, D.C. 20542   (202) 287-5100

National Council on the Aging
West Wing 100
600 Maryland Avenue, S.W.
Washington, D.C. 20024   (202) 479-1200

National Council of Senior Citizens
925 15th Street, N.W.
Washington, D.C. 20005   (202) 347-8800

National Easter Seal Society for
   Crippled Children and Adults
2023 West Ogden Avenue   (312) 243-8400
Chicago, Illinois 60612   (312) 243-8880

National Eye Institute
Public Information Office
9000 Rockville Pike
Bethesda, Maryland 20205   (301) 496-4000

National Foundation for Ileitis and
   Colitis
444 Park Avenue South
New York, New York 10016   (212) 685-3440

National Foundation of the March
   of Dimes
622 3rd Avenue
New York, New York 10017   (212) 922-1460

National Heart, Lung and Blood
   Institute
Public Information Office
Room 5A03, Building 31
9000 Rockville Pike
Bethesda, Maryland 20205   (301) 496-4236

National Homecaring Council
235 Park Avenue South
New York, New York 10003   (212) 674-4990

National Hospice Organization
Suite 902
1901 North Fort Myer Drive
Arlington, Virginia 22209   (703) 243-5900

National Institute on Aging
Public Information Office
Room 5C35, Building 31
9000 Rockville Pike
Bethesda, Maryland 20205   (301) 496-1752

National Institute of Arthritis,
  Diabetes, Digestive and Kidney
  Diseases
Public Information Office
Room 9A04, Building 31
9000 Rockville Pike
Bethesda, Maryland 20205   (301) 496-6110

National Institute of Dental
  Research
Public Information Office
Room 2C35, Building 31
9000 Rockville Pike
Bethesda, Maryland 20205   (301) 496-4261

National Institute of Neurological
  and Communicative Disorders
  and Strokes
Public Information Office
9000 Rockville Pike
Bethesda, Maryland 20205   (301) 495-4000

National Multiple Sclerosis Society
205 East 42nd Street
New York, New York 10017   (212) 986-3240

National Parkinson Foundation
1501 Northwest 9th Avenue
Miami, Florida 33136   (305) 547-6666

National Rehabilitation Association
633 South Washington Street
Alexandria, Virginia 22314   (703) 836-0850

National Rehabilitation Information
  Center
Catholic University of America
4407 8th Street, N.E.   (202) 635-5826
Washington, D.C. 20017   (202) 635-5884

National Safety Council
444 North Michigan Avenue
Chicago, Illinois 60611   (312) 527-4800

National Self-Help Clearinghouse
Graduate School and University
  Center of the City University of
  New York
Room 1227
33 West 42nd Street
New York, New York 10036   (212) 840-1259

National Society to Prevent
  Blindness
79 Madison Avenue
New York, New York 10016   (212) 684-3222

National Spinal Cord Injury
  Association
149 California Street
Newton, Massachusetts 02158   (617) 964-0521

National Support Center for
  Families of the Aging
P.O. Box 245
Swarthmore, Pennsylvania 19081 (215) 544-593

National Therapeutic Recreation
  Society
P.O. Box 161126
Alexandria, Virginia 22303   (703) 820-3993

Office for Handicapped Individuals
Department of Health and Human
  Services
330 Independence Avenue, S.W.
Washington, D.C. 20201   (202) 245-6568

Paralyzed Veterans of America
801 18th Street, N.W.
Washington, D.C. 20006   (202) 872-1300

Recordings for the Blind
545 5th Avenue
New York, New York 10017   (212) 517-9820

Rehabilitation International, U.S.A.
20 West 40th Street
New York, New York 10018   (212) 620-4040

The Self-Help Center
908 Argyle Street
Chicago, Illinois 60640   (312) 271-0300

Sister Kenny Institute
A/V Publications Office
800 28th Street
Minneapolis, Minnesota 55407   (612) 874-4400

Society for the Right to Die
250 West 57th Street
New York, New York 10107   (212) 246-6973

United Cerebral Palsy Association
66 East 34th Street
New York, New York 10016   (212) 481-6300

United Ostomy Association
2001 West Beverley Boulevard
Los Angeles, California 90057   (213) 413-5510

Veterans Administration
810 Vermont Avenue
Washington, D.C. 20420   (202) 393-4120

Appendix E

Special Supplies

The following is a list of companies that sell self-help aids, assistive devices, and equipment for home modifications. Send for their catalogs and use these large supply houses and mail-order companies when you can't find what you want at the local hardware store, pharmacy, plumbing company, fabric shop, or variety store.

AliMed Inc.
297 High Street   (617) 329-1560
Dedham, Massachusetts   1-800-225-2610

American Foundation for the Blind
Customer Service Department
15 West 16th Street
New York, New York 10011   (212) 620-2000

B and B Lingerie Co., Inc.
P.O. Box 5731
Boise, Idaho 83705-0731   (208) 343-9696

Bruce Medical Supply
P.O. Box 9166
Waltham, Massachusetts 02154   (617) 894-6262

Camp International
109 West Washington Avenue
Jackson, Michigan 49204   (517) 787-1600

Cleo Living Aids
3957 Mayfield Road
Cleveland, Ohio 44121   (216) 382-9700

Crestwood Company
P.O. Box 04606
Milwaukee, Wisconsin 53204   (414) 461-9876

Dipsters Corporation
265 Wyndcliff Road   (914) 725-0225
Scarsdale, New York 10583   1-800-431-2660

Enrichments, Inc.
P.O. Box 579
145 Tower Drive
Hinsdale, Illinois 60521   1-800-343-9742

Everest & Jennings
3233 East Mission Oaks Boulevard
Camarillo, California 93010   (805) 987-6911

Fashion-Able
Box S
Rocky Hill, New Jersey 08553   (609) 921-2563

Handi-Ramp Inc.
P.O. Box 745
1414 Armour Boulevard
Mundelein, Illinois 60060   (312) 566-5861

Independent Living Aids, Inc.
11 Commercial Court
Plainview, New York 11803   (516) 681-8288

Jobst
P.O. Box 653
Toledo, Ohio 43694   (419) 698-1616

Lumex
100 Spence Street
Bay Shore, New York 11706   (516) 273-2200

Maddak, Inc.
6 Industrial Road
Pequannock, New Jersey 07440   (201) 694-0500

G.E. Miller, Inc.
484 South Broadway
Yonkers, New York 10705   (212) 549-4850

J.A. Preston Corporation
60 Page Road
Clifton, New Jersey 07012   (201) 777-2700

Rehabilitation Equipment and
    Supply
311 North Western Avenue
Peoria, Illinois 61604   (309) 676-6054

Fred Sammons, Inc.
P.O. Box 32
Brookfield, Illinois 60512-0032   1-800-323-5547

Sears Roebuck & Co.
Home Health Care
(312) 875-2500 Sears Tower
Chicago, Illinois 60684   1-800-323-3274

Swedish Rehab Products
    Corporation
17 Briarcliffe Drive
Scotch Plains, New Jersey 07076   (201) 322-9299

Ways & Means
The Capability Center
28001 Citrin Drive
Romulus, Michigan 48174   (313) 946-5030

Appendix F

Reading Material

Most of the groups listed in Appendix D, "National Resources," publish material on specific disabilities or on aging. Of course, there are thousands of other sources of information. The following is a modest selection of useful books and periodicals. It is not meant to be exhaustive, but it will get you started if you're interested.

BOOKS

Anderson, Sir W. Ferguson, F. I. Caird, R. D. Kennedy, and Doris Schwartz: *Gerontology and Geriatric Nursing*, Arco, New York, 1982.

Breuer, Joseph M.: *A Handbook of Assistive Devices for the Handicapped Elderly: New Help for Independent Living*, Haworth Press, New York, 1982.

Brody, Jane: *Jane Brody's Nutrition Book*, Bantam, New York, 1982.

Cary, Jane Randolph: *How to Create Interiors for the Disabled: A Guidebook for Family and Friends*, Pantheon, New York, 1978.

Crewe, Nancy M., and Irving Kenneth Zola: *Independent Living for Physically Disabled People*, Jossey-Bass, San Francisco, 1983.

Hale, Glorya (ed.): *The Source Book for the Disabled: An Illustrated Guide to Easier and More Independent Living for Physically Disabled People, Their Families and Friends*, Saunders, Philadelphia, 1979.

Klinger, Judith Lannefeld: *Mealtime Manual for People with Disabilities and the Aging*, Campbell Soup Company, Camden, New Jersey, 1979.

Mace, Nancy L., and Peter V. Rabins: *The 36-Hour Day, A Family Guide to Caring for Persons with Alzheimer's Disease, Related Dementing Illness, and Memory Loss in Later Life*, Johns Hopkins, Baltimore, 1981.

O'Hara-Devereaux, Mary, Len Hughes Andrus, and Cynthia D. Scott: *Eldercare, A Practical Guide to Clinical Geriatrics*, Grune & Stratton, New York, 1981.

Sargent, Jean Vieth: *An Easier Way, Handbook for the Elderly and Handicapped*, Iowa State University Press, Ames, Iowa, 1981.

Sine, Robert D., J. David Holcomb, Robert E. Roush, Shelly E. Liss, and Georgianna B. Wilson (eds.): *Basic Rehabilitation Techniques: A Self-Instructional Guide*, An Aspen Publication, Rockville, Maryland, 1981.

Tanner, Fredericka with Sharon Shaw: *Caring: A Family Guide to Managing the Alzheimer's Patient at Home*, The New York City Alzheimer's Resource Center, New York, 1985.

Williams, T. Franklin (ed.): *Rehabilitation in the Aging*, Raven Press, New York, 1984.

Yurick, Ann Gera, Barbara Elliott Spier, Susanne S. Robb, and Nancy J. Ebert: *The Aged Person and the Nursing Process*, Appleton-Century-Crofts, Norwalk, Connecticut, 1984.

PERIODICALS

Accent on Living, P.O. Box 700, Bloomington, Illinois 61701. A quarterly journal on the practical side of living with a disability.

Disabled USA, The President's Committee on Employment of the Handicapped, Washington, D.C. 20201. A monthly journal reporting on employment opportunities for people with disabilities.

Nutrition Action, Center for Science in the Public Interest, 1501 16th Street, N.W., Washington, D.C. 20036. A monthly food and nutrition newsletter published by a nonprofit public interest organization.

Rehabilitation Gazette, 4502 Maryland Avenue, St. Louis, Missouri 63108. An annual international journal and information service for disabled people.

Tufts University Diet & Nutrition Letter, P.O. Box 2465, Boulder, Colorado 80322. A monthly newsletter on diet and nutrition.

University of California, Berkeley Wellness Letter, P.O. Box 10922, Des Moines, Iowa 50340. A monthly newsletter on nutrition, fitness, and stress management.

Appendix G

Nursing Homes

Nursing homes are not the end of the world. They are legitimate living quarters for certain people at special times in their lives. For example, if a friend or relative is living at home with you and deteriorates to the point that his or her needs overwhelm your physical, emotional, and financial resources, he or she might be better served in a nursing home. Likewise, if you should become disabled and no longer able to care for your friend, a nursing home again would become a reasonable option. To plan for the future and avoid making uneducated decisions during a crisis, it's best to learn as much as possible about nursing homes before you need one.

All nursing homes provide medical, nursing, personal, and residential care: Differences lie in the intensity of the services. A personal physician attends to the medical needs of each resident and prescribes the necessary diet, medication, and treatment. Nurses, who are the lifeblood of nursing homes, administer drugs, give injections, do catheterizations, and apply dressings. They keep the residents clean and comfortable and, along with their aides and assistants, provide personal care services by helping with eating, bathing, dressing, and grooming. The rest of the nursing home staff is responsible for the residential services, which include maintaining a clean room, creating a safe and pleasant home environment, arranging for good food, and scheduling appropriate leisure activities.

Nursing homes can be classified according to the level of care they provide. A skilled nursing facility (SNF) provides around-the-clock nursing care and is best suited to people who need constant medical and nursing attention. Intermediate care facilities (ICF) are less intensive. They do not have around-the-clock nursing coverage, and they are most appropriate for people who are ill and can't live alone, but who are not ill enough to need twenty-four-hour nursing care. Rest homes are even less intensive. They are designed for people who are healthy and independent, but who need help with personal care and homemaking chores.

Nursing home costs vary widely from one part of the country to another and even from one nursing home to another within the same city. The differences generally reflect differences in the quantity and intensity of services, the number and training of the staff, and the quality and upkeep of the building and grounds. The nonprofit homes, which are run by religious and charitable groups and government agencies, are usually cheaper than the proprietary ones, which are private businesses run for profit. Don't confuse costs with quality of care, however. They are separate issues.

Daily room rates run from as low as $25 a day to as high as $200 a day, and extra charges are always billed onto this basic rate. The basic rate always covers the room and meals and usually covers housekeeping, linen services, and nursing. The extras include the services of beauticians, barbers, dentists, podiatrists, and physicians, as well as drugs, physical and occupational therapy, and laboratory testing. Nursing homes vary as much in their billing schedules as they do in their charges. Most bill on a monthly basis, but some have a one-time fee for the entire stay, and others bill each time a service is rendered or material is provided.

Don't assume Medicare or Medicaid will pay for everything. It won't. If your friend or relative has recently been hospitalized for at least three days, Medicare will pay for up to 100 days in a skilled nursing facility. But it won't pay for intermediate-level care, and after twenty days of skilled care there is a co-insurance payment. Medicaid is a welfare program, and while it will pay indefinitely for either skilled or intermediate care, the resident must have few or no personal funds. Medicare is a federal program, but Medicaid varies from state to state. It's important to find out about the rules, regulations, and reimbursement schedules in your own locality. If your friend or relative has private health insurance, find out if nursing home care is covered.

Before choosing a nursing home, make sure you thoroughly understand the financial arrangements. Pay particular attention to what the government pays, what the insurance company pays, and what you pay. Get the daily rate clear, especially what it does and doesn't include, and find out about the extra charges. When you finally make your decision, you or your friend or relative will have to sign a contract. Don't sign it until you understand it completely, and it's best to have a lawyer review it as well.

Even before getting to the contract stage, you and your friend or relative should visit several homes to find the safest, most comfortable, caring, and cheerful ones. Visit as often as necessary, but at least once during mealtime. Join the residents for a meal and check out the food, the service, seating arrangements, noise level, and hygiene. Is it easy to get substitutes or seconds? Are staff members courteous and kind, or are they impatient and annoyed? Are the dining room, other public areas, and individual rooms clean? How are the residents dressed? Are they clean? Most important of all, what is the feeling of the home? Is it cheerful or gloomy? Is there a sense of caring or one of neglect? Is there a high energy level or a state of depression? Is there a lot of activity, or have the residents given up?

Don't forget that, more often than not, nursing homes are temporary quarters rather than permanent residences. After a hospitalization, an elderly person can recuperate in one and regain his or her strength before returning home. Likewise, if you are hospitalized and temporarily unable to care for your friend or relative, he or she can live in a nursing home until you return home.

If a nursing home becomes necessary, don't feel guilty or that you have failed as a care giver and provider. Your goal has always been to do what's best for your friend or relative. If at some point he or she would be better served in a nursing home than with you, then a nursing home is preferred. You've tried to keep your friend at home, but nature has insisted that he or she live elsewhere. It takes as much courage and wisdom to admit that as it does to care for a loved one at home.

For additional information on nursing homes, refer to *How to Select a Nursing Home*, a priceless guide published by the U.S. Department of Health and Human Services (available from the Superintendent of Documents, U.S. Government Printing Office, Washington, D.C. 20402, for $4.75, GPO stock number

017-062-00123-5). This booklet provides, among other things, the following checklist of points to consider when selecting a nursing home.

NURSING HOME CHECKLIST

The following is a checklist of important points to consider in selecting a nursing home. You should find the checklist helpful in several ways: for brushing up on things to look for and ask about before you visit a home, for referring to as you talk with staff members and tour a home, and for sizing up a home after a visit and comparing it with other homes you have visited.

There are many items on the list, because nursing homes are complex operations. To cover all the items, you may have to make additional visits or follow-up telephone calls.

Some of the items will be difficult to find out on your own, so you will probably have to ask personnel of the home.

This checklist is offered to serve as a reference guide:

The name of nursing **Home A** is _____
The name of nursing **Home B** is _____
The name of nursing **Home C** is _____

	HOME A	HOME B	HOME C
	Yes/No	Yes/No	Yes/No
Is the home certified to participate in the Medicare and Medicaid programs?	☐ ☐	☐ ☐	☐ ☐
Does the nursing home have the required current license from the State or letter of approval from a licensing agency?	☐ ☐	☐ ☐	☐ ☐
Does the administrator have a current license?	☐ ☐	☐ ☐	☐ ☐
If the person you are placing requires special services, such as rehabilitation therapy or a therapeutic diet, does the home provide them?	☐ ☐	☐ ☐	☐ ☐

	HOME A Yes/No	HOME B Yes/No	HOME C Yes/No
Is the general atmosphere of the nursing home warm, pleasant, and cheerful?	☐ ☐	☐ ☐	☐ ☐
Is the administrator courteous and helpful?	☐ ☐	☐ ☐	☐ ☐
Are staff members cheerful, courteous, and enthusiastic?	☐ ☐	☐ ☐	☐ ☐
Do staff members show patients genuine interest and affection?	☐ ☐	☐ ☐	☐ ☐
Do residents look well cared for and generally content?	☐ ☐	☐ ☐	☐ ☐
Are residents allowed to wear their own clothes, decorate their rooms, and keep a few prized possessions on hand?	☐ ☐	☐ ☐	☐ ☐
Is there a place for private visits with family and friends?	☐ ☐	☐ ☐	☐ ☐
Is there a written statement of patient's rights? As far as you can tell, are these points being carried out?	☐ ☐	☐ ☐	☐ ☐
Do residents, other visitors, and volunteers speak favorably about the home?	☐ ☐	☐ ☐	☐ ☐

LOCATION

Is the home near family and friends?	☐ ☐	☐ ☐	☐ ☐

GENERAL PHYSICAL CONSIDERATIONS

	HOME A Yes/No	HOME B Yes/No	HOME C Yes/No
Is the nursing home clean and orderly?	☐ ☐	☐ ☐	☐ ☐

	HOME A Yes/No	HOME B Yes/No	HOME C Yes/No
Is the home reasonably free of unpleasant odors?	☐ ☐	☐ ☐	☐ ☐
Are toilet and bathing facilities easy for handicapped patients to use?	☐ ☐	☐ ☐	☐ ☐
Is the home well-lighted?	☐ ☐	☐ ☐	☐ ☐
Are rooms well-ventilated and kept at a comfortable temperature?	☐ ☐	☐ ☐	☐ ☐

SAFETY

	HOME A Yes/No	HOME B Yes/No	HOME C Yes/No
Are wheelchair ramps provided where necessary?	☐ ☐	☐ ☐	☐ ☐
Is the nursing home free of obvious hazards, such as obstacles to patients, hazards underfoot, unsteady chairs?	☐ ☐	☐ ☐	☐ ☐
Are there grab bars in toilet and bathing facilities and handrails on both sides of hallways?	☐ ☐	☐ ☐	☐ ☐
Do bathtubs and showers have nonslip surfaces?	☐ ☐	☐ ☐	☐ ☐
Are there smoke detectors, an automatic sprinkler system, and automatic emergency lighting?	☐ ☐	☐ ☐	☐ ☐
Are there portable fire extinguishers?	☐ ☐	☐ ☐	☐ ☐
Are exits clearly marked and exit signs illuminated?	☐ ☐	☐ ☐	☐ ☐
Are exit doors unobstructed and unlocked from inside?	☐ ☐	☐ ☐	☐ ☐

	HOME A	HOME B	HOME C
	Yes/No	Yes/No	Yes/No

Are certain areas posted with no-smoking signs? Do staff, residents, and visitors observe them?   ☐ ☐   ☐ ☐   ☐ ☐

Is an emergency evacuation plan posted in prominent locations?   ☐ ☐   ☐ ☐   ☐ ☐

MEDICAL, DENTAL, AND OTHER SERVICES

	HOME A	HOME B	HOME C
	Yes/No	Yes/No	Yes/No

Does the home have an arrangement with an outside dental service to provide patients with dental care when necessary?   ☐ ☐   ☐ ☐   ☐ ☐

In case of medical emergencies, is a physician available at all times, either on staff or on call?   ☐ ☐   ☐ ☐   ☐ ☐

Does the home have arrangements with a nearby hospital for quick transfer of nursing home patients in an emergency?   ☐ ☐   ☐ ☐   ☐ ☐

Is emergency transportation readily available?   ☐ ☐   ☐ ☐   ☐ ☐

PHARMACEUTICAL SERVICES

	HOME A	HOME B	HOME C
	Yes/No	Yes/No	Yes/No

Are pharmaceutical services supervised by a qualified pharmacist?   ☐ ☐   ☐ ☐   ☐ ☐

Is a room set aside for storing and preparing drugs?   ☐ ☐   ☐ ☐   ☐ ☐

Does a qualified pharmacist maintain and monitor a record of each patient's drug therapy?   ☐ ☐   ☐ ☐   ☐ ☐

NURSING SERVICES

	HOME A	HOME B	HOME C
	Yes/No	Yes/No	Yes/No

Is at least one registered nurse (RN) or licensed practical nurse (LPN) on duty day and night? ☐ ☐ ☐ ☐ ☐ ☐

Is an RN on duty during the day, seven days a week? (For skilled nursing homes) ☐ ☐ ☐ ☐ ☐ ☐

Does an RN serve as director of nursing services? (For skilled nursing homes) ☐ ☐ ☐ ☐ ☐ ☐

Are nurse or emergency call buttons located at each patient's bed and in toilet and bathing facilities? ☐ ☐ ☐ ☐ ☐ ☐

FOOD SERVICES

	HOME A	HOME B	HOME C
	Yes/No	Yes/No	Yes/No

Is the kitchen clean and reasonably tidy? Is food needing refrigeration not left standing out on counters? Is waste properly disposed of? ☐ ☐ ☐ ☐ ☐ ☐

Ask to see the meal schedule. Are at least three meals served each day? Are meals served at normal hours, with plenty of time for leisurely eating? ☐ ☐ ☐ ☐ ☐ ☐

Are nutritious between-meal and bedtime snacks available? ☐ ☐ ☐ ☐ ☐ ☐

Are patients given enough food? Does the food look appetizing? ☐ ☐ ☐ ☐ ☐ ☐

Sample a meal. Is the food tasty and served at the proper temperature? ☐ ☐ ☐ ☐ ☐ ☐

Does the meal being served match the posted menu? ☐ ☐ ☐ ☐ ☐ ☐

	HOME A Yes/No	HOME B Yes/No	HOME C Yes/No
Are special meals prepared for patients on therapeutic diets?	☐ ☐	☐ ☐	☐ ☐
Is the dining room attractive and comfortable?	☐ ☐	☐ ☐	☐ ☐
Do patients who need it get help in eating, whether in the dining room or in their own rooms?	☐ ☐	☐ ☐	☐ ☐

REHABILITATION THERAPY

	HOME A Yes/No	HOME B Yes/No	HOME C Yes/No
Is a full-time program of physical therapy available for patients who need it?	☐ ☐	☐ ☐	☐ ☐
Are occupational therapy and speech therapy available for patients who need them?	☐ ☐	☐ ☐	☐ ☐

SOCIAL SERVICES & PATIENT ACTIVITIES

	HOME A Yes/No	HOME B Yes/No	HOME C Yes/No
Are there social services available to aid patients and their families?	☐ ☐	☐ ☐	☐ ☐
Does the nursing home have a varied program of recreational, cultural, and intellectual activities for patients?	☐ ☐	☐ ☐	☐ ☐
Is there an activities coordinator on the staff?	☐ ☐	☐ ☐	☐ ☐
Is suitable space available for patient activities? Are tools and supplies provided?	☐ ☐	☐ ☐	☐ ☐
Are activities offered for patients who are relatively inactive or confined to their rooms?	☐ ☐	☐ ☐	☐ ☐

	HOME A	HOME B	HOME C
	Yes/No	Yes/No	Yes/No

Look at the activities schedule.
Are activities provided each day?
Are some activities scheduled in
the evenings?   ☐ ☐   ☐ ☐   ☐ ☐

Do patients have an opportunity
to attend religious services and
talk with clergymen both in and
outside the home?   ☐ ☐   ☐ ☐   ☐ ☐

PATIENTS' ROOMS

	HOME A	HOME B	HOME C
	Yes/No	Yes/No	Yes/No

Does each room open onto a
hallway?   ☐ ☐   ☐ ☐   ☐ ☐

Does each room have a window
to the outside?   ☐ ☐   ☐ ☐   ☐ ☐

Does each patient have a reading
light, a comfortable chair, and a
closet and drawers for personal
belongings?   ☐ ☐   ☐ ☐   ☐ ☐

Is there fresh drinking water
within reach?   ☐ ☐   ☐ ☐   ☐ ☐

Is there a curtain or screen
available to provide privacy for
each bed whenever necessary? ☐ ☐   ☐ ☐   ☐ ☐

Do bathing and toilet facilities
have adequate privacy?   ☐ ☐   ☐ ☐   ☐ ☐

OTHER AREAS OF THE
NURSING HOME

	HOME A	HOME B	HOME C
	Yes/No	Yes/No	Yes/No

Is there a lounge where patients
can chat, read, play games, watch
television, or just relax away from
their rooms?   ☐ ☐   ☐ ☐   ☐ ☐

Is a public telephone available for
patients' use?   ☐ ☐   ☐ ☐   ☐ ☐

	HOME A	HOME B	HOME C
	Yes/No	Yes/No	Yes/No

Does the nursing home have an outdoor area where patients can get fresh air and sunshine?   ☐ ☐   ☐ ☐   ☐ ☐

FINANCIAL AND
RELATED MATTERS

	HOME A	HOME B	HOME C
	Yes/No	Yes/No	Yes/No

Do the estimated monthly costs (including extra charges) compare favorably with the cost of other homes?   ☐ ☐   ☐ ☐   ☐ ☐

Is a refund made for unused days paid for in advance?   ☐ ☐   ☐ ☐   ☐ ☐

Are visiting hours convenient for patients and visitors?   ☐ ☐   ☐ ☐   ☐ ☐

Are these and other important matters specified in the contract? (See page 29)   ☐ ☐   ☐ ☐   ☐ · ☐

TRADENAMES AND MANUFACTURERS

Alka Seltzer	Miles Laboratories, Inc.
Artane	Lederle Laboratories Division American Cyanamid Co.
Benadryl	Parke-Davis Division of Warner-Lambert
Bromo Seltzer	Warner-Lambert
Camay	Proctor & Gamble Company
Carter's Little Liver Pills	Carter Products
Chux	Johnson and Johnson
Clyserol	Clyserol Labs
Cogentin	Merck & Company, Inc.
Colace	Mead Johnson Pharmaceutical Division Mead Johnson & Company
Dalmane	Roche Products, Inc.
Darvocet	Eli Lilly & Company
Demerol	Winthrop-Breon
Dr. Scholl	Scholl
Donnatol	A.H. Robins Company
Doriden	USV Laboratories Division USV Pharmaceutical Corp.
Dove	Lever Bros. Co.
Dramamine	Searle Pharmaceuticals
Dulcolax	Boehringer Ingelheim Pharmaceuticals, Inc.
Elavil	Merck Sharp & Dohme Division of Merck & Co., Inc.
Eucerin	Beiersdorf, Inc.
Fleet Enema	C.B. Fleet Co., Inc.
Gelusil	Parke-Davis
Gripmate	Kemplant Limited
Ivory	Procter & Gamble
Kaopectate	The UpJohn Company
KERI LOTION	Westwood Pharmaceuticals, Inc.
Larodopa	Roche Laboratories Division of Hoffman-La Roche, Inc.
Lomotil	Searle & Co.
Lubriderm	Warner-Lambert
Maalox	William H. Rorer, Inc.
Mellaril	Sandoz, Inc.
Metamucil	Procter & Gamble
Motrin	The UpJohn Company
New Balance	New Balance Athletic Shoes, Inc.
Nike	Nike, Inc.

Neutrogena	Neutrogena Corp.
Oral-B toothbrush	Oral-B Laboratories, Inc.
Parlodel	Sandoz, Inc.
Percodan	DuPont Pharmaceuticals E.I. duPont de Nemours & Co. (Inc.)
Pericolace	Mead Johnson Pharmaceutical Division Mead Johnson & Company
Perdiem	William H. Rorer Inc.
Phenergan	Wyeth Laboratories, Division of American Home Products Corporation
Probanthine	Searle & Co.
Py●Co●Pay Softex	Block Drug Co., Inc.
Pyribenzamine	Geigy Division of Ciba-Geigy
Riopan	Ayerst Laboratories, Division of American Home Products Corporation
Seconal	Eli Lilly & Company
Sinemet	Merck Sharp & Dohme Division of Merck & Co., Inc.
Sinequan	Roering Division of Pfizer Pharmaceuticals
Symmetrel	DuPont Pharmaceuticals E.I. duPont de Nemours & Co. (Inc.)
Tab Grabber	Ron Hoffman Group, Inc.
Tinactin	Schering Corporation
Travad	Flint Division of Travenol Laboratories, Inc.
Universal	Universal Gym Equipment, Inc.
Nautilus	Nautilus Sports/Medical Industries, Inc.
UpJohn Health Care	UpJohn HealthCare Services, Inc.
Velcro	Velcro USA, Inc.

Index